Switching to Digital Television
UK Public Policy and the Market

Michael Starks

intellect Bristol, UK / Chicago, USA

First Published in the UK in 2007 by
Intellect Books, PO Box 862, Bristol BS99 1DE, UK

First Published in the USA in 2007 by
Intellect Books, The University of Chicago Press, 1427 E. 60th Street, Chicago,
IL 60637, USA

A catalogue record for this book is available from the British Library

Cover Design: Gabriel Solomons
Copy Editor: Holly Spradling
Typesetting: Planman Technologies

ISBN 978-1-84150-172-7

Printed and bound by Gutenberg Press, Malta.

About the Author

Michael Starks is an Associate of Oxford University's Programme in Comparative Media Law and Policy.

From 2002 to 2004 he managed the UK Digital TV Project, working for the UK Government, planning the UK's full switch to digital television. Earlier, in the course of a long BBC career starting in TV production, he led the BBC's initial feasibility study of digital television. He was the founder Chairman of the UK Digital TV Group of broadcasters, receiver manufacturers, retailers, transmission companies and R&D experts. In 2001 he initiated the BBC's Free-to-View Digital TV Project which culminated in the launch of *Freeview* in 2002.

Michael Starks graduated in History from Cambridge University and studied Political Science at the University of Pennsylvania as a postgraduate. His book on public sector management, *Not for Profit, Not for Sale*, was published in 1991, followed in 2002 by *A Traveller's History of the Hundred Years War in France*.

Contents

Acknowledgements

I have two major groups of colleagues (many of whom became close friends) whose contribution to this book I must acknowledge – those with whom I worked during my years of professional involvement and those who assisted me in my subsequent research.

The professional colleagues are so numerous that to list them all would be impractical. I hope I have given a flavour of their roles in the course of the book. However, the ones who were, in a very real sense, my teachers in the early digital television feasibility study phase included John Birt (now Lord Birt), Bob Phillis, Patricia Hodgson (now Dame), Bob Ely, Martin Bell, Ian Childs, David King, Phil Laven, Henry Price, Gary Tonge, Chris Hibbert, Chris Daubney and Barry Cox. In relation to my subsequent work on free-to-view digital TV several of the same names recur and I must additionally thank Greg Dyke, Carolyn Fairbairn, Andy Duncan, Caroline Thomson, Peter Davies, Andy Townend, Mark Evans, Graham Plumb and David Levy.

Finally, in respect of my switchover work for the Government, I should credit Andrew Ramsay, Catherine Smadja, David Hendon, Jane Humphreys, Ian Dixon, Michael Crosse, Michael Hodson, Greg Bensberg, Danny Churchill, David Harby, Emyr Hughes, Mike Hughes, David Youlton, Marcus Coleman, Peter Marshall, Jane Ostler, Jos Cleare and the leading members of the TV manufacturers' association, including Hugh Peltor and Laurence Harrison. I apologize for not naming the many others with whom I also worked closely.

I am most grateful to the British Academy for the support it gave me to undertake research in 2005 and 2006, including travel to the United States and Japan and within Europe.

In the United States I was greatly helped by Phil Budden and Jennifer Taylor at the British Embassy and by Jonathan Levy, Evan Kwerel and Sherille Ismael at the Federal Communications Commission. I was grateful for the interviews given to me by Susan Eid (DirecTV), Johanna Shelton (House of Representatives staff), James Assey and Rachel Welch (Senate staff), Lynn Claudy (National Association of Broadcasters), John Lawson (Association of Public Television Stations), Gary Shapiro (Consumer Electronics Association), Bob Schwartz (who briefed me on the role of the Consumer Electronics Retailers' Coalition), Matt Polka (American Cable Association), Mark Richer (Advanced Television Systems Committee), Kyle McSlarrow (National Cable and Telecommunications Association), and Janice Obuchowski and John Alden (High Tech DTV Coalition).

In Japan I had invaluable help and advice from Yoshiko Nakamura of NHK's Broadcasting Culture Research Institute and her colleagues. I much appreciated the opportunity to interview Tomohiro Ando, Director of Information Technology at the Cabinet Office of the Japanese government; Madoka Tsuchiya and Maki Shigemori of NHK; Norio Kumabe, visiting professor at Waseba University; Hideki Maekawa of the TBS Media Research Institute; Sadahiro Iehara, Norimasa Okamura, Susumu Masukane, Katsumi Matsumoto and Osamu Inoue of the Japan Electronics & Information Technology Industries Association; and Tetsuo Hamaguchi of the Association for the Promotion of Digital Broadcasting. I was also very grateful for a background briefing by Andrew Dumbreck of Ofcom.

In researching digital television in other European countries, I drew on visits I had made professionally to Germany and Italy. I also consulted Phil Laven and Ed Wilson of the European Broadcasting Union. Peter Scott at the European Commission was very generous in giving me a wide-ranging background briefing. I attended the 2006 conference of the DICE project (digital innovation through cooperation in Europe) in Sweden, learned much about the Swedish experience of switching off analogue television from the team responsible for leading it and, subsequently, consulted Ingrid Walther about Germany's timetable. I also visited Finland in 2006 and was greatly helped by Antti Sillanpää of the Helsinki University of Technology; Tauno Äijälä of the TV2007 project and his colleagues; Katariina Kovistö of the Ministry of Transport and Communications; and Mika Ojamies, Mauri Vakkilainen and Erja Ruohomaa of YLE (Finnish national broadcasting).

At Oxford I greatly enjoyed collaborating with Damian Tambini, then Director of Oxford University's Programme in Comparative Media Law and Policy, and María Trinidad García Leiva, a visiting Ph.D. researcher from the Complutense University of Madrid, analysing different nations' experience of digital television and jointly publishing a journal article. Separately, María Trinidad García Leiva gave me a detailed briefing on digital television in Spain.

Within the UK I interviewed Martin Bell, my former BBC colleague in this field who is also now writing about it. On mobile television developments, I appreciated David Harby's advice and comments on my text.

Any mistakes are, of course, my responsibility.

Finally, I would like to thank May Yao and her colleagues at Intellect Books for all the work involved on the publishing side.

Preface

'Digital switchover' is the term used to convey to the public the compulsory abolition of the conventional analogue television system, to which every household became accustomed in the twentieth century, and its replacement by digital television. It sounds a more positive term than the harsher alternative 'analogue switch-off'. As the policy bites, with implications for all consumers, this account explains why we are all being compelled to switch. It is a story with a cast of politicians and media barons and a good plot with plenty of twists – and is matched by similar experiences in other countries.

The decision-making around switching off the old-style analogue television and converting all television viewing to digital in the UK – and in other nations too – provides an illuminating case study of the interplay between politics and the market. Through a combination of exhortation and regulatory intervention politicians aimed to secure what they wanted from business leaders, and, through a combination of lobbying and commercial action, business leaders endeavoured to achieve their own institutional goals. Both parties knew that at any point the viewing public, as consumers or as voters, could rebel and that consumer persuasion was critical to success.

This is not a technical book, nor am I technically qualified to write one. It is a political and business saga, with analysis and some lessons for the future. I have included some lay explanation of the technology in order to convey a general understanding of the subject, especially where technology was relevant to political or commercial decisions. I hope that this enables the non-technical reader to follow the industrial politics and avoids offending those readers who do have technical expertise.

The political process should be of interest to policy-makers, broadcasters, industry managers and business commentators in the UK and in other countries, while students of politics, regulatory law and media can see how the main themes and conclusions relate to the wider field of telecommunications. For political scientists the story provides a close-up of the complexities and the sophistication of the politico-commercial relationships underpinning change in technologically advanced societies. What we see goes beyond regulated capitalism, falls well short of a planned economy, and has a distinctive character of its own. Here is a slice of the real politics of a modern mixed economy.

For the wider public, viewers and voters, the process is illuminating too. This account shows the points at which the public had opportunities to shape decisions potentially affecting every household. However, the ease with which the general public could access relevant information at virtually every stage of the decision-making process contrasts with the difficulty of grasping the whole plot at any one time. So, as the full implications of digital switchover become more widely understood, it is instructive to look back and see how we arrived here, with consumer and citizen roles intertwined.

*****

Chapter One outlines in general terms the main theme of the interaction of politics and the market in developing digital television and preparing for digital switchover. It includes a brief outline of the underlying technology and a survey of some of the other transitions taking place in the broadcasting world. It identifies the key strategic relationships needed to achieve digital switchover and describes the 'do nothing' alternative. This provides the context for the account of UK developments in the following chapters.

Chapter Two focuses specifically on digital terrestrial television. It addresses the question of who wanted it and why. How far was it a political initiative, not just in the UK but in other countries too, and how far was it market-based? Was the market a free-standing commercial one or, at least in part, a political construct, linked to the public policy goal of analogue switch-off and the Government's desire to reclaim and re-use spectrum?

Chapter Three describes the launch of digital television in the UK and tracks the fortunes of the major players during the first four years when, despite their close involvement in setting the ground rules, politicians were certainly not in charge. It highlights the subsidy-fuelled growth of pay TV and the effect this had on the digital receiver industry.

Chapter Four recounts the crisis of 2002, when ITV Digital went bankrupt and the regulator had to conduct an emergency re-advertising of its digital terrestrial franchise. The BBC led a rescue operation with a vision of subscription-free digital television which depended both on public funding and on collaboration with ITV Digital's principal pay TV rival, and arguably the BBC's own major long-term competitor, BSkyB. The resulting launch of *Freeview* proved a swift commercial success.

Chapter Five covers the work of the UK Digital TV Project when Government, regulators, broadcasters, manufacturers, retailers and consumer representatives implemented an Action Plan to chart the UK's course through to full digital switchover. During 2003 and 2004 a formal Cost-Benefit Analysis was undertaken and the full implications of switching off analogue terrestrial television were articulated to Government ministers.

Chapter Six recounts the political decisions which then followed, setting the framework within which digital switchover could be achieved in the UK by the end of 2012. The political strategy was to place the responsibility for implementation primarily with the broadcasters – giving the BBC a major role, spelling out regulatory obligations for the commercial terrestrial broadcasters and encouraging the formation of a new industry organization, Digital UK, to handle many of the operational practicalities. The role of the licence fee was central.

Chapter Seven goes to the heart of the political challenge of digital switchover – persuading the public to buy new equipment. It looks at the public face of a policy which has to shift from being voluntary in the first instance to becoming compulsory in the end. Any date set for analogue switch-off risks being a government-industry bluff which the consumer-voter can call. Persuasion, assisted by some targeted help, is required to secure public acceptance of the compulsory policy.

Chapter Eight examines the experience of other countries, looking at motivation, launch strategy and switchover policy. It surveys the major advanced television markets across the globe – the United States, Japan and Western Europe – and the varying approaches taken towards analogue switch-off. While subsidiary goals, strategies and timing differ between nations, the governmental aim of making more efficient use of spectrum through digital switchover is a common theme.

Chapter Nine zooms out from digital television to the wider picture of the convergence of broadcasting, telecommunications and computer technology. Possibilities for re-using the spectrum released by switching off analogue terrestrial TV go wider than conventional broadcasting. Broadcasting's interface with the Internet, whose initial development and rapid adoption took place more or less simultaneously with the growth of digital television, is critically important. However, the contribution which digital switchover in the UK can make to the construction of an 'Information Society' is limited.

Now that the UK, the USA, Germany, Finland, Sweden, the Netherlands and other countries have developed realistic strategies for completing switchover – so that it is no longer just a distant hazy goal – it becomes possible to identify some of the essential ingredients for success. Chapter Ten aims to pull the analysis together, not least for the benefit of the many other countries now preparing to embark on a similar journey.

The analysis shows that the full-scale substitution of a new digital television technology for an old requires public policy initiatives. Yet the commercial and political risks associated with public intervention are so great that government and regulatory action can work only in a very supportive set of market conditions.

Even then there are key technical and marketing ingredients which neither governments nor regulators, nor an uncoordinated market, can deliver.

Industry organizations with a coordinating role are also required. Market competitors must collaborate both with one another and with government and regulatory bodies. Ultimately, however, the public needs to be convinced about switchover on citizenship grounds and the political task of making the citizenship case persuasively is vital.

Digital switchover can easily falter or fail. In the UK we saw the financial collapse of ITV Digital and in Spain a major broadcaster suffered a similar fate. Several countries have named digital switchover dates and then postponed them. The recipe for success can be elusive.

To be successful, switchover needs to be a joint project between politicians and the market. The market can grow digital TV services but a coherent, market-based public policy is required; first, to plant the seeds for any digital terrestrial television and then, either a little or a lot later, to harvest the benefits from analogue terrestrial switch-off.

*****

My role in this story is that of a participant. I was involved across a sufficiently broad field to have seen a lot of the action and to have undertaken some of it myself. I led the BBC's feasibility study of digital television in the mid-1990s, when the technology was new and untried. I became the founding chairman of the industry-wide Digital TV Group in the UK. I was involved in the birth of *Freeview* after the collapse of ITV Digital. Finally, having left the BBC to work for the Government at the end of 2002, I managed the UK Digital TV Project, based on the Action Plan which had been drawn up between Government, regulators and industry and consumer stakeholders.

It is, of course, easy to exaggerate the importance of what I saw and difficult to evaluate the significance of what was hidden from my view, but I have endeavoured to give as broad and balanced an account as possible. In completing the later chapters especially, I have drawn not only on visits, conferences and international collaboration in which I was involved professionally but, more importantly, on research conducted with the aid of a grant from the British Academy during 2005 and 2006.

My account ends in 2006, a date I chose because by then the strategy and policy had been very largely constructed, practical implementation was due to begin in 2007–08 and I viewed that as a separate subject for study at a later date. Needless to say, the story of digital switchover continues to unfold, some surprises are almost inevitable, and readers of this book will bring to it extra topical information.

Chapter One

Public Policy and the Market

On Saturday 15th June 1996 the Queen presided over the Trooping the Colour ceremony on Horse Guards Parade, as she did every year. Massed ranks of guards paraded in front of her, perfectly executing their well-rehearsed drill. As usual the pageant was televised, the camera direction as carefully choreographed as the parade itself. But this year there was a difference. The Queen was also presiding over the world's first simultaneous analogue and digital terrestrial widescreen television broadcast.

There were in fact two separate video feeds to two sets of receivers. The BBC's outside broadcast unit fed back conventionally shaped TV pictures for normal transmission to the millions of normal analogue TV sets in households all over the country. Alongside, from the same cameras it fed back a separate stream of widescreen pictures which were processed for digital terrestrial transmission.

The digital widescreen pictures and sound could be received only on two prototype digital receivers, the size of large refrigerators, specially built by research engineers to handle this emerging new technology. One was in the BBC's broadcasting centre in Newcastle, the other was in the BBC's White City centre in London.

In front of the London receiver was a small group of BBC executives and technology experts, headed by the Managing Director of BBC Television, Will Wyatt, whom I had invited to come to work in their weekend clothes for this historic occasion. We were not disappointed. The new technology performed, both for us and for our colleagues in Newcastle. This first 'live' trial was a success.

In the short term all we had to do then was to launch it for real. In the longer term we had to persuade the millions of analogue viewers to switch to watching what for the moment were still 'refrigerators'.

Switching to digital TV

In simple terms digital television involves coding and then compressing the television signal. The benefits of digital transmission are increased robustness, resulting in technical quality improvements, and increased capacity, giving the option of many more programme services.

By 1996 digital coding and compression were in use in the United States and elsewhere for satellite and cable television transmission and, in the UK and elsewhere, for digital audio broadcasting. Digital terrestrial television involved applying the same technology to the more traditional transmission from hilltop masts to rooftop aerials, and thence to digital receivers.

Two years later, in 1998, digital television was formally launched in the UK, with both digital terrestrial and digital satellite broadcasts. Digital cable in the UK began the following year. Offering a panoply of new services, digital TV swiftly began to transform the whole television industry. It gave an immediate boost to the take-up of multi-channel pay TV. It created new relationships between broadcasters and receiver manufacturers, underpinning the marketing of set-top boxes. Its picture format encouraged the growth of widescreen TV sets. It introduced interactive features and services. It further segmented audiences, which in turn affected funding and competitive relationships among broadcasters. It necessitated changes to the statutory and regulatory framework. It gave further impetus to the technology convergence between the broadcasting, telecommunications and computer industries.

Moreover, it gave politicians a new industrial ambition. On 18th September 2003, the Secretary of State for Culture, Media and Sport, Tessa Jowell, was sitting frustratedly in a traffic jam when she was due to give a speech at the Royal Television Society's biennial industry Convention in Cambridge. In her absence her speech had to be read by her deputy, Lord McIntosh. So it fell to him to tell the assembled company of media executives that the Government had definitely decided to switch off the UK's traditional analogue terrestrial TV services and replace them fully with digital television. By 2003 digital television had penetrated around half the households in the UK, most of which had added satellite, terrestrial or cable set-top boxes to conventional analogue TV sets. It now became firm public policy to persuade, and in the last resort to compel, the other half of the population to make the same switch.

The proposed switchover timing – on a regionally phased basis between 2008 and 2012 – was included in the Labour Party's May 2005 election manifesto.[1] On 15th September 2005, with Labour's election victory behind her, Tessa Jowell addressed the next Convention of the Royal Television Society, winningly confessing that she had come to Cambridge a couple of days early to be sure of arriving on time, and announced the detailed switchover timetable, region by region, starting with the (England and Scotland) Border region in 2008.

Although the substitution of digital for analogue television had been envisaged at the outset, this was a significant public policy decision. Its most tangible public policy benefit would be to enable digital terrestrial television to achieve comparable coverage to analogue and allow hitherto under-served parts of the country to receive additional terrestrial TV services. The longer-term goal was to save spectrum at the point of analogue switch-off and re-use it for new services yet to be devised.

The political difficulty was that every household wishing to continue to watch television after analogue switch-off would have to acquire a digital set-top box (as a converter) or a new digital TV set – and that would include a minority, the size of which would not be trivial, who would not otherwise have done so and might well resent the cost and trouble.

Moreover, the consumer implications of this decision extended well beyond a requirement to adapt the main TV set. Switching off analogue transmission would affect all the additional analogue TV sets in the home and the capabilities of analogue video cassette recorders. In some cases new aerials would be required. Communal systems, whether in blocks of flats, hotels, schools or prisons, would all require conversion. Demand for new equipment and for installation services would have sharp peaks, in different parts of the country at different times, distorting normal commercial logistics. The costs of the compulsory element of switchover would be large in total and uneven in their incidence. For the UK – as for other countries pursuing parallel policies – digital switchover was therefore fraught with political, technical and commercial risks.

Analogies tend to be partial. Digital switchover is different from the switch to the 625 line system and colour television in the 1960s and 1970s: in that case, retention of the old 405 line technology was not a barrier to the spread of the new and the timetable for completing the process could therefore be gentle. It differs from the national programme to install North Sea Gas in every household in the late 1960s because that job was done by a central body which supplied and installed the consumer equipment without charge. It is not like the replacement of leaded petrol with unleaded, which has been gradual, without a prominent switching date. The campaign to prepare all computer systems for the Year 2000 (Y2K), with a common date and an onus on every system owner to take remedial action, perhaps provides a closer analogy. However, in that case the switching date was set by the calendar and was not a matter for political decision.

So no analogy is exact. As a public policy challenge, the switchover from analogue to digital television is *sui generis* – difficult to get right, easy to get wrong and one of the major national projects of the early twenty-first century.

Political and commercial interdependence

The whole development of digital television – from its early experimental stage through to completion of the planned technology substitution – involves a complex interplay between technology, commerce and politics. Digital switchover could never have been planned without a major government role and the decision to undertake it was a political one.

Broadcasting has always been political and British broadcasting, editorial independence notwithstanding, is no exception. In the 1920s, 30s and 40s – the period of Lord Reith's 'brute force of monopoly' – the role of commerce had been subservient to public policy. The strategic issues – how many broadcasting services there should be, their remits, their funding – were all decided by the Government. A broadcasting monopoly was entrusted to the BBC as a public corporation, in contrast to the flourishing pattern of commercial radio, and then television, stations in the United States.

In the 1950s, when the British establishment eventually admitted commercial television, the Government placed it too within a strong public policy framework. Initially, the commercial television companies were contractors producing programmes for a new public service body, the Independent Television Authority, to publish.

By the last decade of the twentieth century, the emphasis had shifted. The BBC-ITV duopoly had given way to a much more pluralist pattern, including Channel 4 and Channel Five, Welsh and Gaelic language services, and a lively independent production sector. During the 1980s analogue satellite and analogue cable had developed new multi-channel pay TV businesses as well. Regulators had attempted to take technical decisions on behalf of the satellite industry and had failed. Television was increasingly shaped by commercial forces.

Even so, the UK Government had explicitly decided not to treat television as if it was just like publishing and could be left to the market, operating within the normal laws of competition, fair trading and libel. Politicians regarded broadcasting as special for a number of reasons which gave them an interest in it:

- maintaining a regime of editorial balance and impartiality,
- preserving taste and decency in a medium which entered into every home,
- pursuing educational and cultural goals,
- having a potential tool for government communication in wartime,
- and managing spectrum as a public resource.

So the industry remained regulated within its own public policy and legal framework, set primarily by successive Broadcasting Acts, by the BBC's Charter and Licence, and by the regulations governing the use of spectrum. Analogue terrestrial television broadcasters were therefore not constitutionally free to set up new services without reference to the Government. Nor, of course, could the broadcasters unilaterally decide to replace one television transmission system with another in the way that, for example, the music and consumer electronics industries substituted the CD for the LP. A major technology change in broadcasting such as digital switchover had to involve politicians.

However, the Government could not unilaterally decide that the country was now going to adopt a new broadcasting technology and impose it. No government could sensibly specify the detailed technical standards to ensure interoperability between digital transmitters and receivers. In modern mass communications no country is a technological island, and the television receiver industry in particular had developed into an international market.

Spectrum usage is planned internationally as well as nationally. Within the framework of the United Nations Organization, the International Telecommunications Union (ITU) has a high-level oversight of the way spectrum is used across the whole range of broadcasting, telephony, mobile communications, navigation and astronomy throughout the world. Its aims are to prevent harmful interference and improve effectiveness of use and, by agreement, it allocates particular bands of spectrum for particular purposes to assist compatibility.

This is done within three ITU regions – (a) Europe, the Middle East & Africa (b) the Americas and (c) the Far East & Australasia. Each band of spectrum is given primary and secondary uses, with primary-use services fully protected and secondary-use services protected from one another but not from primary-use services. Within Europe a body called the CEPT (European Conference of Postal and Telecommunications Administrations) coordinates and guides the European countries' governments and regulators and publishes the European Common Allocation Table, listing, for each frequency band, the various services recognized in Europe.

Even if the politicians of the European Union, whose territory constitutes a major regional market in the global business of TV receiver manufacturing, combined to attempt to impose new technical standards for the European market, there could be no confidence that their prescribed solutions would work commercially. Down that road lay the prospect of political embarrassment over alleged responsibility for commercial failure. So, in planning digital switchover, politicians had to work with the market, taking account of the market's European and global dimensions.

This is much easier to say than to do. The television market is open, competitive and international – and regulated to this end. So no individual company could be a monopolistic government 'partner' organizing the end-to-end changes needed to bring in new technology smoothly. Concentrations of ownership and vertical integration could help, but major vertically integrated players in a competitive market face commercial risks and can go bankrupt or undergo major changes of ownership. Public service broadcasters could play a leading role, but they have limited funds, a limited appetite for financial risk and no ability to guarantee receiver supply and purchase. So in pursuing switchover, governments had to work with a diverse and somewhat fluid group of market competitors, many of them international businesses who, before they could work with national politicians, had first to agree to collaborate with one another – up to a point and in some respects.

Even when enough of the key political and commercial decision-makers can agree that collaboration is both desirable and practical for technical purposes – to mark out the digital technology playing field on which competition in services and products can then take place – the issues become much trickier in areas of marketing and communications. Whose job is it to market the new technology as a whole, as distinct from the individual programme channels or receivers and recorders? Whose job is it to explain to the public that digital switchover will, in the end, have to be compulsory? Politicians can be shy here: after all, every reluctant consumer is a voter.

So, as this account of digital switchover in the UK will show, a kind of dance ensued – in which broadcasters took some initiatives but lobbied the Government to take others, while the Government made some decisions and sought to persuade broadcasters and manufacturers to become responsible for others.

Broadcasters and manufacturers not only danced with the Government and regulators, they also danced with one another, with occasional changes of partner. All the time everyone watched the responses of the public – the consumers, licence fee payers and voters. The performance was largely in public, making this period of broadcasting history very different from the 'top-down' decision-making of the early-twentieth-century founders of the BBC or the behind-the-scenes pressure group activity leading to the 1950s launch of commercial television.[2] Ensuring that the policy-making was in the public domain was essential to the goal of public persuasion – and public persuasion was where the dance ultimately had to lead.

What is digital television?

Before any of us could take the first steps in public, however, we had to understand what digital television was and how it worked, most of us from a starting point of almost total ignorance. Specialist experts understood its technical potential but were not judges of its commercial viability. For senior managers and government policy-makers, with varying degrees of technical literacy, digital television was a new subject, and I certainly had to start with the basics.

The term 'digital' had crept into common parlance as the compact disc permeated the music market and as small digital mobile phones replaced the brick-sized analogue models initially in the market. It was a buzzword associated with consumer electronics equipment promising superior technical quality at a neat size.

The two characteristics which, for the non-technical person, most obviously distinguish digital from traditional analogue communications are coding and compression. In digital television the video and audio signals are encoded into a stream of ones and zeros and this provides a robust format which avoids loss of quality between the transmitter and the receiver. The signals are also compressed, which brings the additional benefit of increased transmission capacity. This extra capacity can be used either for a technically richer signal, providing superior technical quality (high definition), or for additional programme services (more channels). From the consumer standpoint, therefore, digital television is potentially 'bigger and/or better'.

Television can be sent from the broadcaster to the viewer in a number of different ways:

- satellite transmission, where the signal is 'up-linked' to a satellite from which it then comes down to a satellite dish;

- through a cable running under the ground and coming up into the house;
- conventional 'through the air' (terrestrial) transmission from a transmitter on a hill to a domestic rooftop or set-top aerial.

Digital coding and compression technology can be applied to all of these methods, giving the three main digital television transmission 'platforms', as they are often known, of digital satellite, digital cable and digital terrestrial television. Although the technology was at a very early stage in the 1990s, coded and compressed digital television signals can also be delivered through a conventional telephone wire. By the early twenty-first century this technology had developed into a fourth platform, broadband, which could deliver not only easy Internet access but television services as well.

At the reception end, once the signal from the broadcaster has arrived, it needs to be decompressed and decoded before it can be displayed on a TV set. For satellite and cable (and telephony), this is normally done by routing it through a set-top box. For digital terrestrial television, a set-top box linked to a conventional analogue TV set is the most widespread arrangement but an alternative is an integrated digital TV, where the digital electronics are built into the TV set and no extra box is required.

Digital television services can use either the conventional picture format (a 4:3 ratio of width to height) or widescreen (16:9). The BBC chose 15th June 1996 as the opportunity to initiate a strategic switch to widescreen, and the widescreen format is now predominant in UK digital television. Virtually all integrated digital TV sets sold in the UK are widescreen.

Digital television services can be either free-to-view (e.g. financed by the licence fee or by advertising, with no charge at the point of consumption) or available on payment of a subscription or a pay-per-view charge (pay TV services). For pay TV services the signal is not only coded and compressed, it must also be encrypted (scrambled). At the receiver end it therefore needs to be decrypted and this is normally done through the provision of a viewing card which is inserted into the receiver. Entitlement to a card is conditional on payment so that, if the bill has not been paid, access to the services can be denied. This encryption-decryption technology is termed conditional access.

Although conditional access is usually associated with pay TV, it can be used for free-to-view services too. On satellite, where the broadcast signal (the satellite 'footprint') may spread over a number of different countries, national broadcasters may choose to encrypt their free-to-view services to prevent feature films and sporting events, for example, being seen in countries for which they have not purchased the broadcasting rights. In such cases access to the services, using a broadcaster-funded viewing card, can be granted only to households within a designated geographical area. This can also enable satellite commercial broadcasters to ensure that viewers in any given region receive only the relevant advertising content. Free-to-view services may also be encrypted to prevent unauthorized copying. This is particularly important for feature films and other high-cost productions, especially if transmitted in high definition.

A key innovation associated with digital television is interactivity – the possibility of two-way services. There are differences here between the platforms. Cable and broadband have the technical capacity for genuine two-way communication. Satellite and terrestrial broadcast transmissions are essentially one-way – as a viewer, you cannot send an electronic message from your satellite dish to the satellite, or from your rooftop aerial to the transmitter, back to the broadcaster. To overcome this constraint the satellite or terrestrial broadcaster can specify a technical link from the set-top box to a conventional telephone point so that the viewers can use their household telephone line as a 'return path', e.g. for voting, ordering pizzas or for pay-per-view transactions.

The other so-called interactivity option for one-way broadcasters is to send extra supplementary programme streams which remain hidden until the viewer selects them. Thus, for coverage of the Olympics, for example, a digital broadcaster might transmit simultaneous coverage of athletics track, field, swimming and sailing events – giving viewers the choice, via the red button on the remote control handset, of the events they wish to follow. This is interactivity of a sort, but between viewers and their receivers, not between viewers and the broadcasters.

The most familiar form of interactivity in digital television is probably the Electronic Programme Guide (EPG) which viewers select via the remote control handset and which lists both present and future programmes for each channel. A well-designed and sophisticated EPG is more than just a useful tool for multi-channel television: for many viewers, being able to navigate around the viewing options and call up information about future programmes is a significant part of digital TV's appeal. Moreover, it can simplify the process of recording.

Interactive television, even in a relatively simple form like a Text service, an EPG or the choice between two athletic events, requires a sophisticated interface between the broadcast software and the receiver. The computer industry, as it matured, came to appreciate the importance of standardizing the interface between popular software applications and a wide range of personal computers. Digital television requires an equivalent standardized interface (an API, or Application Programming Interface) so that the interactive applications can work on a wide range of digital television receivers.

Digital television technology can be either 'open' or 'proprietary'. These are relative rather than pure terms but, in general, open technology is based on published standards and is available for use by any company wishing to enter the market, though there may be licences to purchase. Proprietary technology, on the other hand, is controlled by a particular company, often a pay TV broadcaster and, within the regulatory framework, managed in the interests of its own business. The broadcaster may, for example, restrict the number of set-top box manufacturers it licenses and may require the marketing of the boxes to be linked to signature of a contract or to a commitment to subscribe.

In the areas of conditional access, Application Programming Interfaces, and Electronic Programme Guide design, the adoption of open or proprietary technology is important in allowing, or restricting, the interoperability of consumer equipment within or between platforms. In the UK, given the role of proprietary technology, different receivers are normally required for the different transmission platforms.

Analogue transmission is less efficient and, thus, more wasteful of spectrum, than digital, and replacing analogue terrestrial transmission fully, by some combination of satellite, cable, broadband and digital terrestrial, produces a saving of spectrum which can then be used for other purposes. From a public policy standpoint this is one of the fundamental benefits of digital switchover (or of analogue *terrestrial* switch-off, to be precise).

Switching off analogue terrestrial television to secure a saving of spectrum is a public policy means rather than an end. Lurking behind the goal and the strategies for achieving it is the fundamental question of the final purpose. Windfall auction revenue accruing to a government or regulator does not constitute a full answer. To whom might the spectrum be auctioned or allocated and with what balance of public and private consumer benefits?

Given the long timetable for switchover and the rapid pace of technological change, there are no prizes for deciding too definitively too early. Within broadcasting, potential new users of saved spectrum include mobile television (with reception on hand-held receivers), a fuller commitment to high-definition television, more digital broadcasters and/or more channels, including fuller development of regional and local television. Wireless broadband is another candidate – and broadband may develop into the way many homes will in future receive their television. It is in the wider context of the convergence between digital television and other forms of communication that the future uses of released spectrum will probably be decided.

Compulsory digital switchover

As those of us wrestling with the policy issues acquired our understanding of these basics of digital television, we began to appreciate just how complex all this could seem to the consumer. The central question consumers would ultimately want answered clearly was why digital switchover had to be compulsory. The biggest communication challenge would not lie with retail staff trying to make a sale to potentially interested customers, but with politicians or broadcasters explaining the subject to reluctant viewers.

When the majority of households switched to the compact disc, anyone who wanted to retain their turntable and LPs and go on using them was free to do so with no cut-off point. Typewriters still worked after the arrival of word-processors (even if typewriter repair shops disappeared). Why could digital switchover not be based on letting the market take its course?

For satellite and cable the decisions to switch to digital transmission are essentially commercial: satellite and cable broadcasters can switch at different times of their own choosing. In practice satellite broadcasters have mostly switched, offering their digital customers new receivers, while the cable industry has become a mixed economy of analogue and digital systems.

For terrestrial television, since the allocation of spectrum to broadcasters is made either by government or by a regulatory body with powers granted by government, the decision to end analogue terrestrial transmission is ultimately a political one. It does not have to be implemented across the whole nation on the same day – indeed there are strong practical reasons for designing a phased implementation – but it does ultimately have to be implemented for *all analogue terrestrial broadcasters* in order to realize the full spectrum efficiency benefits. An analogue TV receiver, of course, can only be fully functional if it receives an analogue signal from a broadcaster. Before their local analogue transmitter is switched off, consumers who wish to continue to view television need to have replaced or converted their receivers. In that sense, the switchover policy in the end becomes compulsory.

In a modern democracy, however, compulsory policies have to have a substantial measure of voluntary acceptance to be enforceable – especially in an area like the technology used for television transmission and reception. Broadcasters can be compelled by law and regulation to cease transmitting analogue. However, if a large body of consumers failed (or refused on principle) to spend their own money buying digital reception equipment and then challenged the acceptability of switching off the analogue broadcasts, political opposition would soon gather. No government would be likely to call (let alone win) an election on this issue.

Public resistance had memorably killed off the poll tax under Mrs Thatcher's government. In the field of broadcasting it had only taken a protest march on Broadcasting House in 1991 to overturn a BBC decision to cease transmitting Radio 4 on long wave. A widespread viewer revolt against digital switchover which gathered steam would be difficult to defy.

Free boxes for all?

Could the potential political unpopularity of the policy be averted by some project finance scheme? This was one of the first ideas we explored: look for the end-beneficiaries and find a device for making them pay. After all, in a project to construct a major bridge or tunnel, a toll can be imposed on users following its completion and the anticipation of this revenue stream can allow the project investors to borrow the capital needed upfront.

The simplest application of this line of thought to digital switchover would be a scheme to auction the spectrum released through switchover, using the anticipated proceeds from this auction as the basis for borrowing enough capital to finance the universal supply of digital terrestrial set-top boxes and the creation of the necessary digital transmission infrastructure.

However, while some such approach might help to complete the switchover process in some circumstances, digital switchover was never going to be that simple. The potential costs would be very high, the provision of a set-top box to every household would carry no guarantee of reliable reception (e.g. if there were aerial problems), the timescale could be long, the future uses of the released spectrum unclear and the whole process riddled with risk. In a country like the UK, with a sizeable number of analogue terrestrial homes to be converted, no government or commercial consortium was likely to view this as a workable basis for the entire switchover scheme. The financial and political risks would be prohibitive.

Moreover, such a scheme would needlessly eliminate the enormous contribution the market could make through voluntary take-up. If digital television proved attractive to consumers, most of them would spend their own money voluntarily over time, especially as the average household could be expected to replace its main TV set within a decade. The market could then be the main financial engine for driving the public policy. That way, the number of households for whom the change would be compulsory – at least in respect of their main TV set – could be kept relatively low.

Even so, in the end, the policy would need to be made compulsory and explaining why this was so, and persuading the great majority of the public to accept and support it, was unavoidable. This prospect posed dilemmas both for politicians, whose political survival instincts warned them not to be too evangelical on the subject, and for broadcasters and the receiver industry, who had their own relationships to cultivate with the public and were sensitive to the risks of becoming the bearers of the Government's 'bad news'. Some of the most intricate dance steps by the politicians and the industry leaders proved to be around this issue.

The shifting context

In the UK it took roughly a decade from starting to formulate the regulatory framework for digital television through to the announcement of a firm timetable for switching off analogue – with the actual switchover operation still to follow over several more years. Inevitably, over such a long period, the context for political and commercial decision-making altered. Changes of government took place, new broadcasting organizations were created, and the financial fortunes of the broadcast advertising market and the high-tech industry sector fluctuated significantly.

In the late twentieth century satellite broadcasting, either directly or in association with cable, facilitated the globalization of television. The international news broadcasting services of CNN and BBC World were one facet of this;

imports into the UK of North American channels and programming constituted another; increasing foreign or multinational ownership of UK broadcasting industry companies was a third. Regulatory perspectives needed to widen. Symbolically, the European Union developed a regulatory policy entitled *Television Without Frontiers*.[3]

Some existing broadcasting organizations reinvented themselves during this period. The BBC twice went through Charter renewal processes, with accompanying debates about the justification for and the future of the licence fee – first in the period leading up to the end of 1996 and then again ten years later. Also, during this period, ITV, at the outset a federation of regional companies, transformed itself into ITV plc. Terrestrial transmission operations, both for public service and commercial broadcasters, were privatized and the two companies in charge of them were both subsequently sold, more than once, to new owners.

Within the television receiver industry another form of switchover was occurring – the shift from the traditional cathode ray tube technology of a TV set to plasma and Liquid Crystal Display (LCD) flat-screens. Recording technology was moving away from videotape and into DVD and hard-disc products. Meanwhile the television and video recorder rental business, once prominent in every high street, declined and contracted.

Elsewhere in the communications industry strategic upheavals took place with impacts on the hitherto rather self-contained world of broadcasting. The invention and development of the Internet was by far the most significant. The potential links and synergy which telecommunications and computers might have with digital television excited technical innovators and politicians alike. The growth of the mobile telephone industry not only heightened pressure for the efficient use of spectrum but also opened up the technical possibility of receiving mobile television on portable telephone handsets.

Gazing into the future of the new converged communications systems, enthusiasts started using terms like 'Information Superhighways', the 'Information Society' and the 'Information Revolution'. The prospect was compared in significance to the original Industrial Revolution. Here was a set of technology and commercial forces which would transform society's workings and usher in 'e-learning', 'e-business' and 'e-government'. This vision shaped a political agenda of liberalizing telecommunications regulation and encouraging the take-up of Internet access devices.

The convergence of the broadcasting, telecommunications and computer technologies also created new regulatory challenges. This led to the creation of Ofcom as a new regulatory body, replacing the former broadcasting and telecommunications regulators and encompassing the Radiocommunications Agency of the Department of Trade and Industry. This in turn produced a new agenda for broadcasters, as pricing and auctions were developed as new tools for spectrum allocation.

The nature of broadcasting regulation also altered. Detailed content regulation eased: as the number of broadcasters expanded and more 'niche' services were launched, regulators felt less need to approve the detailed time bands for mixed programming schedules. The importance of competition regulation, however, grew as a consequence of the increased number of competing organizations and the complexity of multiple platforms. Henceforth, before any new development of publicly funded services was authorized, a regulatory assessment of the potential repercussions on commercial organizations operating within the same sphere was required.

So, as politicians, broadcasters and receiver manufacturers strove to assess the significance of the invention of digital television and the practicalities of achieving digital switchover, the context for decision-making was shifting in a complex variety of ways.

In his 2004 study of digital TV in the United States and the UK, Hernan Galperin portrays the transition to full digital television as a public policy response to three main issues, each important in turn. It began, he argues, as an industrially inspired desire to counter the steady decline of the American and European consumer electronics sector. It then metamorphosed into political support for the information revolution. It was finally sustained by the political need for additional spectrum created by the rapid growth of mobile telephony and other wireless telecommunications, coupled with government interest in obtaining revenue from spectrum auctions.[4]

Looking across a wider number of countries, we can add other factors. Generally, motives for introducing digital terrestrial television included preserving a place for terrestrial transmission and reception in a world in which satellite, cable and broadband telecommunications were steadily enlarging their roles. In countries with a strong public service broadcasting pattern, this might be in order to have a reserve government mechanism for communication in wartime and/or for cultural reasons. In countries where incoming globalized satellite services were perceived to be a threat, constructing a new framework to safeguard national broadcasting institutions in the developing new digital era was a way of preserving national culture and language.

While full digital switchover – in the sense of switching off analogue terrestrial transmissions in order to recoup spectrum for alternative uses – was present as an ambition from an early point both in the UK and elsewhere, the political importance attached to it grew. However desirable it might be for spectrum efficiency reasons, it could only become feasible on the back of a successful commercial market. At the outset, therefore, the industry motives – the desire of broadcasters to launch new services, the desire of the receiver industry to manufacture and sell a new generation of products and the desire of governments to protect national culture – were critical. Without a flourishing market, a public policy of switchover was not plausible.

But as the digital switchover goal crystallized, in the UK and in other countries too, a pattern emerged from the apparent flux of a shifting context and an evolving mix of motives. Designing a digital switchover strategy involved three key themes.

(a) Spectrum for incumbent analogue terrestrial broadcasters

Since governments and regulators, whether in the UK or elsewhere, desired digital switchover in order to make more efficient use of spectrum, they needed some form of collaborative relationship with the incumbent analogue terrestrial broadcasters. The latter would be required to surrender frequencies but needed to have an opportunity to migrate their viewers to digital TV first. It therefore suited governments to design some regulatory arrangement whereby the incumbent broadcasters were given (either for free or on terms sufficiently favourable to induce acceptance) new digital terrestrial spectrum in order to duplicate their analogue services for a period – an arrangement termed 'simulcasting' – to provide a transitional phase during which viewers would be expected to acquire new digital receivers.

An analogue terrestrial television broadcaster in the 1990s could understandably have wished that digital television had never been invented, and no doubt this sentiment was uttered in many a boardroom discussion. Major analogue terrestrial broadcasters, public service and commercial, were big fish in a small pond. Their share of audience and, in the case of commercial broadcasters, their share of advertising was relatively large and the number of competitors limited by the scarcity of spectrum. Digital television threatened to bring more channels, even within a reduced amount of broadcasting spectrum, which would mean more competitors, loss of audience share and a probable decline in commercial revenue.

Pessimism was not universal, since some terrestrial broadcasters had ambitions to expand the number of channels they provided, and, in any event, digital television *had been invented* so the issue was how to respond. One attraction of new digital spectrum to incumbent analogue broadcasters was, crudely, that the more they had, the less would be available for potential new market entrants. Part of the appeal to incumbents of coupling switchover to high definition, as in the United States and Japan, was that it required so much digital terrestrial spectrum that new terrestrial market entrants were effectively excluded ahead of switchover.

Because of spectrum constraints, even with digital technology, the total number of competitors would be lower on the digital terrestrial platform than in the multi-channel satellite and cable markets. If it was no longer feasible to be a big fish in an analogue terrestrial pond, then constructing a digital terrestrial lake for medium-sized fish was perhaps preferable to swimming solely in the satellite and cable ocean. Incumbent analogue terrestrial broadcasters therefore tended to try and acquire as much digital terrestrial spectrum as they could sensibly afford to use.

Here was the basis for government-broadcaster collaboration over digital switchover. It could not, however, be a cosy relationship. Governments and regulators needed to be fair to satellite and cable broadcasters with different commercial interests. They also had to consider how much political importance they attached to bringing in new broadcasters, either for social and cultural reasons or to help boost the attractiveness of the digital television consumer proposition.

Moreover, this government-broadcaster relationship was a pragmatic response to the challenge of achieving switchover. Incumbents had no entitlement to longer-term protection. Even if there were spectrum constraints on the number of new broadcasting competitors feasible during the transition period of simulcasting, the whole thrust of the technology development was towards greater pluralism, with greater market competition, post-switchover.

(b) Relationships between broadcasters and the receiver industry

Broadcasters could not make a success of digital television, whether simulcasting or the launch of new services, without an accompanying consumer outlay on the acquisition of new digital receivers. So they needed to work in some form of partnership with the TV receiver industry – both manufacturers and retailers. Although hybrid variations also emerged, there were two main models for this.

The first was the model of a vertically integrated pay TV broadcaster. Here the broadcaster marketed subscription services and took on the responsibility of ensuring that its subscribers acquired the necessary reception equipment, either on a rental basis or as a purchase subsidized through the subscription revenue. In this case the broadcaster's conditional access technology would need to be incorporated into the receivers at the manufacturing stage; the receivers would need to be specified so that they displayed the broadcaster's Electronic Programme Guide (EPG) and could handle its interactive features; and the broadcaster would underwrite orders to manufacturers. The retailer's job would be to sell subscriptions, rather than receivers, and the broadcaster might choose to pay retail staff a commission on every successful sale.

Under this arrangement the broadcaster took on commercial risk on the reception, as well as the broadcasting, side. To make it work, the programme services had to have a high enough premium content to bring in sufficient continuing revenue to cover the full range of costs and risks. The main advantage of this model was that the broadcaster could provide integrated control across the whole business.

The second model was more relevant to the free-to-view market and resembled the traditional division between broadcasters, on the one hand, and receiver manufacturers and retailers, on the other, familiar from the analogue world. Here the broadcaster took responsibility only for the programme content and the transmission, while the receiver manufacturers and retailers carried the commercial risk of marketing receivers, whether through sale or rental. This reduced broadcaster risk and gave the receiver industry control over its own business. The disadvantage of this horizontal market was the lack of integrated control and the accompanying risks of insufficient coordination between transmission and reception.

The practical consequences of such risks could be that, while broadcasters invested in programme content and in transmitting it,

- there might be no receivers available in the shops, or
- the receivers might be unable to display, or provide navigation between, all the services, or
- the receivers might not be able to handle interactive features.

In such circumstances, the retailers might blame any problems on the broadcasters and the broadcasters blame any problems on the manufacturers. It is easy to see how an uncoordinated horizontal market could fail.

The result was that, if vertical integration did not exist, some steps would need to be taken to ensure collaboration and coordination between the broadcasting and the receiver industries. The market could only function smoothly if all, or virtually all, broadcasters collaborated both with one another and with all, or virtually all, receiver manufacturers and retailers. The technical complexity of this, especially at the outset when the technology was still new, meant that old, loose styles of working had to change. The collaborative arrangements required normally stopped short of becoming formal joint ventures but coordination had to go a long way in that direction.

(c) The public policy framework for broadcaster funding

Retailers could only successfully sell receivers to consumers if consumers valued the content of the programme services those receivers delivered. No one would buy a digital TV receiver, however well designed, if it only delivered a digital version of the existing analogue services and nothing else. The 'something extra' could be improved technical quality, or widescreen, or extra channels, or interactive features or, in practice, some combination of these features.

This 'something extra' would inevitably involve broadcasters in extra cost, whether for new programmes on new channels or new production equipment to deliver new technical quality and features – and this cost would be additional to investment in new digital transmission technology. For broadcasters a major challenge in switching to digital was to find sources of revenue sufficient to add real consumer value. Consumer subscription was one possibility, complicated by the strength of established competitors.

Incumbent terrestrial broadcasters, however, were likely to be free-to-view and to wish, to some extent, to remain so. This suited the public policy goal of switchover, since it is politically difficult to compel all viewers to switch to subscription as well as to digital. However, for advertisement-financed terrestrial broadcasters, the costs of switching to digital, especially during a transition period of simulcasting, could easily outweigh any increased revenue. Publicly financed broadcasters also faced funding constraints. So the other major theme which underlay digital switchover was managing the regime of financial regulation.

Existing analogue terrestrial broadcasters normally had to pay a charge for their licence to use scarce spectrum and such charges were set by public policy. Should the charge be reduced during the transition to digital TV on the basis that the value of the analogue spectrum to the broadcasters was diminishing – and would be negligible on the eve of analogue switch-off? Should there be a charge for a digital replacement licence? If so, should it be smaller, to reflect increased competition in the multi-channel, all-digital environment? Other regulatory policies could also have a bearing on revenue, for example, the ground rules for allowing a company to use its analogue channel to advertise its additional digital channel(s).

In the UK a fundamental issue was the extent to which the licence fee should be increased specifically to cope with additional expenditure related to digital switchover. This in turn required a political judgment about how far the funding of digital switchover should be left to the private sector and what role should be assigned to BBC public service broadcasting. Public subsidies were another policy option, used in some countries to help launch digital television, and in the UK and elsewhere to soften the compulsory cost for certain groups of viewers as analogue switch-off neared.

Public policy and the market were thus deeply intertwined. The setting for the story of digital switchover is not the purist market model of a mixed economy, in which the Government role is limited to setting the legal and regulatory framework for commercial activity and funding the provision of a limited number of public services. It is much more complex and potentially contentious.

The 'do nothing' alternative

Was the decision to pursue digital switchover in the first place inevitable and was there a democratic alternative? Certainly in the UK the political options were set out for any interested citizens to find. Public consultation documents, from the Government and from regulators, were published on almost every aspect – from the ground rules for launching digital television at the outset through to detailed technical issues such as how much spectrum to save and how many digital transmitters should be planned. Consumer groups were briefed and consulted and the terms on which, for example, selected groups might qualify for some form of publicly financed assistance at switchover were rehearsed in public ahead of political decisions. The interested parties – most obviously the broadcasters and the receiver industry but a wider group of stakeholders as well – followed the evolving plot closely and had ample opportunity to contribute their views.

Yet, because the policy evolved over time through the interplay of public policy-makers and the market in changing circumstances, the full picture was not easy to grasp. Much of the debate sparked by consultations was about the detail of how and under what conditions to proceed, rather than on the more fundamental question of 'Should we be doing this at all?'

In any project, including digital switchover, there is a 'do nothing' option. In this case it was simply to leave the development of digital television to the market and keep the politicians out of it. Under this scenario, clearly some regulatory framework would be required but this could be constructed in response to market-driven activity – with no public policy goal, no special access to spectrum for incumbent analogue terrestrial broadcasters, no special action on broadcaster funding, no discussion of the possibility of publicly assisting certain groups of viewers and, above all, no compulsion to switch.

Under this option, if there was a commercial market for digital terrestrial television under a regime of spectrum pricing, it would develop, but if it never happened, or if it misfired and failed, so be it – at least no public money would have been spent. Analogue terrestrial television reception would probably shrink and be largely replaced by digital satellite and cable, increasingly supplemented by broadband, but why not? Why should politicians meddle with, or attempt to manipulate, the platform configuration the converged communications market might produce in the future.

The 'do nothing' option had one articulate advocate from the start – David Elstein, Head of Programmes at BSkyB and, subsequently, from 1996 to 2000, chief executive of Channel Five. His view, as expressed in 2002, was that digital terrestrial television 'would not exist at all in the UK but for political intervention', that it could be viewed as 'a political project designed to protect public service broadcasting', and that it was at best 'an intermediate technology'. He judged the switching off of analogue terrestrial transmission to be hugely expensive, low on benefits and likely to take a very long time, if, indeed, it could be achieved.[5]

The 'do nothing' alternative is normally the benchmark against which any development proposal should be evaluated. In this case, as the digital switchover policy gathered momentum in the UK and in other advanced industrialized nations, and the prospects for saving spectrum and incorporating public policy objectives into the digital broadcasting pattern became real, the appeal of the 'do nothing' option diminished over time. However, at the outset – in the mid-1990s when the whole subject of digital television was completely new and the feasibility of the switchover goal very uncertain – this approach was a serious alternative.

It is back in this period that, in the next chapter, the saga of the UK's public policy collaboration with the market starts.

Chapter Two

Who Wants Digital Terrestrial Television?

In the mid-1990s digital television jumped onto the policy agenda of ministers, civil servants and broadcasting industry managers in the UK. The focus was on digital terrestrial television. It was relatively easy to predict that digital television had a promising future. The more difficult question was whether digital terrestrial technology had a viable role within it. The technical and financial risks were high and investment seemed to involve hybrid political-commercial decisions. I led the BBC's feasibility study on the subject.

Runt of the family

Digital terrestrial, at the time, was very much the runt of the digital television family. Digital cable and digital satellite were its elder siblings, already establishing themselves in the market. Digital terrestrial television, after an initial technology breakthrough in the United States, was still being invented. Its inferior status was not just a matter of age, though; digital terrestrial technology seemed to have far less potential.

Digital cable had the greatest technological sophistication, with its ability to be used for two-way interactive services such as video-on-demand. Cable could also carry Internet and telephony, as well as broadcasting, services.

Digital satellite had enormous breadth – plenty of capacity for carrying lots of channels and easy, economic coverage of large areas. It was pioneered in the United States for feature film subscription services. It had enough capacity to stagger several start times for each film, so that it could offer 'near-video-on-demand' on a pay-per-view basis. It was a rival not only to cable but also to the video shop. The shop might have a few bare shelves on weekend nights: digital satellite had no constraint on the number of people who could watch the same film at the same time.

Digital terrestrial transmission had far less capacity than digital satellite and cable and very limited scope for interactivity. However, it could work with the existing rooftop, and even set-top, aerials which nearly all households already had for analogue television. So it was potentially of appeal to consumers who did not wish to have a dish or a cable installed and simply wanted a fuller choice of what they regarded as normal television.

Its main political interest was as a more efficient substitute for the near-universal analogue terrestrial television. In doing their homework and assessing its prospects, policy-makers not only needed to know the characteristics of the different types of digital television platforms, they also had to grasp the rudiments of the terrestrial television transmission system.

The band of spectrum used for broadcasting terrestrial television in the UK is divided into 46 frequency channels, each with a number between 21 and 68 (channels 36 and 38 are excluded). In analogue television one frequency channel carries one television service channel (e.g. BBC One) at one transmitter – so, at each transmitter, five different frequency channels are required to broadcast five analogue services. To avoid interference, they should not be immediately adjacent to one another nor too close to the frequency channels used by neighbouring transmitters.

To cover the whole UK, over 1100 analogue transmitters are used, each with a different set of frequency channels, chosen carefully to avoid interference with one another and interference with those used by nearby transmitters (including some transmitters in France, Belgium and Ireland). Spectrum planning for broadcasting is therefore a complex art.

Using digital terrestrial technology, one frequency channel could accommodate at least three programme channels equivalent to BBC One (subsequent technical progress increased this to at least four). Digital services are more rugged than analogue, so using adjacent frequency channels would be much less of a problem and they could be transmitted effectively at lower power. Covering the country digitally would therefore require far fewer frequency channels than the total used for analogue television. Thus, a full network of digital terrestrial television could provide several times as many services using substantially less spectrum.

If the digital broadcasts included digital versions of BBC One, BBC Two, ITV, Channel 4 and Channel Five, then, once the public had acquired digital receivers, the analogue services could be switched off and the spectrum saved could be used for other purposes. The 'killer' argument in favour was: why would anyone ever contemplate replacing the analogue transmitter networks, as they aged, on a like-for-like basis when digital terrestrial transmission could be so much more efficient in spectrum usage?

The snag in the UK was that digital terrestrial television could only perform consistently well once analogue terrestrial was discontinued and there were no analogue constraints on digital frequency configurations and transmission power. The total spectrum band available for terrestrial television already accommodated a UK-wide system of analogue television; it could accommodate a UK-wide system of digital television *instead* far more efficiently; but accommodating *both* side-by-side was a different matter.

In the short term, digital terrestrial transmissions would have to be squeezed into the spectrum in gaps between the analogue frequency channels and kept on excessively low power to avoid interference with analogue. This would limit total digital coverage and some digital frequency channels would have better coverage than others.

These spectrum planning considerations militated in favour of introducing digital terrestrial *instead of* analogue terrestrial television, because of the spectrum efficiency gain – and against designing a system in which digital terrestrial and analogue terrestrial would coexist on a continuing basis (in the way that AM and FM radio coexist, for example), since, under this scenario, digital terrestrial would forever technically underperform.

Looked at from a commercial investment perspective, digital cable and satellite could work as consumer-based business propositions regardless of the future of analogue terrestrial television. Digital terrestrial television, on the other hand, might not be commercially viable, other than perhaps for limited low-cost purposes, if the analogue system was to remain permanently in place. So the prospects for the runt of the digital family were linked from the outset to the public policy goal of switching off analogue television.

Industrial policy context

On a broader, international level industrial policy was an important driver for digital television – cable, satellite and terrestrial – for reasons which went wider than spectrum efficiency.

In the United States the consumer electronics industry was fighting a rearguard action against the Asian invasion of its domestic market for TV sets. Back in 1964 American companies had accounted for 94 per cent of the US colour TV market; for 1987 the figure was 16 per cent. Although the French purchase of the major American manufacturer provided part of the explanation for such a dramatic fall, Japanese companies' share had risen to 34 per cent.[1] By the 1990s this had become a political issue.

Most American consumers already had some form of multi-channel television, so increasing the number of TV channels was a lower priority than improving technical quality, particularly as the prevailing analogue transmission system in the United States offered relatively poor picture quality. The future of television sets in the US market was perceived to lie with high definition (HDTV) – offering 'cinema quality in the home'. In the 1980s the Japanese national public service broadcaster, NHK, in conjunction with Japanese manufacturers, had developed an analogue version of HDTV, termed Hi-Vision. Japan wanted to establish Hi-Vision as a global market for its consumer electronics exports. For the United States this was seen as an industrial threat.

American electronics manufacturers, R&D companies and government policy-makers therefore saw the development of digital HDTV – to a US technical specification – as a way of retrieving the initiative. As Hernan Galperin characterized it,

> The Japanese efforts in the late 1980s to gain worldwide adoption of the NHK system set off an international arms race to develop HDTV.[2]

The European perspective was different. Japanese competition was a concern for the two major European TV manufacturers – Philips, in the Netherlands, and Thomson, in France. However, the European consumer electronics industry was licking its wounds after a commercially disastrous attempt to introduce a new set of European analogue technical standards, known as MAC (multiplexed analogue components), designed for both high and standard definition analogue satellite transmissions.

The lesson European companies drew from this was that technical standards for the future had to be more firmly based on consumer demand and consumers in Europe were not at that time asking for HDTV. However, with a history of national public service broadcasting, many European countries still had a relatively small number of TV channels. There was a market in Europe for an expansion of multi-channel television which digital television – cable, satellite and, perhaps, terrestrial – could potentially meet.

The UK no longer had British-owned TV set manufacturers. The companies operating in the UK market were mainly European, Japanese, or other Asian. Some had factories in the UK, especially in South Wales, but, with cheaper labour, Eastern Europe, Turkey and Asia were steadily taking over mass production. However, the production of high-tech components, the development of software and the production of set-top boxes were activities in which digital television could bring economic advantage to the UK. The UK's strengths were technology know-how and R&D skills. Moreover, the UK had a worldwide reputation for the quality of its television programme content. For these reasons, keeping abreast of a new generation of broadcasting technology was important for 'UK plc'.

While these broad industrial policy factors generated an interest in digital television in general, they did not point specifically to digital terrestrial television. Here the spectrum efficiency consideration was critical. Spectrum management was at that time the responsibility of the Radiocommunications Agency, under the Department of Trade and Industry, and spectrum was increasingly seen as a scarce and valuable public resource.

Broadcasting's own requirements for spectrum were expanding, with the arrival of new TV channels and radio stations and ever more ambitious 'live' feeds into programmes. Transportation users, from the civil aviation industry to taxi companies, generated growing demand. Military needs continued. Growth in mobile telephony was dramatic, with 1.9 million subscribers in 1994 rising to 3.5 million in 1995.[3] Reinforcing the perception of spectrum as a vital resource for the future lay a budding political interest in the Internet and the infrastructure of a new Information Society, associated with the convergence of the telecommunications, computer and television technologies.

During the twentieth century the UK had ceased to be the world's leading economy. Its traditional Industrial Revolution industries of coal and steel had declined; so, too, had its engineering-based manufacturing of ships, cars and even TV and radio receivers. But British broadcasting was still world class and digital television could build on this strength. The first country in the world to switch off analogue terrestrial television might seize the lead in digital technology for the new Information Society of the twenty-first century. UK companies in this sector would be able to flourish in export markets on the strength of the UK's advanced home market. A new national ambition was in the making.

Broadcasting policy context

The industrial policy push towards digital terrestrial television had a good fit with broadcasting policy. The long-term structural change which the Government was managing in the UK's broadcasting system was in the direction of greater pluralism and increased competition.

British broadcasting had started with a BBC monopoly but, from the perspective of the mid-1990s, that was history. The policy commitment to a strong BBC public service remained but it was widely accepted that the arrival of competition had been good for the BBC. Further television competition for the BBC, ITV and Channel 4 was about to arrive in the form of Channel Five. Because of spectrum constraints, its UK coverage would be incomplete. So it was easy to see that Channel Five would be the UK's last terrestrial TV channel on analogue. Future expansion would have to be on digital.

In broadcasting funding, again, the trend was towards competition. The 1970s philosophy of encouraging competition for audiences but not for funding now seemed slightly quaint. With Channel 4 selling its own advertising independently and with the creation of Channel Five, ITV's monopoly in the sale of terrestrial television advertising came to an end. The BBC licence fee remained intact but, while the 1986 report of the Peacock Committee recommended against advertising on the BBC, its long-term vision included funding the BBC largely by subscription.[4] Neither the Government nor the BBC accepted this for the BBC's main public service channels, but the idea of extra BBC subscription services providing supplementary revenue was part of the dialogue about the BBC's post-1996 new Charter. Digital television, with conditional access, could clearly have a role here.

Subscription funding at the time was almost entirely limited to analogue satellite and cable multi-channel television, in which the dominant player was BSkyB. Digital television offered a policy opportunity to introduce pluralism and competition here too. BSkyB's dominance of the analogue satellite market would give it a huge advantage in the field of digital satellite. The cable companies already depended on BSkyB for much of their programming and this could well continue as digital cable developed. However, digital terrestrial television could bring a new pay TV operator who might challenge BSkyB and prevent digital television becoming a BSkyB monopoly. This was not just an abstract Government or regulatory idea – it engaged BBC and ITV strategists as well.

After a very tough start during the 1980s, Rupert Murdoch's UK company BSkyB had become a powerful new player in UK television, with a management led by Sam Chisholm, whose ambition, drive and ruthless competitiveness had become legendary. The terrestrial broadcasters – the British broadcasting 'establishment' as Murdoch saw them – viewed Sky with a mixture of awe and fear. They had been humiliated by Sky in the analogue satellite market and they now saw a risk that Sky digital satellite could completely dominate the emerging technology of digital television and the potentially huge pay TV market.

This theme is so important that it is worth recounting the early history of satellite television in the UK and the traumatic commercial crisis which led to the creation of BSkyB. These events alone do not explain why the UK went into digital terrestrial television – as discussed above, spectrum management policy played an important part. However, they do explain why the UK went into digital terrestrial television *in a hurry*.

Revenge of the terrestrials?

Back in 1980 the BBC had expected to be the nation's first and foremost satellite broadcaster. The UK had been allocated spectrum for five channels of direct-to-home analogue satellite broadcasting. The BBC swiftly applied for two. Satellite was clearly a key distribution method for the future, offering new programme opportunities and, added Director-General Alasdair Milne, some additional money:

> not a lot, nothing that could come near replacing the licence fee, but additional money that might help to reduce the necessary increments in the licence fee which seemed to be a growing political worry. This satellite operation would, we were clear, be quite independent of the licence fee. It would be an additional service, paid for either by regular subscription or on a 'pay-per-view' basis.[5]

In 1982 the Government gave approval for two new BBC satellite channels to be launched on a British-made satellite by 1986, with no Government funding. The technical standard was to be the new European MAC, firmly backed by the European Commission, who hoped that it would supersede the PAL system operated for analogue terrestrial broadcasting by the UK and most of Europe and the SECAM system used by the French.

However, no arrangements for manufacturing receivers could be agreed. The commercial sector would not risk producing them and the Government would not underwrite them. The BBC decided that, on that basis, its own financial risk would be too great. An attempt then to enter the satellite market with a broader coalition, including ITV and others, known as 'The Club of 21', also foundered.

So in 1985, before any British satellite had been launched, the BBC and most of the ITV companies pulled out – retreating back to the familiar and more comfortable analogue terrestrial business. Alasdair Milne acknowledged:

> It was one of the chief failures in my time as Director General of the BBC.[6]

The commercial broadcasting regulator, the Independent Broadcasting Authority (IBA), then advertised a UK satellite franchise to commercial bidders. The strongest bid came from a new consortium, called British Satellite Broadcasting (BSB), whose principal members were Pearson (publishers of the *Financial Times*), Virgin and Granada, one of the major ITV companies. In 1986, BSB defeated a rival bid spearheaded by Carlton and won the franchise. BSB would use a high-powered satellite capable of being received on small square aerials – the 'squarial', as it was known – and the new MAC technical standard as required by the IBA. The services would be encrypted and marketed on a subscription basis. BSB aimed to launch in 1989 and it expected to have a monopoly of the brand new UK satellite TV market.

In 1988 Rupert Murdoch announced that Sky Television, at that time running a small operation in Europe, would launch a rival satellite service in the UK. It would use a Luxembourg-based Astra satellite outside the IBA's technical remit; it would stick with the well-tried PAL technology; and its channels would initially be free, relying on advertising, with subscription to follow later. Murdoch's aim was to 'keep it simple' and be first-to-market.

In 1989 Sky launched four channels and, frustrated by lack of retail support, took direct control of the marketing, sale and installation of receivers and dish aerials. Costs were kept low. Programme quality was judged by many to be thin – though in Rupert Murdoch's view:

> Much of what passes for quality in British television is no more than a reflection of the values of the narrow elite which controls it and has always thought that its tastes were synonymous with quality.[7]

Even so, after the start-up investment, the bidding war with BSB for Hollywood film rights and the marketing investment, Sky went deep into the red. In 1990, with the station losing about £3 million a week, New Zealander Sam Chisholm, who had built a 'tough guy' reputation in Australian television, arrived as chief executive at Sky's low-cost premises at Osterley in west London and announced:

> You bastards are draining the group's reserves. This can't bloody well go on. This bloody operation has got to come under control.[8]

Meanwhile, BSB, led by Anthony Simonds-Gooding, was spending on a much greater scale. Based first in Knightsbridge, then in the palatial Marco Polo House in Battersea, BSB topped up its capital with new loans and invested heavily in films, programming and marketing. It then discovered that the MAC receiver microchip, technically the key to reception, was still in development – no working version existed, or could exist in time for a 1989 launch. The 'squarials' also had technical teething problems. So BSB did not launch until 1990. Arriving second as a more expensive buy, BSB then subsidized consumer take-up. Its losses in 1990 ran at about £8 million a week.[9]

The *dénouement* followed swiftly. Without telling either Anthony Simonds-Gooding or the IBA, BSB agreed merger terms with Sky which were tantamount to a Sky takeover. The new company, BSkyB, would be headed by Sam Chisholm, based at Osterley, and would use the Astra satellite and PAL technology. The BSB equipment, including MAC receivers in which major manufacturers had invested substantially, would be withdrawn. The UK's satellite slot and the BSB satellite were no longer required.

Recounting the history in 1991, authors Chippindale and Franks judged the UK's satellite venture

> one of the greatest commercial disasters in British history and certainly the greatest in the history of the British media.[10]

For a while the newly merged company continued to make losses but, now that it had a monopoly satellite subscription service, the turnround could start. BSkyB (or 'Sky' as it remained in common currency) built a customer base towards the tabloid end of the market. Then, in 1992, it bought the rights to live coverage of Premier League football – in alliance with the BBC, who could use the Highlights, outmanoeuvring and outbidding an ITV Sport team led by London Weekend Television's Greg Dyke. This deal laid the foundations of BSkyB's financial fortune.

By the mid-1990s, when digital TV technology arrived, BSkyB was a powerful force in British broadcasting, an outsider with the financial strength and business acumen to do a lot more competitive damage to the British establishment.

The appeal in the United States of the digital satellite pay TV service Direct TV, based primarily on movies, was closely watched by UK broadcasters. BSkyB saw in it a possible model for a Sky digital satellite TV in the UK – and was interested. The BBC, ITV and Channel 4 saw in it a possible model for a Sky digital satellite TV in the UK – and were alarmed. Were they to leave BSkyB to develop multi-channel subscription television unchallenged? Or did digital terrestrial technology offer them an opportunity for a return match in which they might play on their own, more familiar ground?

It is easy to portray the instinct to challenge BSkyB as part of a wider anti-Murdoch sub-culture, with roots in the history of takeover and union confrontation in the newspaper industry. Looking back on the early history of satellite, Rupert Murdoch recalled:

> When we started Sky, everybody in Britain was against us. The whole of the media was against us. The British establishment was against us, and remains hysterically against us.[11]

However, amongst the main terrestrial broadcasters, attitudes were more commercially hard-nosed. None of the main terrestrial broadcasters wished to see digital television become a *de facto* BSkyB monopoly in the way that analogue satellite now was. Equally, none of them was spoiling for a head- to-head competitive fight with the risk of emulating the sad history of BSB and the 'squarial'. The BBC had already allied tactically with BSkyB over football negotiations, and Granada, a shareholder in the merged BSB-Sky company, was on good business terms with BSkyB management. The terrestrial broadcasters did not approach digital television on the basis of emotional hostility to Sky.

They were, however, concerned not to be competitively disadvantaged by allowing BSkyB several years' head start in the digital TV market. They assumed BSkyB could launch a digital satellite service at almost any time – the technology was proven and BSkyB had the necessary financial resources. If the analogue terrestrial broadcasters were going to launch digital terrestrial television to preempt a *de facto* BSkyB monopoly, they (and for me, this soon became 'we') would need to move swiftly.

Getting into 'start' position

We were not starting cold. I had first heard of the USA's digital terrestrial television in 1991 when I was leading a BBC Task Force on technical innovation, part of the BBC's preparation for renewing its Charter. We recommended switching BBC R&D effort into digital transmission. ITV had also grasped the importance of the subject. Barry Cox of London Weekend Television and his ITV colleagues took a close interest in United States developments and their relevance to the UK.

The Independent Television Commission (ITC), successor to the television arm of the IBA, commissioned the newly privatized transmission company NTL to conduct a digital terrestrial television research project. This work, spearheaded by Gary Tonge of the ITC, showed how new digitally transmitted terrestrial channels could be woven into the existing analogue spectrum, in between the analogue channels but at much lower power.

A seminal ITC discussion paper, published in June 1993, outlined a range of implementation strategies and scenarios, including the option of simulcasting (duplicating) the analogue channels on digital until such time as the analogue could be discontinued. Simulcasting alone, the ITC recognized, would not drive digital take-up, so additional options should be considered including widescreen picture format and new digital-only services.

Reflecting the budding interest of the UK's terrestrial broadcasters, the ITC pressed for political decisions and action. It firmly rejected the alternative, the *status quo* model:

> Under this model there would be no digital terrestrial television developments at all, and all digital advances would take place only on satellite or cable. There would be no promise of greater spectrum efficiency in the long-term future (unless terrestrial services were to slowly 'wither on the vine'). Although this might provide a simpler and less disruptive outlook for viewers who remained content to receive only the existing terrestrial services, a strategy of this kind would be seen by many as defeatist and unacceptable.[12]

At the Royal Television Society and in other industry gatherings, David Elstein, then Head of Programmes at BSkyB, tended to champion the 'do nothing' terrestrial option. Why did we need digital terrestrial at all if digital satellite and cable had so much more potential? If analogue terrestrial had no long-term future, then why not just let it wither naturally as satellite and cable developed? I argued that there would have been similar arguments about whether trains would still be needed in the 1920s and 30s, when the steam train was being challenged by the arrival of cars and airplanes. But modern diesel and electric trains turned out to have a complementary role alongside air and road travel – similarly, modern terrestrial transmission would have a continuing future in television distribution.

Behind the strategy debates in the UK and in other countries, technical standardization work proceeded at European level, in parallel with the formulation of a different set of technical standards in the USA.

Under the technical leadership of a German academic, Professor Ulrich Reimers, whose chairmanship of meetings of diverse interested parties was brilliant, the European broadcasters, manufacturers, regulators and governments hammered out standards within the framework of the Digital Video Broadcasting (DVB) project. This process encompassed standard-setting for satellite (DVB-S) and cable (DVB-C) as well as digital terrestrial (DVB-T). Learning the lessons from the disastrous MAC analogue standard, the DVB was adamant that the proposals it made for endorsement by the official European standardization bodies should be *commercially viable* – over-priced technical perfectionism would not be acceptable.

The European standardization process ran into one argument, reflecting a difference of view within the UK. The ITC, NTL and ITV proposed interleaving new digital channels between the analogue ones, using different frequencies for different parts of the country as for analogue transmission. BBC R&D, however, at that time argued for a technically more efficient method, originally developed for digital audio broadcasting, called a 'single frequency network', which used the same frequency throughout the UK. BBC management was attracted to this and had its eye on a vacant frequency, channel 35, which might otherwise go to Channel Five.

Single frequency network broadcasting would deliver a uniform programme service throughout the UK and was thus unsuitable for ITV's regionally varied structure. Moreover, a chip with the capability of handling single frequency networks would be more complex and would therefore take longer to bring to market. In the end the DVB allowed for both the simple chips adequate for interleaved frequencies, based on 2000 carriers (in shorthand, called '2k') and those with the ability to handle single frequency networks, requiring 8000 carriers ('8k'). Significantly, technical standard-setting in Europe was no longer based on striving after the best technical solution. The DVB approach here was that the market could choose.

Against this background, in July 1994, the Conservative Government announced a plan for twelve UK digital terrestrial television services. Four of these could be broadcast as a single frequency network, using frequency channel 35, and another eight would be constructed on an interleaved basis. The existing analogue channels would be simulcast and, if a sufficient number of viewers switched to digital, then it might be possible, after a transitional period of perhaps fifteen years, to switch off and re-use the analogue frequencies.[13]

The BBC's senior engineer, Phil Laven, convinced Patricia Hodgson, the BBC's Director of Policy & Planning, and John Birt, the director-general, that the BBC should be a prime mover in UK digital terrestrial television. They boldly told the Government that, subject to a feasibility study, the BBC would begin experimental digital terrestrial television in 1995 with the aim of launching services in 1997. No one knew for sure when BSkyB would launch a UK digital satellite service, but the BBC was not going to sit back and wait. I was put in charge of the feasibility study and I set up the BBC Digital Broadcasting Project to carry it out.

Like the ITC, the BBC favoured broadcasting digital versions of the analogue services (digital simulcasts), so that the latter could ultimately be withdrawn, as well as introducing new services, such as a 24 Hour News channel. The digital simulcasts offered the opportunity to switch the BBC's television services to widescreen. The task we faced in our BBC Digital Broadcasting Project was to assess whether this development would work – or whether UK digital terrestrial television risked failing and becoming another 'BBC satellite' or, worse still, another BSB.

The technical model the BBC had in mind at that time was a single frequency network, using frequency channel 35. It became clear to me that this approach would not work – for three reasons.

First, a single frequency network, broadcasting a uniform service across the whole UK, had no technical advantage over satellite. Moreover, not only was the ITV network regionally structured, but so was BBC One which, for important parts of the day, broadcast different output to different parts of the UK. Channel 4's advertising was also regionally varied. So the whole idea of using a single frequency to simulcast the main analogue services was flawed.

Second, channel 35 was widely used as a frequency for video recorders and anyone awarded the use of it would have to incur a sizeable bill for re-tuning them. We subsequently undertook practical work to confirm this, scoping the task and its cost by carrying out a trial at a small relay transmitter in Wales. (Channel Five later acquired both frequency channel 35 and the re-tuning cost).

Third, as the BBC's experience in digital audio was clearly demonstrating at that time, the receiver industry would not manufacture receivers for BBC services alone, especially if much of the content was simply a copy of analogue. Lack of receiver investment had helped render the BBC's satellite venture abortive. The BBC would not wish to enter the receiver market itself. The commercial TV manufacturing and retail industry would only take the risk of investing in receivers itself for a much richer service offering. The BBC, in my judgment, would get nowhere by quarrelling over technical standards with the ITC, NTL, ITV and Channel 4.

We could have left it there, warning the BBC off making an expensive mistake – and leaving the digital television field to satellite and cable. However, although I thought that the BBC was looking at the wrong technical model, it did not follow that digital terrestrial television as such would not work. On the contrary, our project team's work convinced me that developing digital terrestrial TV in the UK was feasible, provided:

- we made use of the technology's ability to provide regionally varied output, using the interleaved frequency planning approach favoured by commercial television;
- we persuaded ITV and others to join in;
- there were enough new services to support a market for digital receivers;
- widescreen simulcasts of the main analogue services drove a market for new widescreen digital TV sets.

After extensive consultation and debate, our project team endorsed the feasibility of the development in a broadly supportive report, including an outline Critical Path, which I knew the BBC would pass on, with prudent caveats, to the Government. We did not try to deal with all the issues immediately but recommended a step-by-step approach both to completing the technical investigation and to sounding out other broadcasters and receiver manufacturers. The central message was that, as a programme service provider, the BBC should be willing to act as a catalyst for a technically and commercially successful launch of digital terrestrial TV in the UK (with various provisos about technical feasibility, value for money, receiver manufacturer undertakings and relevant evidence of public support).

Having visualized the opportunity the BBC had here both for widescreen and for new channels, I wanted to demonstrate the technology – to show it in action technically, in line with the BBC's offer of providing an experimental service in 1995. By showing real digital television to senior executives and politicians who had never seen it, we could build enthusiasm and commitment, internally and externally.

With a joint effort between BBC R&D, the BBC's transmission department and some French colleagues, we mounted an experimental demonstration in spring 1995. With the French colleagues and a whole battery of equipment hidden 'behind the arras' in a next-door room, we assembled some widescreen TV sets in the BBC's White City building and gave a convincing series of illustrated talks on the technology's potential to BBC, industry and government audiences. Separately NTL organized its own demonstration.

The main BBC work was led by Bob Ely and Martin Bell. Phil Laven, his colleague Henry Price and I gave the presentations. We were under strict instructions on no account to give any public impression that the extra channels we illustrated would be BBC channels – but we all knew that we were looking at the prospect of multi-channel BBC TV. However, the star feature of the show was Phil Laven's live demonstration of digital set-top aerial reception.

In mounting these demonstrations and, in effect, selling digital terrestrial TV technology, we had answered 'Yes' to the question 'Would it work?', knowing that, if it subsequently transpired that the verdict should have been 'No', a great deal of investment would turn out to have been wasted. I was to live with the responsibility for that answer for the rest of my working life.

The BBC was too canny to put all its eggs in the digital terrestrial basket and, in line with advice which a young McKinsey consultant called Michael Ross had given me almost at the outset, we advocated broadcasting the BBC's digital services on satellite and cable, as well as on digital terrestrial television. Patricia Hodgson's Policy & Planning team made sure, during the course of our feasibility study, that we paid full attention to the potential of these other platforms. This was not just prudence: until such time as analogue terrestrial could be discontinued, digital terrestrial, on its own, could not achieve universal coverage and would need to be complemented by other forms of digital distribution.

The proposed regulatory framework

In August 1995 Virginia Bottomley, Secretary of State at the Department of National Heritage in John Major's Conservative Government, published proposals for launching digital terrestrial broadcasting in the UK – television and radio – and invited comments. The Government's aims for television were to

- ensure that viewers could choose from a wide variety of terrestrial television channels;
- give existing national broadcasters the opportunity to develop digital services and safeguard public service broadcasting into the digital age;
- give terrestrial broadcasters the opportunity to compete with those on satellite and cable;
- help a fair and effective market to develop;
- help UK manufacturers and producers to compete at home and overseas;
- make best use of the available spectrum.[14]

On the issue of switchover, the Government added:

In the long term the Government wishes to do all it can to release spectrum by switching off existing analogue transmission signals, should digital broadcasting be successful enough to allow it.[15]

It now appeared that eighteen or more digital terrestrial TV channels would be possible. The ITC had done further planning work, leaving the BBC idea for using channel 35 as a single frequency network out of the equation. It had found six frequencies which, on an interleaved basis, could have

potential coverage in the medium term ranging from 60–70% to over 90% of the UK population. Each frequency channel will be able to carry at least three television channels.[16]

These six frequency channels, each capable of carrying at least three digital TV services in the spectrum normally required for one analogue service, were termed 'multiplexes'. Technically the different services within any one frequency channel needed to be 'multiplexed' into a single digital signal as part of the coding and compression process before transmission.

The Government proposed that the ITC hold a competition to award licences to organizations willing to bid for the right to manage a multiplex. Selection would be on the basis of:

- investment in the transmission infrastructure;
- investment in promotion, including encouraging the take-up of receivers;
- the variety of programme services to be transmitted.

Significantly, there was no proposal to charge for spectrum. The Government was more interested in practical results than in revenue.

Broadcasters would only be licensed to provide programme services if they had a contract with a multiplex provider. Thus the broadcasters were not, at this point, pictured as being the multiplex providers themselves. However, guaranteed places would be offered for BBC One, BBC Two, Channel 3 (ITV), Channel 4, S4C (the Welsh-language service in Wales) and Channel Five

> to maintain public service broadcasting and ultimately to allow analogue signals to be switched off.[17]

Switchover was thus built into the design, by a Conservative Government, from the start.

If the BBC decided to take up its guaranteed slots, its existing services would be carried on the multiplex with the widest coverage. The Government, having already privatized the transmission arm of the old IBA, was considering privatizing the BBC's transmission department in the context of its post-1996 Charter. There was an assumption that the BBC might seek a contract with a multiplex provider company focused on transmission infrastructure and willing to invest in promoting the take-up of new digital receivers. The private sector would be expected to carry the main investment risks.

Subscription funding was assumed to be fundamental to the business of launching new channels and multiplex providers could offer conditional access (encryption and decryption) and subscription management services. Encouraging the take-up of receivers – one of the selection criteria for multiplex providers – was widely interpreted as code for subsidizing receivers for subscribers.

The industry was given a couple of months to comment on the Government's proposed structure, after which the key provisions would be incorporated in a new Broadcasting Bill. To help stimulate enthusiasm, Virginia Bottomley hosted 'a sumptuous dinner at Hampton Court for all the moguls' of the broadcasting world.[18]

The BBC's strategy

The BBC welcomed the opportunity to shift to widescreen and to introduce new digital TV services – it had ideas for 'spin-off' material from BBC One and BBC Two and was particularly keen to launch its own 24-hour News service. I suggested that the BBC bid for the whole of the best multiplex, aiming to manage the multiplexing operation ourselves – and we did. The risks of adopting an untried technology with limited capacity were weighed. John Birt, the director-general, judged that, while cable and satellite would appeal to viewers who particularly valued breadth of choice, DTT 'might appeal to conservative viewers' and could be 'an important counterweight to Murdoch', diminishing the dominance which BSkyB's digital satellite system would otherwise have.[19]

The BBC was also interested in using its commercial arm, BBC Worldwide, to market BBC archive-based subscription channels, with a joint venture partner to put up the risk capital. The Deputy Director-General Bob Phillis, who was in charge of BBC Worldwide, led the negotiations here. After exploring the alternative of a deal with BSkyB, BBC Worldwide entered into partnership with the cable channel company Flextech to form the UKTV joint venture. UKTV would use BBC content for its services but, to distinguish them clearly from the BBC's core public services, these pay TV channels would not be BBC-branded.

The BBC proposed to broadcast both its public service and its UKTV channels on all three digital platforms – terrestrial, satellite and cable. The cable companies had an obligation to carry the BBC's public services and would be pleased to offer their subscribers the UKTV channels. The BBC's big issue, therefore, was how to get its digital services onto satellite in a way which was compatible with Sky receivers but did not make the BBC part of BSkyB.

At the end of a conference session at which he had been speaking in London, I approached Romain Bausch, the director-general of Astra, and suggested that we talk. He was keen. Early one morning in April 1996 a BBC Worldwide colleague and I flew to Luxembourg and returned that evening with the offer of two transponders' worth of capacity – enough for our known plans at the time – on the new Astra satellite which BSkyB would be using for the UK. Astra wisely put a deadline of the end of July for acceptance, which focussed the BBC on a decision, and I then led the team which negotiated our contract. After the sad history of the BBC's first venture into satellite, this was, in its way, an historic moment, though tricky negotiations with BSkyB still lay ahead to achieve full compatibility with BSkyB-specified and subsidized receivers.

Meanwhile our Digital Broadcasting Project team set out to undertake the first real digital terrestrial broadcast using the newly agreed DVB European standard – this time without the French engineers 'behind the arras'. We aimed to demonstrate the programme-transmission-reception chain in full working order, while the Government was setting the regulatory framework, in order to give the whole technology commercial credibility ahead of the point at which the existing analogue broadcasters would need to commit to taking up their guaranteed digital spectrum.

It was a stressful task. The DVB technical standard for digital terrestrial television had been the subject of so many revisions and adjustments that no one had actually made the final version work. My nightmare was that, having said the technology would work and having encouraged everyone else in the business to share this judgment, I would discover some unexpected technical flaw. Much to my relief and theirs, the R&D team cracked the final technical problems by May. That made it possible for Bob Ely and Martin Bell and a team of production, technical and transmission colleagues to mount the landmark *Trooping the Colour* broadcast on 15th June 1996.

The Government awarded the BBC the whole of the digital terrestrial multiplex with the best coverage so, by the summer of 1996, with both that and the signed Astra contract, the BBC was in a position to begin implementing its strategy.

The commercial players

The Government offer to potential multiplex organizations was of free spectrum under a licence for twelve years with an option to renew (though not necessarily without charge at that point). The politically designed regulatory framework was intended to be commercially attractive.

Nonetheless, private sector appraisals of the prospects for digital terrestrial television were mixed. With low consumer take-up of receivers inevitable at the outset, the principal revenue stream was unlikely to come from advertising. Subscription finance would almost certainly have to feature in any funding model. That would require some brave group of entrepreneurs to venture back down the road which had led the BSB satellite venture to commercial disaster.

BT, initially thought of as a possible multiplex partner for the BBC, drew back. Rupert Gavin (later to join the BBC from BT) chose instead to open discussions with BSkyB about a partnership in digital satellite. Digital satellite set-top boxes would almost certainly be connected to householders' telephone lines – with the telephone connection used for on-screen automated bookings for pay-per-view programmes. BT wanted to exploit the synergy between this new form of television and its own core business, the telephone. Once installed, a telephone connection could be used for telephone shopping for a wide range of other services, similarly driven by broadcast on-screen displays and menus. Digital satellite would have far more capacity than digital terrestrial for the broadcast component of such interactive services, and the telephone connection was likely to be integral to the satellite consumer proposition. So BT would not be a bidder for a terrestrial multiplex.

Charles Allen, then chief executive of Granada and a leading figure within ITV, had declared back in 1994:

We believe that digital terrestrial could offer the greatest potential of all.[20]

It was an opportunity for ITV to tap into subscription revenue through a transmission technology suited to the regionally structured ITV network, though, meanwhile, Granada, a minor shareholder in BSkyB, was also developing collaborative channels with Sky (Granada Sky Broadcasting). The other major ITV player, Carlton, was keen on digital terrestrial. At Virginia Bottomley's Hampton Court dinner in September 1995, by John Birt's account,

Michael Green of Carlton strutted his stuff and said he was up for it.[21]

Channel 4 also saw digital terrestrial television as an opportunity for growth, as did S4C.

Channel Five, however, as a new analogue channel, had no wish to see early competition from a host of new digital channels. Greg Dyke, then at Pearson Television and Channel Five's chairman, canvassed a scheme to fund the whole digital terrestrial television development from the projected proceeds from the sale of released spectrum once the analogue signals could be switched off. I had looked at this idea in my BBC work and concluded it was not feasible, at least at that early date. I was not sure whether Greg Dyke believed in it or whether he had simply calculated that the immediate practical effect would be to delay all the broadcasters from committing to the costs of taking up their guaranteed spectrum. I took his consultant to see the major telecommunications company which he thought would pay a very large sum of money for the released spectrum. The company quickly torpedoed such optimism, after which this initiative fizzled out.

BSkyB was publicly sceptical about digital terrestrial but privately very industrious in doing its homework on the subject.

The other enthusiasts were the terrestrial transmission companies – NTL and the BBC's transmission department, shortly to be privatized – for whom digital terrestrial would mean extra sales in the short term and the continuation of their key business of terrestrial transmission in the longer term. Receiver manufacturers and their silicon chip providers were also positive.

It was obvious to all interested parties that the technology could only work through planned collaboration – among broadcasters, between broadcasters and transmission companies, and between transmission companies, broadcasters and receiver manufacturers. We agreed, initially with BT and then with a wider group of companies, to found the industry-wide Digital TV Group, mainly to collaborate technically. I became its first chairman, with Chris Daubney of Channel 4 as vice-chairman. We held a major conference, attended by the Government Broadcasting Minister Lord Inglewood, to promote the new technology. Working with Ed Wilson of the European Broadcasting Union, we also created a forum (with the somewhat inelegant name of 'Digitag') in which UK organizations could share experiences with other European colleagues, particularly in Spain and Scandinavia where digital terrestrial was also taking seed.

By October 1996, ITV, Channel 4, S4C and Channel Five had to decide whether to take up the guaranteed spectrum the Government had enabled the ITC to offer them. While there would be no charge for the digital spectrum, there would, of course, be substantial programme development, transmission and marketing costs. All the companies, including Channel Five, said 'Yes'. Leslie Hill, chairman of the ITV Association, said that ITV

> welcomed the chance to put the UK in the forefront of the digital TV revolution.[22]

With the BBC on the first multiplex, ITV and Channel 4 shared the whole of the second, and Channel Five and S4C were guaranteed some of the space on a third. In accordance with the new 1996 Broadcasting Act, the ITC then invited competitive bids for operating this partly tenanted third multiplex and for operating the three further available multiplexes.

The responses to the opportunity to develop a wholly new digital broadcasting proposition on these three vacant multiplexes would show the market's verdict on the commercial viability of digital terrestrial television.

The DTT multiplex awards

The first task any prospective bidder would undertake would be an assessment of digital terrestrial's technical performance. Our *Trooping the Colour* digital TV broadcast in June 1996 had demonstrated the technical feasibility of the technology – but there was obviously still a long way to go to reduce receivers from refrigerator size to small set-top boxes or modules for incorporation into television sets.

Coverage too would remain an issue, especially after the ITC decided to maximize the number of services per multiplex.

The technical parameters for digital terrestrial television recommended by the BBC's R&D experts (multiplex capacity of 18 Mbits per second and 16 Quadrature Amplitude Modulation, known in shorthand as the 16 QAM mode) were set to maximize coverage and reception quality. As a public service funded by licence fee payers, the BBC naturally wanted to reach as many people in the country as possible.

However, a different formulation (24 Mbits per second and 64 QAM) would allow for a larger number of programme services, at a cost to the robustness of the signal. The drawbacks were a reduced coverage area and increased risks of interference. However, the more services broadcast, the greater the potential revenue from the sale of advertising and the more attractive the subscription package – key factors for commercial broadcasters. This was the approach the ITC adopted, with BBC senior management agreement.

The 64 QAM standard sounded commercially attractive, in that there was now scope for over 30 programme services across the six multiplexes, but, for the three fully vacant multiplexes on offer, the effective coverage to roof-top aerials, we estimated, was reduced to less than 70 per cent, less than 55 per cent and less than 45 per cent. Set-top aerial reception could not be reliably predicted.

The UK industry agreed to opt for the 2k chip, in order to make an early start, since, with interleaved frequency planning, it had no requirement for the 8k chip needed for single frequency networks. The technical experts advised that the 8k version, once it became available, would be technically superior in any event but the terrestrial broadcasters were not in a waiting mood.

Remembering the history of the 'squarial', they did not want to allow BSkyB a significant head start.

In our BBC project we had done enough market research to be confident about our proposed switch to widescreen:

> Our research shows that overall 77% of the audience prefer this format when they see purpose-made widescreen programmes displayed on a widescreen set. Widescreen is closer to the shape of the cinema, it is closer to the shape of the football or the rugby pitch, and it is closer to the shape of people's field of vision. Making the transition is difficult, but simulcasting makes it easier. It enables us to avoid the prominent letter-boxing effect on 4:3 sets which has been the inhibiting factor until now.[23]

Working with a consultant from Arthur Andersen, Jolyon Barker, we had also modelled the big commercial picture. In this we were merely shadowing the real work being done elsewhere by, for example, John Egan of Carlton and Jeremy Thorp of NTL, who were preparing competitive bids for all three of the fully vacant multiplexes. I made our analysis public in 1997:

> We modelled the economics for the whole industry: we knew it wouldn't work for the BBC if it didn't work for others. I can confidently tell you that there are very many ways of modelling a negative cashflow for DTT (digital terrestrial television). There are relatively few ways of modelling commercial success. Without giving away any trade secrets, three of the essentials are: avoiding a hardware war between rival receivers; tapping the TV set replacement market as well as the set-top box market; and offering a mix of free-to-air and pay TV services, with at least some of the pay services also carried on at least one other means of distribution.[24]

Some in the industry fondly hoped that all the digital terrestrial television pay services could be 'exclusive'. But that would mean too many pay channel providers waiting too eagerly for the first cheque signed by the first digital terrestrial TV subscriber before being able to build a customer base. This in turn would limit channel providers' investment in quality, which would limit consumer appeal. Some of the pay services would therefore have to rest on an existing cable or satellite customer base. Any commercially successful multiplex licensee would need some measure of collaboration with cable and/ or satellite. 'Platform wars' could lead swiftly to disaster. Indeed the BBC would ideally have liked to see a single set-top box design for all three platforms.[25]

The concept of tapping the TV set replacement market was linked to the assumed public policy of digital switchover. If the aim was to switch off analogue terrestrial television in the long term, there would come a point at which it would no longer make commercial sense to manufacture analogue TV sets. Digital television sets would become the norm and the annual TV set replacement market, with around 5 million sales p.a., would then act as an engine driving digital take-up. The business case therefore had links with Government policy.

Over the 1996–97 winter the commercial bids took shape. A new commercial company called SDN was formed to bid for the multiplex which included Channel Five and S4C and in due course it was awarded this licence.

The real fight was for the three fully vacant multiplexes, which could be bid for *en bloc*. Whoever secured these would dominate the digital terrestrial television platform.

A consortium called the Digital Television Network (DTN), headed by the American-based cable company Cabletel who had just bought NTL, was one of the two main contenders. In content terms, its bid was judged by many to be the more innovative, in that it exploited telephone and cable technology to offer interactive services.

Its rival was the British Digital Broadcasting consortium, BDB, with a more orthodox programme service line-up but representing a partnership of three of the best known brands in television. The first was Carlton, with Michael Green's early enthusiasm undimmed. The second was Granada, who must have needed some persuasion in that Charles Allen, initially keen, had stated rather mystifyingly in December 1996:

I would argue that DTT is dead technology.[26]

However, Granada's re-conversion was probably helped by a well-kept secret, the participation of the third partner, BSkyB.

When the bids and the bidders' names were published, BDB seemed the safer commercial choice. Digital terrestrial pay TV was much more likely to succeed commercially if BSkyB were an ally and not a head-to-head competitor. The terrestrial pay TV channels could then be presented as a *table d'hôte* alongside the much more extensive *à la carte* of BSkyB's digital satellite service.

BDB was further strengthened by a last-minute promise of support from BBC Worldwide's pay TV joint venture, UKTV. Thus the consortium brought together an alliance of the most powerful organizations in British broadcasting – Carlton, Granada, BSkyB and the BBC. Faced with a choice between competing directly with BSkyB or collaborating with it, the major terrestrial broadcasters had all opted for collaboration.

BDB's programme service proposition was therefore strong, if familiar, bringing together films from the Carlton library, sports based on BSkyB's contracts, and documentary programmes supplied by the BBC-Flextech UKTV channels. In terms of broadcasting experience and knowledge of the

British market, BDB looked a winner and was seen to reduce the commercial risks. In June 1997, after a period of public consultation, the ITC accordingly decided in favour of BDB.

There was just one snag. In a last-minute development the European competition authorities advised the ITC that BSkyB's membership of the consortium could be considered an anti-competitive arrangement because of its dominance in the field of pay television. So the ITC required BSkyB to leave BDB and become purely a programme service provider. BSkyB withdrew, with the promise of a £75 million compensation payment, and the ITC was then able to award all three multiplexes to BDB.

It was a dramatic change in the plot. The commercial relationships between BSkyB and the major terrestrial broadcasters would now be very different – as would the risks of launching digital terrestrial television, with untried technology, on a hybrid politico-commercial basis.

The stage was set for the launch of digital television in the UK.

Chapter Three

Digital = Pay TV?

The pre-launch phase of digital television in the UK had been, to a significant extent, the work of 'hands-on' politicians and civil servants. They had proposed the public policy framework, consulted upon it in draft form, and then turned it into legislation and regulation.

Now, in the aftermath of the launch, the Government stood well back. There remained the public policy goal – to switch off analogue terrestrial in the long term. However, the Government was understandably reluctant to name a target switchover timetable for the UK before digital television had even been launched. Instead, Virginia Bottomley had promised a review of the date for switching off analogue

> once 50 per cent of UK households were able to receive digital terrestrial television, or after five years of the first multiplex licence period, whichever was the sooner.[1]

At this stage, therefore, there was no public policy strategy charting a course to switchover. It would be for the market to drive sufficient consumer take-up to make the policy goal credible – and how the market did that was not for the Government to decide. The key players had now been selected and the politicians disengaged.

The multiplex licensees were not exactly as first envisaged by the Government. Essentially they were now the main analogue terrestrial broadcasters in one guise or another. Multiplex 1 was licensed to the BBC. Multiplex 2 was licensed to a company called D3&4 formed by ITV (Channel 3) and Channel 4 and with no resources other than those supplied by these two broadcasters. Multiplex A, as the third one was known, was licensed to a new, small company called SDN, based around the Welsh service S4C, United Business Media (one of the ITV companies), and the transmission company NTL and was required to provide guaranteed capacity to Channel Five and S4C. The other three multiplexes – B, C and D, as they were termed – were licensed to BDB which now consisted of the two biggest ITV companies, Carlton and Granada.

Now that BSkyB had been ejected, the BDB consortium was not exactly as envisaged either. It was now BDB's job to launch digital terrestrial television in an essentially competitive relationship with BSkyB and the cable companies. The fortunes of digital television as a whole in the UK would hinge on the relative success of, and the relationships between, these three platforms in their race to sign up potential pay TV customers.

Digital satellite

When BSkyB started work on digital satellite, it was with confidence and high ambition. Geoff Walters, BSkyB's chief technology officer, paraphrased the brief he and his team were given by Sam Chisholm as:

> Here are many millions of pounds. Go away and build a digital broadcasting system with a complexity of technology unseen anywhere else in the world and make sure it's ready by September 1997.[2]

Although BSkyB had a flourishing analogue satellite business, the company could see the limitations of analogue technology and the attractions of a digital system which offered greater capacity, lower running costs per channel, interactive services and the ability to automate pay-per-view booking and billings.

BSkyB's aim was to switch the whole of its analogue satellite customer base to digital, and recruit new subscribers, so that it could achieve the equivalent of the Government's ambition for terrestrial – the switch-off of analogue satellite. The business case rested on being able to make the analogue satellite savings without a prolonged period of duplicated analogue-digital transmissions.

A key ingredient was BSkyB's head start in conditional access technology, for encrypting and decrypting programme services. For its analogue services BSkyB had a proven proprietary system of its own, developed by a News International sister company which was well placed to provide a robust system for digital satellite.

The ground rules for the regulation of conditional access were set at European level, though their detailed application in the UK was the responsibility of the telecommunications regulatory body Oftel. The outcome of a prolonged political wrangle over common, open systems versus proprietary systems had left proprietary systems dominant in the field. While idealistic politicians and public service broadcasters had argued for open systems which did not imprison the consumer within the technology of one particular commercial company, the economics of the pay TV business pulled the other way. The emerging model was for pay TV providers to subsidize set-top boxes and recoup part of their subsidy by licensing their proprietary conditional access technology to other programme service providers.

So, while the European Union mandated a common interface in integrated digital TV sets to allow for the use of different conditional access systems, there was no such requirement for set-top boxes. BSkyB was free to commission its own set-top boxes designed to work with its own proprietary encryption system – to which other broadcasters had to be given fair access.

BSkyB negotiated a new satellite with Astra, at a new orbital position – so even their analogue customers would need a new satellite dish (smaller in size) as well as a new set-top box. The enticement was a line-up of some 200 broadcast services, with a strong reliance on sport and movies, a steadily improving Sky

News, the BBC's digital services and the UKTV channels. The new automated pay-per-view system and the interactive features relied on a telephone 'return path'. In other words, the system design involved two-way communication – from BSkyB to its customers via satellite broadcast and from its customers back to BSkyB, or to third parties offering interactive shopping and other services, by a conventional telephone connection.

The whole BSkyB service proposition was neatly brought together on a well-designed – and proprietary – Electronic Programme Guide which enabled the customer to navigate around this 'digital supermarket' of choice.

BSkyB's dialogue with BT about potential collaboration around the telephone-based interactive services came to fruition. The two companies, together with the Midland Bank (which later became HSBC) and the Japanese electronics manufacturing giant Matsushita, formed a joint venture called British Interactive Broadcasting. It had two roles, carefully designed to conform with competition regulations:

- to provide a set of interactive shopping and other services, under the umbrella brand of 'Open…'
- to provide a subsidy for every set-top box connected via the telephone to give access to these revenue-earning interactive services.

This meant that the satellite set-top box could be offered at a price of £200 when the full price would have been around £500.[3]

In deciding to make its own digital services available by satellite, the BBC had to grapple with what was for it the novel issue of encryption. Pay TV services were, of course, encrypted to ensure that only those who had paid for them could receive them. The BBC decided, however, that it would also have to encrypt its free-to-view public services to prevent them being accessed by viewers in other countries covered by the satellite footprint for which the BBC did not have the broadcasting rights. This meant doing a deal with BSkyB. While the BBC's satellite transmissions could be arranged direct with Astra, their reception, especially if they were to be encrypted, was dependent on BSkyB technology.

After protracted haggling and the threat of regulatory intervention, Patricia Hodgson, the BBC Director of Policy & Planning, concluded a deal – reportedly for one-seventh of Sky's original asking price.[4] Channel 4 and Channel Five had a similar need to encrypt. ITV, however, chose not to have its services carried on satellite at all, not wishing to help what it now viewed as a rival platform to digital terrestrial.

Geoff Walters, with David Chance, Robin Crossley, Ian West and other BSkyB colleagues, and with James Ackerman managing 'Open…', duly delivered Sam Chisholm's vision. Not least because of the regulatory issues surrounding the subsidy and joint venture, BSkyB's satellite service did not launch in

September 1997 – indeed it did not launch until October 1998. It was still ahead of the BDB digital terrestrial launch and, more importantly, it worked.

Sam Chisholm may have been bold in his aim but he was also cautious in its execution: 'Digital is a theoretician's delight and a practitioner's nightmare', he observed.[5] The whole BSkyB operation, technically and commercially, was highly complex. Taking that extra year proved a good decision, though it meant that Sam Chisholm was not around when the launch took place. He and David Chance left BSkyB at the end of 1997, and Mark Booth took over as chief executive.

Following the launch, customer take-up of the BSkyB service was swift, passing the million mark within six months,[6] and providing a steady stream of subscription revenue. In a dramatic move, from the summer of 1999, BSkyB then offered potential subscribers the set-top box for free. Take-up accclerated in response. BSkyB had achieved a technical and commercial triumph.

Digital terrestrial

Meanwhile the disparate digital terrestrial broadcasters collaborated to launch the first digital terrestrial service in the world. The coordinating framework was provided by a new body embracing all the multiplex licensees, called The Digital Network (TDN), which – prior to moving to a new job as the BBC's Director of Customer Service in 1997 – I had founded with Barry Cox of ITV and Frank McGettigan of Channel 4.

The complex technical side of the launch was led, highly effectively, by an external project manager, Charles Evans, whom the BBC had contracted, with Ian Jenkins and Bob Ely as the BBC's technical experts and Chris Hibbert and Mike Hughes prominent among the technical chiefs of the commercial broadcasters. The Digital TV Group's technical publications assisted greatly. The transmission network was based on 80 transmitters – enough to achieve a very high proportion of the coverage possible within the constraints posed by analogue terrestrial television.

While the technical planning and implementation was impressive, digital terrestrial technology was still very immature. Spurred on by BSkyB's public commitment to launch on digital satellite, the UK's terrestrial broadcasters had been in a hurry throughout the later stages of the R&D work. The calculations of national coverage for each of the multiplexes were untested. In practice, actual coverage turned out to be less than predicted: the levels of transmitter power initially chosen through a hyper-cautious desire not to cause interference with analogue television were simply too low. Similarly, issues of local interference arose which had not been anticipated.

Aerial issues were also significant. Many TV aerials are designed to handle only the frequency channel groups used in the area in which they are sold. However, the search for frequency channels for digital terrestrial which would not cause analogue interference had led the frequency planners to select 'out-of-group' frequencies for some areas. Many viewers in such areas would need to replace their existing aerials with new wideband aerials capable of handling the full range of frequencies, but this was not fully appreciated at first either.

Not only was technical performance disappointing, so too were the programme services. A cautious protection of the familiar analogue world manifested itself on the editorial side as well. The widescreen strategy was implemented but not widely publicized, to avoid alienating the great majority still viewing on the conventional 4:3 receivers.

Early BBC thinking on new services had focussed on 'side-channels', which would be auxiliaries to BBC One and Two rather than anything bold and new enough to become an internal rival for audience. Funding was a constraint, though the BBC was permitted to use the proceeds of the privatization of its transmission department for digital investment and received a short-term above-inflation boost on the licence fee. In the event the BBC launched a rather incoherent mix of programmes branded BBC Choice, a learning channel called BBC Knowledge, which mixed education and documentary repeats, and the 24-hour-news channel, News 24, plus an audio feed of Parliament and a digital Text service.

ITV, with little prospect of any major new flow of advertising revenue at the outset, launched a modestly funded ITV 2, with variations for Scotland and Northern Ireland. Channel 4 launched a well-regarded subscription movie channel, FilmFour, which, like the BBC's services, was also broadcast on satellite and cable. Then there were Digital Teletext, a new S4C service for Wales covering the Welsh Assembly, Gaelic programmes for Scotland and Channel Five.

The three BDB multiplexes carried a portfolio of subscription services under the brand of 'ONdigital'. ONdigital's channel line-up included BBC Worldwide's UKTV services (but not exclusively, since they were also available by satellite and cable), some lifestyle channels from Carlton and Granada, some Sky sport and movie channels and a pay-per-view offer. Unable to compete with satellite on channel quantity, ONdigital desperately needed some compensating distinction – but it was hard to detect.

Nor could ONdigital offer a major price advantage. Its fullest basic package was priced at £9.99 per month but initially only offered 12 channels, while BSkyB's fullest basic offer, the 'Family Package', delivered 40 channels for £11.99 per month. The cheapest ONdigital package on offer cost £7.99 per month but BSkyB's entry point cost was £6.99 per month.[7]

Headed by a new chief executive, Stephen Grabiner, ONdigital unsuperstitiously housed itself in Marco Polo House in Battersea, the somewhat grandiose building in which the ill-fated British Satellite Broadcasting (with its 'squarials') had gone bankrupt in the 1980s. From here, ONdigital – with John Egan in a leading role – led the commercial and operational side of the digital terrestrial launch. It was ONdigital who would commission – and subsidize – digital terrestrial set-top boxes.

The problems created by BSkyB's eviction from the BSB consortium were serious. Steve Morrison of Granada was to remark much later, with hindsight, that Carlton and Granada should have refused to proceed at that point:

The minute that Sky wasn't allowed to stay in, it became the enemy and it was much bigger… We should have got out… We should all have taken a deep breath when the regulators said, 'OK, go out there and fight a well-established pay provider with less programming, less good equipment and less bandwidth'. At that point what we should have asked was: 'Is it likely to be successful?' We didn't because we had just won the franchise. We were carrying on against unbeatable odds.[8]

ONdigital concluded that it had to free itself from dependence on BSkyB in order to avoid being left behind when BSkyB launched on satellite. So any idea of sharing the same encryption technology or benefiting from BSkyB's expertise in running customer service centres was abandoned.

Where BSkyB used its News International sister company's Videoguard encryption system, ONdigital bought an incompatible alternative from Canal Plus in France called MediaGuard. Where BSkyB had adopted a tailored proprietary product to support its interactive services, ONdigital chose a rival Canal Plus product called MediaHighway. Manufacturers of subsidized digital terrestrial set-top boxes, or of integrated digital TV sets, would need to incorporate this technology in their products.

Thus, as a result of commercial circumstances it regretted and over which it had no control, ONdigital led digital terrestrial television into a position of full-scale rivalry with BSkyB's satellite service. The battle was not just between rival programme service offers, it was between technologies as well. Consumers would not be able to switch from one pay TV provider to another without, in effect, junking their reception equipment.

Whether ONdigital's November 1998 launch was a success subsequently became the central issue of an industrial tribunal case. Set-top boxes were initially in short supply; there were technical difficulties in preparing pay modules for insertion into integrated digital TV sets; an unexpectedly large number of consumers had reception problems, associated either with coverage or with aerials; and ONdigital's call centre had teething problems.

Subscriber numbers grew in response to promotion and subsidy, but so did the company's debt. When BSkyB announced that it would give away set-top boxes free, ONdigital felt it had to follow suit. The business plan was rewritten and any idea of floating the company was postponed. Stephen Grabiner was replaced as chief executive by Stuart Prebble from Granada, who had some pay TV experience from Granada Sky Broadcasting.

Other senior managers, including John Egan, also departed – without receiving any performance bonuses. Embarrassingly, ONdigital declared that it was withholding payment because its launch had been 'unsuccessful'. John Egan and a departing colleague contested this, arguing that although there had been 'some hiccups', they had taken a new technology from the research bench into commercial implementation in a remarkably short time and that the company certainly had not described its launch as unsuccessful in any of its public pronouncements.[9] John Egan won his industrial tribunal case – but the verdict could not restore an aura of success to ONdigital.

Digital cable

Digital cable was not ready to launch until 1999 and, even then, the industry structure was unsettled. Cable had long had the ability to inspire political enthusiasm as the most exciting technology for the long-term future. Back in the early 1980s, Mrs Thatcher's government had commissioned a report from its Information Technology Advisory Panel, which pictured the cable industry not simply enlarging the choice of broadcast services but ushering in the new consumer electronics era of home shopping, home banking and other forms of interactivity. Alasdair Milne records that

> The Prime Minister was, by all accounts, fired by their enthusiasm. Kenneth Baker, then Minister for Information Technology at the Department of Trade & Industry, was aflame.[10]

Looking at the long-term prospects for the BBC's system of financing in the mid-1980s, the Peacock Committee was treated to Peter Jay's vision of a deregulated world of electronic publishing, based on a fibre optic, national grid in which

> the nation's viewers could simultaneously watch as many different programmes as the nation's readers can simultaneously read different books, magazines, newspapers etc. In other words, a television set (or radio) would be like a telephone in that the user would select for himself the connection he wanted.[11]

Professor Peacock's Committee uncoupled its recommendations from the specific idea of a national fibre-optic grid but pictured future technology providing the basis for a market based on consumer sovereignty, multiple payment arrangements including subscription and pay-per-view, no licence fee and virtually no regulation.

In the United States and in Germany, Holland and Belgium, for example, the cable television infrastructure – initially analogue – was extensive. The UK's cable industry, however, had a different history and had trouble keeping up with the exciting future politicians and others envisaged for it.

Historically, a number of small analogue cable companies had grown up to relay the terrestrial transmissions of the broadcasters but with limited cable capacity and a limited commitment to developing new content. BT, which originally had small networks in Swindon, Westminster, Milton Keynes and Aberdeen, but was constrained by the regulator from entering the broadcasting business at that time, gradually withdrew from the cable market. The remaining companies were very fragmented. A new Cable Authority, set up to oversee the industry after the Thatcher government's initial burst of enthusiasm in the 1980s, was quietly folded into the wider regulatory body, the ITC, in 1990.

So, when digital technology first came on the horizon, the UK cable industry was in no shape to handle it. Accordingly, a period of major restructuring and consolidation followed, with American capital doing much of the driving.

The detail of takeovers, mergers and re-christenings is worth re-telling only to convey the industry's extraordinary volatility.

In 1998, when digital satellite and digital terrestrial TV launched in the UK, there were three major cable players. The first was Cable and Wireless Communications – which had been formed by a merger between BT's main telephone competitor, Mercury, and the North American owned operations of Nynex, Bell Cable Media and Videotron.

The second was the recently formed American company Cabletel, headed by Barclay Knapp. It had acquired Insight Communications and British Cable Services and, more significantly, had bought NTL, the privatized former IBA terrestrial transmission business. It then adopted NTL's name for the whole business and proceeded to purchase Comcast, Com Tel and Diamond Cable in a further act of consolidation.

The third player was Telewest, the offspring of the US giants TCI and US West, which had taken over the UK franchises of Southwestern Bell and Maclean Hunter.

By the summer of 1999 this drastically reorganized cable industry was ready to launch its digital television. Cable & Wireless Communications began converting its analogue cable infrastructure to digital and marketed a subscription offer designed to compete with BSkyB's and ONdigital's. NTL and Telewest followed. Programme content was highly dependent on the services supplied by BSkyB.

However, the restructuring saga continued. Cable & Wireless decided to sell off its cable operations and concentrate on telephony – so it sold them to NTL. This made NTL the UK's major cable company. Meanwhile Telewest acquired General Cable, Birmingham Cable and Cable London (the last from NTL), becoming the industry's only other player of any size. Telewest then merged with the cable channel company Flextech (BBC Worldwide's partner in UKTV), which strengthened its access to programme content.

It was really only in 2000, therefore, that the shape of the UK's digital cable industry, centred on NTL and Telewest, became clear.[12]

Both companies began to drive up digital subscriber numbers with consumer packages combining digital TV, interactive services and telephony. By then digital satellite was well out in front, in terms of take-up, with digital cable jostling with ONdigital for second place.

Pay TV colonizes the market

By the end of 2000 digital TV take-up exceeded 6.5 million – a much higher figure than our BBC Digital Broadcasting Project had forecast (we had not predicted set-top boxes being given away 'free'). Precision about the exact total was complicated by the phenomenon of 'churn' – subscribers who signed up and then subsequently stopped subscribing. However, BSkyB, now under a new chief executive, Tony Ball, had, impressively, achieved around 5 million;[13] ONdigital claimed around 1 million;[14] NTL reckoned to have 500,000 and Telewest 350,000.[15]

As well as rapid take-up, the UK digital TV market had two other characteristics. Virtually all the receivers – satellite, terrestrial and cable – were subsidized set-top boxes and, a closely connected phenomenon, virtually all the digital households were pay TV subscribers.

Pay TV had in effect colonized the digital TV market. Pay TV companies specified the set-top boxes, complete with their own branded Electronic Programme Guides. They either placed orders direct with manufacturers or underwrote orders placed by retailers. The boxes were then given to the customer 'free'. Retailers were incentivized to market pay TV subscriptions.

In analogue television, it was normal for the consumer to buy (or rent) the receiver and for the programme services to be free, apart from the compulsory licence fee payment to the BBC – and subscription, in the analogue world, was a minority activity. In the digital TV industry which the UK had launched, the norm was the exact opposite – the set-top box receiver came 'free' but the customer paid a subscription (as well, of course, as the licence fee). The broadcasting economy envisaged by the Peacock Committee, in which the role of direct consumer payment became so dominant that the licence fee system became unsustainable, seemed to be fast arriving.

While cable was exclusively subscription-based, it was possible for digital satellite customers to have a subsidized set-top box without subscribing. This had been one of the conditions on which the competition authorities had finally approved the British Interactive Broadcasting consortium and its subsidy arrangements. However, non-subscriber customers paid more for installation and had to sign a contract with BSkyB undertaking to have the box linked to their telephone line for a year so that they could access the interactive services (since the subsidy came from the interactive services joint venture).

Non-subscription digital satellite customers were a small minority, however. Because the BBC, Channel 4 and Channel Five had encrypted their free-to-view services on satellite, to avoid copyright problems from the satellite signal spillover into other countries, these non-subscription customers also needed a viewing card to decrypt the free services. These cards were provided without charge (i.e. paid for mainly by the BBC) but, by the end of 2000, only 30,000 households had chosen to register for one. Digital satellite was in practice predominantly a subscription service.

For digital terrestrial, where the free-to-view services were not encrypted, the only set-top boxes available on any scale were rented by ONdigital to its subscribers. It was possible to purchase an integrated widescreen digital TV set without subscribing – but the early models suffered technical teething problems, they were not well supported by retail customer service and sales were low.

Thus in 2000, two years after its launch, digital TV in the UK had become virtually synonymous with pay TV. The so-called platform operators – BSkyB, ONdigital, NTL and Telewest – were perceived as the providers of digital television. In order to have it, you needed to sign a contract subscribing to one of them, in much the same way that you needed to subscribe to a telephone company in order to have a phone service.

From many perspectives, the UK's digital TV launch had been a triumph. The UK had been first in the world with digital terrestrial. Digital services had been launched on all three platforms. Digital TV penetration, in terms of the percentage of households taking it up, was – mainly through BSkyB's success – the highest in the world.

My own perspective was very different. I had invested three years' work on the BBC's feasibility study for digital television, between 1994 and 1997, and had championed digital terrestrial technology – but I had not done it for this. Our BBC project had not pioneered digital terrestrial in order to create a world in which BBC viewers had to sign a contract to subscribe to one of our rivals before they could watch our BBC digital services! However, the BBC was not in the driving seat.

Fortunes and misfortunes of the pay TV rivals

The economics of pay TV, in outline, were very simple. Pay TV companies needed to spend under the headings of programme content, transmission and distribution and customer acquisition – this last covering marketing promotions and receiver subsidies. Their principal revenue was a function of the number of subscribers (minus those who ceased subscribing or 'churned') multiplied by the expenditure per subscriber on subscriptions, pay-per-view and other purchases. Advertising made a modest contribution.

In the start-up years the number of subscribers – and hence both the subscription revenue and the value of advertising – was inevitably low. The cost of customer acquisition was high, especially with three platforms in competition for potential subscribers – in excess of £180 per customer. So the early years would inevitably involve high debt and risk. To be a player at this table, you needed deep pockets and a strong nerve.

BSkyB had both, plus experience. It drove up subscriber numbers on the strength of Premier League football, feature films and the 'supermarket' breadth of channel choice, plus a news channel with a growing reputation. The churn rate was around 10 per cent.

In 2001 BSkyB faced some financial issues. Interactive revenues were disappointing. The purchase of the Sports Internet Group proved a mistake.

The 'Open…' consortium was closed: BSkyB bought out the partners and took direct control of subsidy policy. It was nonetheless a year of achievement. BSkyB persuaded virtually all of its old analogue satellite customers to switch across to digital. This enabled the company to close its analogue service and reduce its cost base, setting an example to the rest of the industry.[16]

NTL and Telewest, having spent heavily first on industry consolidation and then on the launch of digital, plunged deeply into debt. Constructing digital cable infrastructure was costly. By comparison with BSkyB's, their customer service was patchy. NTL's churn rate was 16 per cent, and Telewest's higher. NTL's debt, around £12 billion in 2001, kept the company on the edge of financial crisis. A plan to sell the broadcast transmission business was announced but then postponed.[17] Job cuts reduced staff numbers from over 20,000 to around 13,000. Management pay was frozen. Middle managers came and went.

ONdigital had the hardest struggle. Its churn rate was over 20 per cent, due largely to coverage, reception and aerial difficulties. The problem of ambient noise interference, the scale of which was a surprise, had been aggravated by the removal of technical 'safety features' in the haste to launch.[18]

While BSkyB, NTL and Telewest were vertically integrated organizations able to manage the full consumer proposition – from programme acquisition, through marketing, scheduling, transmission and receiver supply – ONdigital had to try and lead the loose federation of multiplex licensees which made up TDN. Its attempts to improve the digital terrestrial offering as a whole by equalizing the coverage of the different multiplexes, so that a consistent package of services could be more effectively marketed, were frustrated by the conflicting financial priorities of the different TDN members.

ONdigital also lobbied hard to convince government, regulators and industry of the urgent need to improve coverage by increasing transmitter power. Good simple 'plug'n'play' reception, without the need for a new aerial installation, was limited to less than half of UK households. As a basis for a pay TV business, this was not viable.

Giving away set-top boxes was never part of the original business plan and was becoming financially crippling. Stuart Prebble therefore enthused about the potential of integrated digital TV sets (iDTVs). Customers had to buy these and the sets could then be converted for subscription by the addition of a module which only cost ONdigital £20. He stressed the importance of iDTVs in reaching the goal of analogue switch-off. While the suggestion that they be made mandatory made no headway, he did persuade the Department of Trade and Industry to launch a 'Kitemark' for digital TVs, using the DVB logo.

ITV agreed to provide some free advertising for DVB-badged TV sets and ONdigital then paid for DVB display material to go into high street shops all over the UK. Unfortunately, reception and aerial problems gave these digital TVs, many of them very expensive, a poor reputation with both consumers and retailers. The BBC, Channel 4 and Channel Five stood back from joining this 'DVB campaign' and, amid a certain amount of ill feeling, it petered out.

Nor was ITV flourishing in the digital world. Its decision not to transmit ITV 1 or ITV 2 by satellite, because of ONdigital's platform rivalry with BSkyB, disadvantaged it, compared to the BBC, Channel 4 and Channel Five, in audience share in satellite homes. This had an impact on its advertising revenue and it had another adverse financial effect too. In designing the regulatory framework for digital television, the ITC had agreed to reduce the commercial terrestrial broadcasters' payments for their analogue licences as they switched their audience across to digital reception. The more digital viewers they could claim, the lower the charge they paid for their analogue spectrum – the so-called 'digital dividend'. The aim was to incentivise digital switchover. Under this scheme Channel Five was able to benefit from its audience on digital satellite: ITV's finances were much more closely tied to the performance of ONdigital.

In April 2001 ITV, largely owned by Carlton and Granada, decided to rebrand ONdigital, owned by Carlton and Granada, as 'ITV Digital'. Stuart Prebble, who had proved a great fighter against the commercial odds, was promoted to be chief executive of both ITV and ITV Digital. If the future of commercial television revenue lay in subscription, or at least in a shift away from total dependence on advertising, then this made sense strategically. ITV's brand could help support the struggling pay TV infant. Heavy promotion, featuring a toy stuffed monkey, heralded a new start.

However, Stuart Prebble set out to challenge BSkyB's domination of televised football. To the family of brands of ITV 1, ITV 2 and ITV Digital, he added a new subscription sports channel, ITV Sport. Unable to prise away the Premier League from BSkyB, ITV Digital paid £315 million for the rights to the Nationwide League. The audiences for these second-rank matches proved tiny and it steadily became obvious that this contract had been a disastrous mistake. A match that cost ITV Digital £1.2 million might be viewed by an audience as low as 1000.[19] The company's troubles were compounded by a flourishing black market in pirate viewing cards.[20] Few people were watching and even fewer were paying to watch.

Carlton and Granada had originally calculated that they would need to invest about £300 million before their pay TV operation could reach breakeven. They now faced the prospect of having to spend at least four times that figure. Granada's nerve cracked first. Its chairman, Charles Allen, wrote to the Prime Minister, following a delay in the legislation on media ownership which might have allowed Carlton and Granada to merge, warning of the possibility of closing ITV Digital. Carlton, who had apparently not been consulted, dismissed his letter publicly as 'hysterical scare-mongering'.[21] In truth both companies were desperate, especially as a major recession in the advertising industry was hitting their main ITV business.

Attempts to find a partner willing to share ITV Digital's financial burden and risk failed. Complaints about unfair competition from BSkyB produced a protracted investigation by the Office of Fair Trading (OFT), an interim report critical of BSkyB, but no result. ITV's war against the satellite platform was called off and, in November 2001, Stuart Prebble reluctantly agreed to pay BSkyB around £17 million p.a. for encryption and other services so that ITV 1 and ITV 2 could finally be broadcast by satellite and augment ITV's 'digital dividend'.

As ITV Digital's commercial problems grew, so did its interest in the public policy goal of digital switchover. If ITV Digital's pay TV proposition was not working in the market, could the prospect of a compulsory national switch to digital television help drive consumer take-up of digital terrestrial equipment and thus rescue the company's fortunes? Political lobbying became a key strand in ITV Digital's survival strategy. Wasn't it time that the Government developed a 'road-map' and a timetable for achieving digital switchover? How about appointing a 'Digital Csar' to champion it?

New Labour

Although the framework for the launch of digital television in the UK had been created by a Conservative administration, by the time of the various digital TV launches Tony Blair's New Labour had come to power following the election of May 1997. Labour replaced the Department of National Heritage with the Department for Culture, Media and Sport (DCMS) and Chris Smith was appointed Secretary of State.

Policy on digital television was characterized more by continuity than by change. The public policy goal of switchover remained but the Government 'supped with a long spoon'.

In 1998 the Government published the report of a study conducted by NERA (National Economic Research Associates) and Smith System Engineering Ltd carried out for the DCMS and for the Radiocommunications Agency on *The Economic Impact of Policies for Digital Television and the Closure of Analogue Transmissions.*[22] In respect of digital switchover the report addressed three main issues:

- estimating the cost of moving all TV households from analogue to digital reception under various scenarios;
- evaluating how the Government might encourage a mixture of consumers, industry and the taxpayer to bear this cost;
- evaluating how the Government might deliver analogue switch-off in 5, 10 or 15 years' time and the implications of naming an analogue switch-off date 5 or 10 years in advance.

The study viewed the key drivers of take-up as, first, pay TV and, second, the gradual process of TV set replacement, noting that the average set replacement time was 8 years and assuming that digital TV sets displaced analogue TV sets in the new-purchase market. It concluded that 10 or 15 years was a much more realistic timetable for completing digital switchover and analogue switch-off than 5 years. Its other main conclusions were:

- there are likely to be significant benefits from an early announcement of a closure date for analogue services, in terms of a more rapid fall in the price of digital reception equipment and a corresponding increase in the rate of consumer take-up;
- the most promising options for completing the digital coverage of the main terrestrial services were to extend the number of transmitters on at least three multiplexes or to ensure satellite provision, or a mixture of the two approaches;
- some of the funding for completing digital coverage and shutting the analogue services could come from an auction of the released spectrum.[23]

In March 1999 the ITC had commissioned the Genesis Project – again involving the Smith Group, this time with NTL – to study frequency planning options for a post-switchover all-digital pattern of UK television. It produced a set of technical scenarios in a report of February 2000.[24]

However, the idea of making an early announcement of the switchover date was a political hot potato. Chris Smith consulted consumer representatives and positioned the Government carefully. The timing of switchover would be based on meeting criteria designed to protect consumers, especially those who simply wished to continue receiving their traditional channels and did not wish to subscribe. The Government would not, therefore, announce a commitment to a specific switchover timetable at this point.

In a speech to the broadcasting industry in 1999, Chris Smith spelled out his criteria:

> I want to set out two crucial tests that must be met before the analogue signal is fully switched to digital: availability and affordability…
>
> At the moment, the main free-to-air channels, including teletext, reach virtually everyone in the UK (99.4% is the conventional figure). Ensuring that these same channels are available in digital form across the whole country, including in remote and rural areas, will be no easy task… and we will need to look carefully at harnessing the various different ways of delivering TV to the home in order to do so…
>
> Second, switching to digital must be an affordable option for the vast majority of people… What does affordable mean in this context? It means prices which are within the reach of people on low and fixed incomes, particularly elderly people for many of whom television is the most important and reliable companion in their daily lives…
>
> The degree of take-up of digital equipment in households (either through a set top box or a digital TV set) will, of course, be a key measure of

progress to set alongside the affordability test. When 70% of consumers have access to digital equipment, we will know that a significant milestone has been passed, and can clarify the timetable further. But I want to make sure that 95% of consumers have access to digital equipment before switchover is completed.

Full switch-over will take place when and only when these two tests of availability and affordability are met.[25]

The message for the management of ITV Digital was not *mañana*, however. Chris Smith added that he believed his criteria could be met so as to allow switchover to start to happen 'as early as 2006 and be completed by 2010.' He set up a Viewers' Panel to advise him further.

Government enthusiasm for getting on with the task was briefly kindled in 2000 when the UK auctioned the spectrum allocated to third generation (3G) mobile telephone systems for over £22.5 billion. Political advisers, recalling the Thatcher government's proceeds from privatization and North Sea Oil, thought that an early sale of the analogue television spectrum might give them another windfall, reportedly perhaps as high as £50 billion. The Downing Street policy unit was reported to be 'horrified' by the prospect of the money falling into the hands of a subsequent Conservative government:

> Senior Labour advisers are determined to speed up the sell-off... The new timetable could potentially see Labour announcing a sell-off within months of winning the next general election, scheduling an auction for 2004 or 2005, to smooth the way for a third term.[26]

However, the Treasury was unconvinced. The proponents of switch-off consulted it about the concept of using a portion of the anticipated auction proceeds to fund vouchers to subsidize the many consumers who could not be expected to have switched to digital on that timescale. Treasury officials regarded the idea as an open-ended risk, compounded by the uncertainty surrounding the commercial future of digital terrestrial television.

Nor was consumer support likely. During the course of 2000, at the Government's request, the ITC, Oftel and the OFT carried out a consultation into consumer perspectives of digital television. Their report, in November 2000, noted a number of barriers to consumer take-up.[27] These included the high cost of integrated digital TV sets (which the Consumers' Association would not recommend in any event because of their lack of technical maturity), coverage and aerial issues, and the lack of inter-operability between the receivers for the different platforms.

The DCMS Viewers' Panel reported in 2001. Taking a traditional view, it expressed concern about the possibility of broadcasters relying exclusively on cable or satellite for their coverage in some parts of the country and argued that terrestrial television should continue to have a universal service obligation in an all-digital world. On timing, the Panel was in no rush:

> The Panel considers that analogue broadcasts should not be switched off until virtually all areas of the country and all sections of the population have switched to digital.[28]

It also became clear that the telecommunications companies, BT prominent among them, who had paid so much for the 3G spectrum in 2000 had misjudged the value and created major commercial problems for themselves. The bubble of expectation about a broadcasting auction was pricked.

Following the 2001 election, Chris Smith was removed from the Cabinet. His successor as Secretary of State at the DCMS was Tessa Jowell, who signalled a note of political caution: an early Government-driven initiative on digital switchover was off the agenda for the present. The Viewers' Panel was judged to have completed its work and was disbanded. The message from Whitehall now was that there was 'no chance' of a switch-off by 2006 and that even 2010 looked optimistic.[29]

So no early announcement of an accelerated timetable for switchover would come to the rescue of ITV Digital.

A shifting political focus

As its focus on switchover softened, the Government gave more emphasis to a wider, more generalized view of digital television as part of the infrastructure of a modern Information Society.

The growth of the Internet and the convergence of the broadcasting, telecommunications and computer industries as digital technology spread had been an emerging political theme during the 1990s. In the United States Vice President Al Gore had popularized the concept of Information Superhighways and President Clinton had set up an Information Infrastructure Task Force. In Europe the EU Commissioner Martin Bangemann had spearheaded the work behind a report on *Europe and the Global Information Society* advocating various regulatory initiatives.[30] Against this background the Conservatives had liberalized the regulation of the telecommunications industry in the UK and Virginia Bottomley had made the connection with digital broadcasting's potential for interactive services:

> For the viewer and the listener, the digital revolution will create a huge increase in variety and choice. There will be more channels, better pictures and sound and a whole new range of services. The digital format will underpin the convergence of broadcasting, telecommunications and computer technologies, speeding the arrival of the information superhighway. Digital broadcasting will offer many people their first experience of the new

information society. It will help develop interactive services like home shopping, home banking, information and education services.[31]

With the spread of the Internet beyond academic and business communications into widespread domestic use as well, interest in technology convergence grew. The Information Society theme and the vision of interactivity linked to electronic shopping and electronic services exerted a powerful gravitational pull on New Labour's thinking about both broadcasting and telecommunications. Chris Smith threw into his 1999 Cambridge speech, as an enthusiastic aside:

> Wouldn't it be wonderful if, after switch-over, we could guarantee as part of the core package of services that every home in the country with a television and telephone could have access to the Internet?[32]

Over the next couple of years Labour Government rhetoric focussed on the role of digital television as a surrogate computer, its cable or telephone return path bringing e-commerce and e-services to households which had not yet bought, and might never buy, a computer. Internet access for all by 2005 started to overshadow analogue switch-off as a Government aim.[33]

Special digital TV channels with interactive capability were envisaged for Government services. A Cabinet Office report published in 2000 declared:

> The introduction of DTV – and in particular the use of such technology to provide interactive services – represents a major new opportunity for the delivery of government and information services directly to the household... Many public sector organisations will find that DTV is an increasingly significant factor in the realisation of their service delivery strategies.[34]

A new regulatory body for the world of convergence, Ofcom, was proposed, to bring together the functions of the broadcasting regulators, the spectrum management role of the Radiocommunications Agency, and the telecommunications responsibilities hitherto carried out by Oftel.

In 2001 the Department of Trade and Industry published a White Paper which set a new public policy goal for digital television:

> Our aim is for the UK to have the most dynamic and competitive market for digital TV in the G7, as measured by take-up, choice and cost.

Britain would lead the world in the development of digital television with every community sharing the benefits:

> Digital television will transform the communications services available in the home. Using technology that people understand and are comfortable

and confident with, we will be able to provide a learning resource and communications centre in every living room. It puts control of viewing in the hands of viewers rather than broadcasters. Choice will increase, and the potential of teletext will be unleashed by use of graphics and high speed updates. Combined with a phone line, it can give everyone access to the Internet in their living rooms, stimulating computer literacy in the population as a whole. It will offer new Internet-based learning opportunities and interactive services, making e-shopping and e-banking more attractive for many people and opening up new opportunities for business products and services.[35]

'Interactivity' beneath the rhetoric

There were elements of political fantasy here. In 2001 interactivity on digital television was still at a very early, and somewhat cumbersome, stage of development. In reality most digital television viewers mostly watched one-way television.

Such interactivity as there was had little or no connection with delivering Government services. The BBC, for example, transmitted, in hidden form, a wide range of extra material – which could be video, audio and/or text – and the viewer could choose, by following the on-screen instruction to 'Press Red' on the remote control, which elements to select. Thus there could be a choice of tennis matches from Wimbledon, a choice of commentaries for a documentary, and optional background material about how a programme was made. Satellite, with its ample bandwidth, was better suited for this than digital terrestrial – and the BBC annoyed Stuart Prebble by its willingness to work with BSkyB on interactive enhancements for BBC digital programmes.

The next level of interactivity involved using a telephone 'return path'. BSkyB's subsidized set-top boxes all contained a modem for connection to a telephone line. Connection was a contractual obligation – providing a gateway to the 'Open...' range of banking, travel booking, pizza ordering and other interactive shopping services. This electronic shopping mall was termed a 'walled garden'. In other words, it was not 'open' at all – it was a closed service area cut off from the genuinely open world of the Internet. This, together with a slightly clunky performance, limited both its appeal and its commercial performance. Gambling proved a better bet.

The broadcasters had their own separate websites and the BBC's had grown rapidly from its launch in 1997 into one of the leading Internet sites in Europe. For the most part website access via the personal computer and a telephone line remained a quite separate activity from digital television viewing, though the BBC subsequently bracketed its Internet services and its digital television interactive features under the common brand 'BBC-i'.

Channel 4 meanwhile pioneered its multi-media *Big Brother* show, a TV programme shaped by telephone, digital interactive and online voting, which was a popular and commercial triumph with feedback techniques which were subsequently utilized by the other broadcasters. Significantly, however, viewers did not need to have a digital television in order to participate in it.

ONdigital/ITV Digital offered its customers direct access to the Internet if they chose to subscribe to an extra ONnet service, with an extra piece of equipment linked to a telephone line. Again the appeal was limited – normal Internet text was not a comfortable read on a TV screen across the room. Both ITV Digital and BSkyB customers could also send e-mails via their digital TV equipment, with some restrictions, using a laptop keyboard.

As the popularity of the Internet grew, the cable companies adapted their sales proposition to the 'Triple Play' of digital television, telephony and the Internet. The demand for faster access fostered the development of broadband, essentially immediate Internet access and sufficient capacity to allow a richer mix of graphics, audio and video services to be available at speed. Generally, the different services – television, telephony and Internet – used the same cable into the house but were then routed to different devices, the set-top box for the TV, the telephone and the PC.

In the telecommunications industry, BT, sensitive to growing cable competition to its telephony services, had been prevented during the 1990s from responding by directly entering the field of television. In 2001 it applied for a licence to broadcast but emphasized that this was largely a formality to widen its options.[36] Technically it was possible to upgrade existing copper telephone lines, using a technology called ADSL (Asymmetric Digital Subscriber Line), to allow them to carry video services. However, after an early experiment with video-on-demand in Colchester, BT was cautious about investing heavily in this.

Within London an independent commercial company, Video Networks, offered a *HomeChoice* video-on-demand service of around 1000 feature films, using BT ADSL capacity.[37] Kingston Communications in Hull offered a range of local and educational interactive services on its local telephone network and attracted both BSkyB support and a *BBC Hull Interactive* trial. Cable television too developed on-demand access to films.

As interactivity initiatives proliferated in the market, the technical planners began to see the need for some further standardization beyond the established DVB (Digital Video Broadcasting) satellite, cable and terrestrial standards for digital TV in Europe. Led by Graham Mills of BT, one of the founders of the UK's Digital TV Group, they sought to develop something they termed the European Multi-media Home Platform (MHP) to provide a standard Application Programming Interface (API).

Market forces had produced the opposite result. Within the UK, BSkyB, ITV Digital and the cable companies had each adopted different interfaces, obliging broadcasters who wanted to broadcast on all platforms to 'author' their applications in three different ways. These differences within the UK were compounded at European level. For a major television receiver manufacturer wishing to sell across the European market, these incompatibilities were a nightmare. It was rather like the early phase of railway development in the nineteenth century when every railway company used a different gauge track.

The DVB did its work: MHP became the open standard recommended (but not mandated) for use across Europe. MHP, the DVB proudly announced,

> defines a generic interface between interactive digital applications and the terminals on which those applications execute. The standard enables digital content providers to address all types of terminals ranging from low to high end set top boxes, IDTVs (integrated digital TV sets) and multimedia PCs.[38]

The only snag was that its complexity made it expensive to implement. So the UK digital TV platforms, like their counterparts in many other countries, paid it lip service, promised vaguely to 'migrate' to MHP at an unspecified time in the future and carried on with their established incompatible systems. The broadcasting, telecommunications and computer industries might be converging, but the UK digital TV industry was not. UK consumers had only the proprietary interface technology on offer from their pay TV provider – still at a relatively early stage of technical development.

The newly created – and short-lived – Office of the E-envoy, which had been set up to pioneer e-government, initially enthused about digital TV but, generally, the link between the promotion of digital communications and the aspiration to give citizens access to electronic public services lay through the Internet. Digital television's relevance as a service provider remained marginal, except in a miscellany of local authority schemes (described more fully in Chapter Nine).

In August 2001 a research report for Oftel painted a picture of interactive services on digital television which put the subject into perspective:

> There were mixed to lukewarm reactions to interactive services, with some subscribers unsure whether they had interactive services at all as part of their package... Such services were generally seen as 'an interesting extra', and were not part of the justification for, and value in, their digital subscription... Most respondents had experienced technical difficulties with interactivity: freezing, having to reboot, PIN code problems; but the most common complaint was the speed of the interactive services.[39]

On the specific services where the digital television set could in theory offer a substitute for the computer, the Oftel research results were damning:

> Respondents were very confused indeed about the home shopping offer. Most felt it was a significantly limited offer, with only a few retailers subscribing to the service... On-line banking was almost universally rejected. Those who wanted to bank remotely already did so (via telephone and

internet banking), and those who did not already have 'remote' accounts were extremely uncomfortable with the idea of managing their account on a large screen TV in the middle of their living room. E-mail also has very limited appeal, and those who had tried it out once or twice had experienced technical difficulties and had simply given up. In any case most already had at least one e-mail address and they were extremely concerned about the lack of compatibility with PCs (personal computers), particularly in relation to the management of attached documents.[40]

Digital television in the UK in its early years was a hard-nosed pay TV business. Its mainstream role was not to deliver a political vision of the Information Society. Arguably, the reason the UK led the world in digital television in 2000/2001 was primarily due to BSkyB's success in selling contracts to watch football. If politicians wanted to imagine that this constituted a potential 'learning resource and a communications centre in every living room', they could. But beneath the political rhetoric the reality of digital television in the UK was head-to-head competition for pay TV subscribers, with rival companies offering rival and incompatible technologies and the growing possibility that not all of them would survive.

Indeed the political posturing about digital television, interactivity and the Information Society cloaked a growing apprehension that the public policy of digital switchover might founder.

Limitations of the Pay TV market

Digital television could not have been launched in the UK without reliance on receiver subsidies provided by the rival companies engaged in pay television. However, there would be a ceiling on the number of subscribers whom BSkyB, ITV Digital and the two cable companies could ever recruit. In offering the Government their advice in 2000, the ITC, Oftel and the OFT noted that digital television take-up in the UK was 'a major international success story', but pointed out:

> Despite this very positive start, estimates by consultation respondents suggest that market developments could drive the digital penetration upwards to reach between 55 and 79 per cent of homes by 2008, but not the 95 per cent needed to meet the Government's... test for switchover.[41]

A substantial body of consumers would resist the idea of subscription for the foreseeable future and, even in subscriber households, pay TV was not necessarily appropriate for every set in the home. Accordingly, the ITC, Oftel and the OFT advised the government to coordinate a generic publicity programme, in conjunction with the industry, to stress the benefits of digital television and get over the message that digital television is not synonymous with pay TV.[42]

This was not a task which could be left to retailers who may have

more incentive to gain commission from pay TV sales than to provide information on free-to-air only reception.[43]

In response to this recommendation, the DCMS convened a series of inconclusive industry meetings, a couple of which I attended, but differences of interest among the major business rivals frustrated any joint action.

One fundamental problem was that, although virtually every calculation of the commercial viability of digital terrestrial television or of the feasibility of switchover had assumed a significant and growing role for integrated digital TV sets (iDTVs) in the TV replacement market, there was no serious sign of this developing. The number of iDTVs bought – and indeed made – remained tiny in proportion to the continuing booming sales of analogue TV sets. The reasons for this were several:

- immaturity of the digital terrestrial technology;
- retailer reaction against digital terrestrial coverage and reception problems (the cost of a set-top box which did not work was ITV Digital's problem, taking back a large TV set was a different matter);
- the satellite and cable companies' focus on set-top boxes and lack of commercial interest in the growth of integrated digital TV sets (which opened up the purchasing household to their ITV Digital rival);
- uncertainty about the long-term commercial viability of ITV Digital;
- the lack of a clear Government timetable for switchover;
- the fact that the UK market was only part of the wider European market where switchover policy, in general, was even less clear.

In March 2001 the Consumers' Association published a research report focussed on those who had *not* adopted pay TV. Its key findings included:

Non-adopters do not seem to be in any particular hurry to go digital. Two thirds (66%) have not even looked into the possibility of getting it... Just under a third of non-adopters (32%) said they would never get DTV, and 50% of older and retired people never want to switch... There are low levels of awareness about the benefits of digital television. 56% of non-adopters feel they don't know enough about the current digital television offering and even a quarter of adopters feel this way.[44]

Then in April 2001 the DCMS published a research report carried out by MORI, commissioned to complement the work of the Government's short-lived

Viewers' Panel. It too concluded that ignorance was a major barrier, including ignorance of the Government's switchover policy:

> Less than half (44%) of the population say they are aware of the switchover... This is a key driver for viewers who predict it is 'likely' they *will* switch in the next five years. However, they will only switch as part of the natural upgrade of their television, whenever that may be at this stage. Knowledge of the switchover is a long-term encouragement, but does not encourage *immediate* adoption of the technology...
>
> The overall conclusion to be drawn from the data on 'possible' and 'unlikely' digital television viewers, is that they do not say they will never get digital television: rather they simply do not know what digital television has to offer...
>
> 'Existing' digital television viewers have switched because the service offers something they want – more channels. To move to a position where *most* of the population has digital television, more information needs to be made available on the costs and benefits of the service. This is the *biggest* concern that non-digital households have about digital, and is the key to understanding why 70% of the population has not yet switched to digital.[45]

In June 2001 the National Consumer Council published the results of a 'Mystery Shopping' exercise it had carried out among the retailers of digital television. Its survey highlighted evidence of poor consumer advice from shop assistants, including inaccurate information about potential switch-off dates, incomplete and partial advice about digital platform choices, and misleading information on technical issues. It concluded:

> The patchy quality of retailer advice is alarming given that many consumers rely on it to make purchasing decisions. As we approach switch-off they have a responsibility to raise their game, ensuring all consumers are getting the accurate information they have a right to expect... But the government should take the lead, providing consumers with the facts they need, in what is a complex and evolving market place... A comprehensive and high profile public information campaign should be implemented as swiftly as possible.[46]

So by 2000/2001 the public policy which underlay the launch of digital terrestrial television looked unconvincing. The market and public policy – which the mid-1990s design for the framework of UK digital television had aimed to align – had come apart. The market had delivered pay TV and pay TV had delivered consumer take-up. However, pay TV could not deliver the policy goal of digital switchover – let alone universal access to the Internet for the Information Society. Nor – as ITV Digital's troubles were by now clearly demonstrating – was this policy goal free from major commercial risk.

Chapter Four

Shipwreck and Rescue

UK digital terrestrial television – the six multiplex convoy designed and assembled by the Government and the ITC – had not fared well in the open waters of the market. By the end of 2001 the ITV Digital flagship was listing badly and its captain was appealing for Government help. It was unclear whether the whole voyage to digital switchover was misconceived or whether the convoy simply needed new commanders and a fresh course. The events of 2002 would answer that question.

ITV Digital calls for help

ITV Digital's financial position was dire. In December 2001 it announced a cut of 550 jobs at its customer service centre in Plymouth.[1] New subscriptions in the last quarter of the year, at around 46,000, totalled only about a third of the 134,000 subscribers recruited in the equivalent quarter in 2000. Nor did subscribers stay subscribed: one in every four ITV Digital customers now 'churned' – declined to renew their subscriptions. Share prices for Carlton and Granada, already hit by the advertising recession, suffered as both companies reported major losses. Break-even plans for the digital operation were revised but, against a trend of falling subscription numbers, high 'churn' rate and a continuing bad press, they looked unconvincing. ITV Digital's prospective losses for the year ahead were estimated at over £200 million.[2]

Stuart Prebble began to lose the initiative to the boards of Carlton and Granada, now desperate to find a way of staunching the ITV Digital financial drain. David Chance, formerly Sam Chisholm's deputy at BSkyB and now a non-executive director at Granada, advocated re-positioning ITV Digital's pay proposition as 'Sky-lite' – offering fewer premium channels and cutting both costs and prices.[3] Exploratory talks along these lines started with BSkyB. In parallel, discussions continued with the BBC and other companies about a possible 'Digital Coalition'. Ed Richards, a former BBC policy strategist and now the media specialist at 10 Downing Street, convened meetings of the industry's major players to see what could be done[4] – aware that one of the casualties of an ITV Digital collapse could be the Government's policy of switching off analogue terrestrial TV.

Prompted partly by Stuart Prebble's pleas, in the autumn of 2001 the Government drew up a list of tasks which would need to be completed for a full switch-over to digital to become feasible. Bill Macintyre, a senior DTI civil servant, convened an industry brainstorming session, pulled the results into a draft set of tasks and then consulted the industry on them. For ITV Digital this work was desperately urgent. Testifying to a Commons Select Committee in January 2002, ITV underlined what it hoped would prove, in effect, a Government rescue plan for ITV Digital

- a clear target date for switch-over (ITV recommended a 2006 start);
- a 'route map' and a 'Digital Champion' to spearhead the switch;
- increasing the digital terrestrial transmission power to improve reception;
- mandating digital TV sets.[5]

The Government consolidated its list of tasks, dubbed them an Action Plan, and began to tackle them methodically, but the pace was cautious, not least because of ITV Digital's difficulties. The broadcasters collaborated in a transmission power increase and a degree of coverage equalization between multiplexes. However, there would be no Government rescue operation.

Tony Ball, BSkyB's chief executive, told that same Commons Select Committee that ITV Digital's problems were of its own making, that the organization was unlikely to be around in its current form in a year's time, that its spectacular mistakes would provide a case study for business schools on how not to run a company, and that its management 'couldn't run a bath'.[6]

Meanwhile at the BBC

The BBC meanwhile monitored and analysed the market. Having been in the vanguard of the technical development of digital television in the mid-1990s, it had subsequently allowed commercial broadcasters to take the lead. Financially risk averse, protective of its traditional analogue channels, and in no hurry to see its heartland of analogue-only homes switch to multi-channel, it was content to let others set the pace and run behind them. ITV Digital's evident difficulties tended to confirm the wisdom of this caution.

Financially, however, the BBC had become digital television's sleeping giant. During the years of Conservative government, the licence fee had been held strictly in line with the Retail Price Index. The Conservative government had granted a modest two year increase for 1998/99 and 1999/2000 to cover the launch of the digital services but planned to offset it by two later years of reduction.[7] John Birt aspired to overturn those planned reductions and to secure a real increase of substance and, with the arrival of a Labour Government in 1997, the prospect of achieving this rose.

In its publication *The BBC Beyond 2000* the BBC appealed to nascent millennial enthusiasm for a digital economy and a digital society:

Three major converging industries, broadcasting, telecommunications and computing, are sources of great value and opportunity... Between them they are now set to transform the world in which we live. The potential benefits of this technological and social transformation are enormous... The BBC has a role to play in ensuring these benefits accrue to the UK. Making sure that the information society is fully shared by all in the UK and that we are in the vanguard of the digital revolution will be essential parts of guaranteeing the health of our society and the nation's long-term competitiveness.[8]

Faced with a BBC bid to reverse its predecessor's decision to have two years in which the BBC income fell below inflation, the Labour Government set up an independent funding review. A specially appointed panel of inquiry would look into the digital crystal ball, assess the strength of the BBC's case and advise the Government in setting the BBC's licence fee increases from 2000/01 up to 2006/07.

The panel was headed by Gavyn Davies, an economist who had worked for earlier Labour governments and then joined Goldman Sachs. He and his colleagues essentially accepted the BBC's arguments for increased public service funding for the Information Society, though not to the full extent of the BBC's wishes. In its report the Panel proposed funding an increase through a supplementary digital licence fee for households with digital receivers: those able to enjoy the BBC's digital services should fund them. The idea was then to taper off this supplement and continue to increase the conventional analogue licence fee, so that there would be a single level again by 2010. This related to the Government's supposed timetable for switching off analogue: any financial deterrent to consumer digital take-up which the supplement might represent would disappear by the time that switching became obligatory.[9]

BSkyB, ONdigital, the cable companies and others with a financial stake in the speed of digital take-up objected vociferously to a supplementary digital licence fee. They had made their bids and investment calculations at the start of digital TV on the basis of the Government framework presented to them then: a supplementary digital licence fee would introduce a wholly new factor, a deterrent to take-up in the short term which would heighten their risk and deepen their debt. The BBC sat on the fence in respect of the Panel's digital licence fee proposal: it just wanted the money.

The Government wanted to strengthen digital television and it wanted the BBC to do the job, bringing quality services and new educational content to the fledgling industry. In February 2000, the Government announced that it would give the BBC a significant licence fee increase – inflation plus 1.5 per cent. However, it did not want to alienate the commercial broadcasters who had taken the main financial risk in launching digital television, so there would be no digital supplement. The boost would be achieved within the annual increases of the basic licence fee. Under Labour's funding arrangement the BBC received its additional income regardless of whether it switched its predominantly analogue audience across to digital.

However, the BBC was dreaming of launching new services. With Greg Dyke now director-general and Mark Thompson in charge of BBC Television, the BBC rethought its digital service proposition. Instead of trying to add channels like BBC Choice and BBC Knowledge which had no real impact on its two main channels, the BBC took a fresh view across them all and began to plan them as a whole. Just as BBC Radio had changed, very controversially, in the 1960s from the mixed genre services of the Home, the Light and the Third, into Radios 1, 2, 3, 4 and Local Radio (and later Radio 5), with different services appealing to different tastes and audience moods, so BBC Television would now become multi-channel.

The plan was trailed in a speech Mark Thompson gave in Canada:

> We are looking hard at the shape of the two networks which are seen by both analogue and digital viewers, BBC ONE and BBC TWO, as well as at our newer digital channels...[10]

Then Greg Dyke set out the full vision in his James McTaggart Memorial Lecture at the Edinburgh Television Festival in August 2000:

> We believe we should have a portfolio of seven services across five channels. Five because this is the maximum number we believe we will be able to deliver on our digital terrestrial multiplex, the platform with the least capacity. Of course, we could do more on satellite and cable but this would mean abandoning our aim of universality.
>
> Incidentally, seven services across five channels is also the number we believe we can afford to fund. Together, they will enable the BBC to meet the needs of our increasingly diverse audiences.[11]

The seven channels started with BBC One and Two, which would evolve to become part of the new digital pattern as digital take-up grew. BBC Choice would be abolished and replaced by a new BBC Three, aimed at a young adult audience (BBC Television's equivalent to Radio 1), broadcast in the evenings only. BBC Knowledge would also end and be replaced by a new cultural and intellectually demanding channel, BBC Four, also confined to the evenings. During the daytime their digital-only frequencies would be used to carry two new children's services, one for the pre-school age group and the other for an older audience. BBC News 24 would continue. In addition to this pattern of seven services on five channels, the BBC would also provide BBC Parliament and BBC Text (later, with interactive features and the BBC's website, branded BBC-i).

This was a vision of BBC multi-channel television with each service focussed on a more segmented audience. Whereas, in analogue, everyone was expected to use both BBC One and BBC Two, not everyone would be expected to watch *all* the BBC's digital-only channels: BBC Four viewers might not like BBC Three any more than Radio 4 listeners liked Radio 1.

Government approval was required for the introduction of new BBC services. When the BBC put forward these proposals, supported by consultation documents indicating public support, opposition came from three directions:

- those who did not want BBC One and Two to change and, in particular, did not want to see arts programmes moved off the mainstream channels on to a digital-only BBC Four (whose availability many associated with pay TV);
- critics of the BBC like David Elstein who argued that the consultations had never asked the most basic question – 'would you rather have these two digital services or have the cost of them removed from the licence fee?'
- commercial companies, like BSkyB, Nickelodeon and Disney, who did not want additional, publicly funded, competition to their own multi-channel services.

ITV Digital, who, one might have imagined, would have wanted the launch of the BBC digital channels with all the associated publicity to drive the take-up of digital TV sets, also joined this last set of objectors.

In September 2001, nine months after the BBC's formal application, having weighed all the objections, Tessa Jowell, the Secretary of State, approved all the BBC's new services (including those for new digital radio services) except for the proposed BBC Three digital TV channel. She laid down a number of conditions in giving approval, one of which was that the BBC publish a plan for promoting digital services and

> commit to and undertake a vigorous and continuing campaign to promote the uptake of digital TV and radio services and equipment generally.[12]

Early in 2002 the BBC was therefore able to launch its two new BBC children's channels – CBBC and Cbeebies – and BBC Four. A revised application for BBC Three was submitted and, after a further round of objections from commercial broadcasters (including, this time, Channel 4, to which Mark Thompson had moved), was eventually approved.

Responding to the heavy political hints, the BBC increased its on-air promotion for digital TV at the end of 2001, giving out a phone number for viewers to ring in order to be sent an explanatory booklet. BBC publicity for digital television still remained muted, however, and, speaking at a Royal Television Society occasion in March 2002, the Broadcasting Minister, Kim Howells, remarked:

> So far, Sky, ITV Digital and cable have done a remarkable job in selling their product. The BBC is beginning to motor but it has been a difficult and steep learning curve which still looks precipitous.[13]

'Free-to-view': a strategy in waiting

In September 2000 I had returned to the digital stage. As the BBC's Director of Customer Service, I was responsible for managing the contract which the BBC had negotiated with BSkyB for issuing BBC-funded viewing (decryption) cards for satellite viewers who did not want pay TV. While this small group of viewers seemed somewhat anomalous on this predominantly subscription platform, I regarded them as the thin end of a potentially very large wedge which could be driven into the digital TV market.

From the BBC's standpoint, developing a non-subscription audience was an important strategic goal. New BBC digital services were being developed and the BBC did not want licence fee payers to see them simply as an optional extra that accompanied BSkyB, cable or ITV Digital pay TV. The other traditional analogue broadcasters agreed but were happy to see the BBC carry the bulk of any costs. With ITV, Channel 4, Channel Five and the Welsh channel S4C, we produced a leaflet to explain to consumers that digital TV did not have to be pay TV, and we put on a small exhibition to accompany its publication.

We had to decide what to call the concept we wanted to develop. 'Non-subscription digital TV' was clumsy and negative; 'free TV' was not strictly true, since viewers would have to pay for new digital reception equipment; 'free-to-air' was the broadcasters' conventional term, but we did not think it conveyed much to the consumer; so we hit on 'free-to-view'.

We set out a clear explanation of how you could be a free-to-view digital TV customer. Back in 2000 this involved either buying an integrated digital TV set or acquiring BSkyB reception equipment and getting the necessary viewing card for decryption (there were virtually no digital terrestrial set-top boxes available without subscription and all the cable services involved a continuing payment). Integrated digital TV sets were generally expensive, in the range £500–£1000 or more, but if households were willing to have a satellite set-top box linked to their phone (and thus to their interactive services) BSkyB would (at that time) give them a free dish and box and simply charge £100 for installation. Although BSkyB was not itself investing in publicity for this free-to-view option, it was content for us to do so – we were, after all, encouraging the take-up of satellite.

Early in 2001 I persuaded the BBC to release me from the Customer Service job and to second me to a new project in which I could concentrate full-time on developing the free-to-view proposition. The project came under Carolyn Fairbairn, the BBC's Director of Strategy. We did some audience-share modelling, comparing the BBC's likely audience share when the nation went fully digital under two scenarios:

- if the pay TV character of the industry remained so dominant;
- if the free-to-view proposition developed and appealed both to those who did not want to subscribe and to subscribers who wanted free-to-view for their second and third TV sets.

It is not difficult to guess which scenario better suited the licence fee-funded BBC.

During 2001, I stimulated a series of initiatives to build awareness for free-to-view: briefings of retailers and manufacturers, a free-to-view display at an Earl's Court technology exhibition, a free-to-view consumer website run by the

Digital TV Group which publicized best retail practice, and a cross-industry conference to launch both the website and a Digital TV Group retailer training booklet. The Government was interested too: the DCMS and DTI civil servants could see that free-to-view digital TV had an essential place in any plan for switching off analogue.

The theme caught on and I was invited to speak at a number of industry conferences. At one, in November 2001, I asserted that the whole digital TV industry was constructed on an unstable structure of subsidies:

> If you're a consumer, a pay TV company will give you a set-top box free (you just need to agree to their terms). If you're a TV or set-top box manufacturer, a pay TV company will place an order for your receivers and put its own electronic programme guide inside them, so you don't have to do that work for yourself. If you're a retailer, a pay TV company will give you an extra payment every time you sell a contract to a pay TV customer.[14]

It was just too good to be true and it could not possibly last. In my view none of the pay TV companies could afford to sustain the current level of subsidy indefinitely, though ITV Digital's problem was the most acute.

At the end of 2001 BSkyB sharply raised the free-to-view price: its £100 free-to-view satellite offer was replaced by a charge of £215 plus £100 for installation.[15] The number of free-to-view satellite consumers had risen substantially during 2001, especially after the Government's agreement to the BBC's new channels. If there was to be a new free-to-view receiver market stimulated by the BBC's new services and a greater BBC willingness to promote digital TV, BSkyB was wary about subsidizing it.

While digital satellite gave us a point of entry, our free-to-view project's central interest lay in remedying the market's lack of free-to-view digital *terrestrial* set-top boxes. We wanted retailers to sell boxes which consumers could buy, at a reasonable price, without having to sign a contract with ITV Digital.

When Greg Dyke arrived at the BBC as director-general, in his memory was the work he had commissioned when chairman of Channel Five to explore funding upfront digital television costs by anticipating the proceeds from auctioning the released analogue spectrum. Could this facilitate the production of a free-to-view digital terrestrial television set-top box? Early work swiftly ruled out anticipating any proceeds from switch-off at that stage – or doing anything involving public money (whether the BBC's or the Government's) which could be construed as discriminatory support for one particular digital platform. However, Greg Dyke kept up the pressure to solve the problem. If a public subsidy would not work, could the BBC find commercial partners who might be willing to subsidize the development for commercial reasons?

Discussions began between the BBC commercial subsidiary, BBC Technology and potential set-top box manufacturers – Pace was interested – and also with telecommunications companies who might secure revenue through a return path. High-level dialogue with ITV executives began in parallel, since ITV Digital was clearly unable to continue subsidizing set-top boxes at full cost for much longer. Suppose a commercial consortium came together to subsidize the development of a free-to-view set-top box which would be sold for a one-off price to free-to-view customers – and, if they wished to subscribe, ITV Digital could give them a subsidized module to add to the box? BBC research suggested that, at a target price of £99, a free-to-view set-top box would sell on the strength of the free-to-view digital services. For ITV it would be a lot cheaper to subsidize an add-on module than to subsidize the whole box. Closer broadcaster collaboration, and cost-saving, on the transmission side was also investigated.

So, from autumn 2001 through the winter into 2002, the BBC conducted negotiations with a number of other major industry players and kept the Government informed. In November 2001 press stories began to appear, heralding the formation of a new 'Digital Coalition'.[16] One newspaper pictured the BBC cavalry coming to the rescue of ITV Digital:

> Who is this mysterious figure, cutting a dash on the plains of digital television? None other than Greg Dyke, director-general of the BBC. He is the leading figure in the creation of *Boxco*, a scheme involving free-to-air broadcasters – including the BBC, ITV, Channel 4 and possibly Channel 5 (though Channel 5 reckons that it is the least involved so far) – to kick-start digital television by offering viewers a cheap set top box providing access to 20-odd free-to-air digital channels with no subscription payments.[17]

'Boxco' was a piece of shorthand for a possible BBC commercial joint venture which, in the end, proved abortive. Philip Langsdale of BBC Technology told the press in December 2001:

> We have looked at launching a set top box in the past but have now ruled it out.[18]

But the quest for a free-to-view digital terrestrial box continued, as did the dialogue with manufacturers. The BBC market research helped create confidence. In January 2002 Pace announced that, without any subsidy from broadcasters or telecommunications companies, it would launch a digital terrestrial box by April.[19]

Once it was clear that BBC Technology did not wish to proceed with a commercial joint venture, I became the main BBC point of contact for the set manufacturers. I organized a series of demonstrations at which Pace and others could show the BBC digital terrestrial set-top box prototypes which they were serious about launching into a free-to-view market. The most striking finding was that Pace was by no means alone: we saw around half a dozen companies, some of whom had been making products for the ITV Digital market and some of whom were new to the business. We asked questions about their pricing and the components which determined their costs and we asked whether they had any orders from retailers. Then we saw all the major retailers and learned how the market looked from their perspective. The answers were very promising.

Meanwhile, Carolyn Fairbairn, with BBC colleagues Charles Constable and Peter Davies, conducted a continuing negotiation with ITV Digital and its Carlton and Granada backers. The ITV side was keen to see free-to-view set-top boxes enter the market, but only if they included the conditional access facility needed for subscription. The conditional access system could either be built-in or the box could contain a common interface into which a conditional access module financed by ITV Digital would fit. Conditional access became a 'must have' for the commercial broadcasters.

The BBC view was that, since conditional access was not required to access BBC digital terrestrial services funded by the licence fee, the BBC had no reason to require this feature. It was prepared to recommend the 'common interface' but not to require it, since it added cost and complexity to the receiver and made it more difficult, at that time, for manufacturers to hit the £99 target price which our consumer research told us was important.

This became a sticking point on our side. Underpinning it was our awareness that ITV Digital's technology was still, in certain respects, tied into the proprietary technology of Canal Plus. I worked closely with a technical colleague, Graham Plumb, on identifying the technical features of receivers which were important to the BBC from a public service broadcasting standpoint. We wanted an open market in which different manufacturers could produce their own products without having to pay Canal Plus or queue up waiting for their technical approval. In particular, we wanted manufacturers to build a version of the interface for interactive services which was free from any links to Canal Plus' MediaHighway system. This was required for viewers to access BBC Text and all the BBCi features associated with BBC digital services.

We also wanted manufacturers and retailers to ensure that, when free-to-view digital terrestrial boxes were sold to the public, consumers were told about the restrictions on digital terrestrial coverage and advised of a post-code checking system to see whether or not a satisfactory signal could be obtained at their address. Moreover, we wanted consumers to be warned of the possibility that some would need a new aerial. We were trying to avoid the reception frustrations which had plagued ITV Digital and undermined the reputation of the early integrated digital TV sets.[20]

In February 2002, ahead of the launch of the Pace box, Carolyn Fairbairn and I convened a meeting in the Langham Hilton hotel of all the potential digital terrestrial box manufacturers, plus interested Government, broadcasting and retailer representatives. We set out, in a consultative manner, what we saw as the

BBC's needs for the successful launch of a free-to-view receiver market and what we were prepared to do, through BBC services and promotion, to support such a launch. Our list of technical requirements was short. After all, the BBC was not proposing to place any orders – we saw that as the retailers' job. The contrast with the much more prescriptive approach ITV Digital had historically taken, for receivers which it specified, ordered and subsidized, was very apparent.

ITV Digital was present. Our relationship with Stuart Prebble and his colleagues was friendly. However, ITV Digital entered a note of dissent over conditional access. It was clear to the manufacturing community that the broadcasters were unlikely to agree and that the prospects for a 'Digital Coalition' were receding. Indeed, Greg Dyke subsequently revealed that, as early as December 2001, the managing director of Carlton, Gerry Murphy, had warned him to be careful about this coalition approach. Even if a BBC-ITV Digital agreement did prove possible, 'he doubted whether there was enough money to keep ITV Digital going.'[21]

ITV Digital's final crisis

At the end of February 2002 Carlton and Granada brought in Deloitte & Touche, the accountancy firm, to review ITV Digital's cost base. Given Deloitte & Touche's experience in handling insolvency, this decision was read in two different ways. Some saw liquidation as now inevitable; others believed ITV Digital's claim that Deloitte & Touche were there essentially to help re-negotiate a number of its major contracts. The underlying point was that unless ITV Digital's suppliers were prepared to take on a major share of its losses by 'taking a hair cut' and lowering their prices then ITV Digital would collapse – and that threat would be explicitly used in the contract re-negotiations.

BBC Worldwide and Flextech, as suppliers of the UKTV channels, and BSkyB, as a supplier of premium movies and sport, were therefore asked to reduce their charges to help rescue ITV Digital. They could see the public relations risk in refusing to talk. However, they were able to take their time since it swiftly became apparent that ITV Digital's primary aim was to escape from its misjudged £315 million contractual commitment to Nationwide League football. Nationwide League matches were broadcast on the ITV Sport channel. Although ITV 1 and ITV 2 were now carried on satellite, Stuart Prebble had been unable to agree terms with BSkyB to carry ITV Sport so its subscriber numbers remained small. Huge sums were therefore being paid for tiny audiences to watch second-rank games. The contract now looked like a financial disaster and it was due to run until 2004.

The position in March 2002 was that, £137 million having already been paid, ITV Digital was due to pay the Nationwide League a further £178 million in two further instalments in the summer of 2002 and 2003. Carlton and Granada decided they simply could not afford this. So Stuart Prebble offered the Football League a mere £50 million instead.[22] The League was told that it could either accept the loss of £128 million or see ITV Digital go bankrupt – in which case TV coverage would cease and it would receive nothing, since Carlton and Granada would not, in those circumstances, be liable for ITV Digital's debt.

The Football League bridled at these negotiating tactics and refused to re-write the contract. League Chairman Keith Harris and Chief Executive David Burns knew that the Nationwide League football clubs would be taken by surprise by such a sudden sharp cut. The clubs had in many cases already spent the money to which ITV Digital was contractually committed, on players' salaries, for example. Keith Harris estimated that, if the League accepted Stuart Prebble's proposal, perhaps 30 of its 72 clubs could face bankruptcy.

All this was played out in public. If ITV Digital had had a bad press over the preceding months, this was nothing compared to the publicity which now ensued. On 21st March, Keith Harris was quoted as having said:

> When major public companies enter into contracts through subsidiaries or in their own right, the counter-parties are entitled to expect those contracts to be honoured.[23]

The headlines included 'ITV crisis threatens lifeblood of League' and 'Footy clubs face ruin in ITV crisis'.[24] The conflict was all the more bitter because neither party had a workable Plan B. Carlton and Granada were quite serious about closing ITV Digital if the League would not renegotiate but the more they threatened, the more likely this outcome looked – which, of course, deterred new subscribers and compounded their business problems. The Football League was prepared to call their bluff by threatening to sue Carlton and Granada if they reneged on ITV Digital's commitment, but their contract was with ITV Digital and they were on legally weak ground here.

At the end of March ITV Digital went into administration. The Football League became one of the creditors. On 2nd April, Stuart Prebble resigned and 1500 ITV Digital staff all feared for their own jobs. Then the pay-per-view film service was withdrawn. Thousands of ITV Digital customers sought to cancel their subscriptions and demanded refunds. The administrators, Deloitte & Touche, put the company up for sale, but they were unable to sell the business as a going concern. While the free-to-view services could continue, the pay TV providers would clearly soon withdraw their services. The ITC therefore made plans for revoking and re-advertising ITV Digital's licences. Finally, on 25th April the administrators announced that they were preparing for the short-term sale of the business and of its assets.

It was the end. The next day Tessa Jowell, the Secretary of State for Culture, Media and Sport, stated in Parliament:

Yesterday's announcement represents the collapse of a brave commercial enterprise to launch an entirely new digital platform. The business has made commercial judgements which have turned out to be unsuccessful. There is always a risk in such ventures, especially in relation to markets built on new technology...

The success of DTT (digital terrestrial television) should not be equated with the position of one commercial operator. The fact that ITV Digital has not succeeded will not deflect us and the broadcasting industry from making a reality of the digital future. Digital TV and the promise it holds is more than ITV Digital.[25]

Thereafter the ITV Digital wreck sank steadily beneath the waves. The pay TV services swiftly ceased and the three digital terrestrial multiplex licences were surrendered to the ITC. The majority of the staff based at the ill-fated Marco Polo House headquarters in London and those in contract call centres were given notice. A skeleton staff remained to keep the free-to-view services on air, but Marco Polo House itself – owned by BSkyB who had inherited it from BSB – was an expense which could only continue on a temporary basis while the ITC re-advertised the three multiplex licences.

The casualty list went beyond the company. The Football League took Carlton and Granada to court in an attempt to recover their lost contract money – and failed. Owing to the form of contract the League had signed, ITV Digital's parent companies were not liable for their bankrupt subsidiary's debt.[26] Keith Harris and David Burns both resigned.

For the present, customers were allowed to keep their ITV Digital set-top boxes, on which they could still receive the BBC's digital channels, ITV 2 and a few other free-to-view services – but, strictly speaking, these receivers were part of the company's assets, which the administrator was obliged to consider re-possessing. The other assets were sold at auction.

ITV Digital's management looked back to see where they thought their venture had gone wrong. Michael Green's verdict was:

Did we make mistakes? Definitely. But the basic problem was that the black boxes didn't work. The signal was weak because civil servants were frightened to interfere with signals for conventional television and mobile phones. Screens would go fuzzy during a drama's crucial kiss. This is not an excuse, but if I did it again I would check all the technology worked first.[27]

John Egan, a leading Carlton founder of ONdigital, felt the consortium would have worked if BSkyB had been allowed to remain a member, and that

It failed because the original forecasts of coverage were not as robust as expected. We were assured of 70% coverage. The ITC had done tests and the

BBC engineers had a lot of expertise, but in real life there are buildings and mountains to interfere with signals. We thought 10–15% of existing aerials would need modifying to receive DTT, but it was closer to one in four.[28]

Stuart Prebble, while acknowledging mistakes, came out fighting:

Sky's Tony Ball famously accused ITV Digital's executives recently of being unable to run a bath. The problem wasn't running the bath, it was that some bastard kept on pulling the plug out.

While Prebble's 'bastard' might be thought to have been BSkyB, he put the blame elsewhere:

Sky is the scorpion: you know what it is capable of when you go near it – you cannot blame the scorpion for stinging. Do I blame the regulators? Absolutely.

And he also blamed the Government:

For giving digital terrestrial bandwidth to the free-to-air broadcasters but putting them under no obligation to develop anything that would attract audiences. For failing to respond speedily to our frequent complaints about the Kafkaesque process of the signal roll-out or the need for power increases. For leaving us bound up in a regulated system while our barely regulated competitors cut our throats.[29]

Speaking at a later date to Peter Goodwin of the University of Westminster, Stuart Prebble reflected that the causes of ITV Digital's collapse had been multiple – pioneering new technology, BSkyB's programme supply pricing, piracy, regulatory limits on cross-promotion by ITV, the Football League deal and the impact of the advertising recession on ITV: 'There were probably half a dozen major problems. We could have survived any three or four of them, but not all six.'[30]

What am I bid for these three multiplexes?

In the aftermath of ITV Digital's failure, the ITC gave the market the opportunity to give a fresh verdict on the underlying commercial viability of digital terrestrial television. At the beginning of May 2002, the ITC invited applications for the three former ITV Digital multiplex licences and, under the leadership of Patricia Hodgson (who had moved to the ITC from the BBC), set an accelerated timetable designed to minimize the period of industry uncertainty and instability.

Industry morale was certainly low. The cable companies were in financial crisis. NTL had run up £12 billion of debt and in January 2002 had called in specialist advisers to restructure its finances and had sought legal bankruptcy protection.[31] In April it announced that its biggest creditors had agreed to wipe out over £7 billion of debt in return for control of the company in a debt-for-equity swap.[32] In May, Telewest announced a cut of 1500 jobs.[33] It subsequently changed its chief executive, made further job cuts and began talks to restructure its debt.[34] For both companies, holding digital TV customers was a struggle.

The failure of ITV Digital and the problems of the cable industry dented the business of the receiver manufacturing sector and retailers were gloomy about the prospects for the digital TV industry as a whole.

At an industry conference at the end of April, David Elstein, a longstanding critic of digital terrestrial television (DTT) and prominent sceptic of the Government plan to switch off analogue, argued that commercial reality had now punctured the unrealistic dreams of a politicized digital TV industry:

DTT has turned out to be rather like the tar baby in the Brer Rabbit story. Every attempt to engage with it has simply entangled the participants in mounting difficulties. Meanwhile, the industrial strategy associated with DTT has crumbled, and the disarray in which ministers now find themselves – almost entirely of their own making – looks impossible to put right.[35]

In collaboration with the Digital TV Group, the ITC carried out tests on some of the technical variables, reviving the early technical debate over the channel capacity of the terrestrial multiplexes. Essentially the technology offered a trade-off between maximizing the number of services in a multiplex (e.g. six TV channels instead of four) and optimizing the robustness of the signal to enlarge the reception area and reduce interference. Bidders for the vacant multiplexes were free to make their own proposals for the technical standard for the future. The BBC's technical experts were convinced that ITV Digital had been short-sighted in cramming so many services into their three multiplexes and that this had been a major contributory factor in the reception difficulties their customers had experienced.

The main, bold commercial reappraisal came from the BBC director-general, Greg Dyke. He argued that the principal lesson to be drawn from the UK digital TV saga from 1998 to 2002 was that having competing pay TV operations on three separate platforms could not work. It had failed in the UK and no other country had made it work either. It was possible to have pay TV on digital terrestrial television but only if it was run in collaboration with another platform, not in direct competition.

Given the parlous state of NTL and Telewest, the only serious candidate for a pay TV partnership was BSkyB, but the regulators had thrown BSkyB out of the ITV consortium in the first place on competition grounds. Therefore, if BSkyB's involvement with digital terrestrial pay was ruled out,

> I suspect there is only one other way to make DTT work and that is to make the platform a free-to-view only service…
>
> At the BBC we have a lot of evidence which suggests that some 35 to 40 per cent of the population don't want pay TV and don't intend to get it. Given that research shows most people confuse 'digital' with 'pay TV', this is a real problem for the Government's plan to switch off the analogue signal by 2010 and make Britain 100% digital.
>
> However, the same research suggests that there is a demand from some of these same people for more channels as long as they are good quality and free-to-view.[36]

The BBC recipe was, therefore, fewer channels, better coverage, quality services and no subscription – and a BBC expression of interest in bidding for some of the vacant digital terrestrial capacity went into the ITC in mid-May.

From my standpoint, having led the BBC's free-to-view digital TV project over the preceding year, the moment of opportunity had come. An editorial in *Broadcast* magazine commented:

> For the first time the BBC's long-suffering free-to-air champion will have a whole multiplex to talk up, rather than a handful of channels nobody really wants.[37]

My principal concern at the time was to support the launch of free-to-view set-top boxes – through publicity, information about the BBC's digital services and access to the BBC's transmission experts. I knew that no bid on a free-to-view basis would be convincing without unsubsidized receivers in the shops to complement the programme service proposition. We hosted a digital industry meeting in early May, and I said firmly that the BBC was in digital terrestrial television to stay and that 'with no if's and but's, we would make it work.'

We underlined the importance of retailers being straight with their customers – not pretending they were within a reception area if they were not, and not pretending that they did not need a new aerial if it was obvious (from the selection of digital frequencies for their area) that they probably would. We agreed, in our own publicity, to advise potential customers to use the Digital TV Group's postcode database to check coverage for their own area. I provided a manager to help train retailers and manufacturers in the characteristics of digital terrestrial reception and funded a special telephone service for retailer staff to call to check the postcode database before they clinched a sale. It was very gratifying to see Pace, Nokia, Grundig, Goodmans, Panasonic, Daewoo and Hauppage boxes come into the market, alongside the integrated television sets, to make free-to-view a practical reality during this commercially unsettled spring and summer.

Meanwhile, led by Carolyn Fairbairn, a BBC team spent long hours talking to all the potential partners with whom the BBC could bid for the vacant licences. The natural candidates were ITV, Channel 4 and Channel Five, all of whom, like the BBC, continued to broadcast free-to-view services on their multiplexes after the ITV Digital multiplexes were surrendered. However, whereas the BBC had a free-to-view agenda, ITV and Channel 4 remained committed to the inclusion of a significant element of pay TV. At the same time the commercial broadcasters viewed the BBC Worldwide-Flextech UKTV channels as commercial competitors.

No agreement had been reached by the mid-May ITC deadline for the expressions of interest. So the BBC and ITV and Channel 4 submitted separate letters. Other expressions of interest came from Crown Castle (formerly BBC Transmission before it was privatized), SDN (the multiplex licencee for Channel Five and S4C), former Mirror Group boss David Montgomery, a venture capital grouping, a Scottish call centre and a shopping channel. BSkyB did not express an interest.

Partly to allow enough time for the technical testing, the ITC extended the timetable by two weeks, setting a closing date of 13th June for bids, with an ITC decision on the awards on 4th July. However, more time did not produce agreement among the terrestrial broadcasters, whose differences soon found their way into the press:

> Plans to relaunch a new digital terrestrial television service out of the ashes of ITV Digital are in disarray because of a row between the BBC and the ITV companies… With ITV at loggerheads with the BBC, Channel 4 wanting capacity for its pay channels… and Channel 5 not keen to come up with any money for the venture, the chances of success seem slim. The Government in particular is desperate to save digital terrestrial from total collapse because of its plans to switch off existing analogue broadcasts between 2006 and 2010.[38]

Greg Dyke's 'Plan B' was to talk to Crown Castle and BSkyB. Crown Castle could bring technical expertise and commercial investment to a new consortium but lacked experience in commissioning and marketing broadcast services. BSkyB was the UK's leading digital TV company, with a formidable reputation for marketing and customer support, but could be viewed as too dominant unless positioned very sensitively.

BBC-BSkyB collaboration for a specific purpose, at ITV's expense, was not unprecedented. There was an *ad hoc* alliance as far back as the 1992 Premier

League contract, with Greg Dyke, negotiating for ITV, on the receiving end. In 1998 BBC and BSkyB experts had worked closely together to launch BBC services on digital satellite. BSkyB had worked hard in recent years to overcome the broadcasting establishment's tendency to stereotype the company as the industry 'bad guys'. It had recruited Sheila Cassells, formerly at the ITC, as head of Economic Policy. It was making progress in overturning a critical interim report arising from an Office of Fair Trading investigation of alleged uncompetitive behaviour. BSkyB's buccaneering culture was still there but it was now overlaid with a layer of political savvy.

The focus for a potential BBC-BSkyB alliance was free-to-view digital terrestrial. Greg Dyke had already concluded that the concept of three competing pay TV platforms was commercially unworkable. He wanted a free-to-view digital terrestrial display within which the BBC's public service digital channels would be the jewels: on satellite and cable they would always be outshone by the premium sports and film services. For BSkyB free-to-view digital terrestrial meant the removal of any terrestrial pay TV competitor. If BSkyB was only an ally, not a bidder for a multiplex licence, and since its potential dominance was in pay TV which, in this case, would not be involved, the alliance ought to pass muster with the competition regulators.

So, behind the scenes, work began on a BBC bid for one of the three vacated multiplexes, a Crown Castle bid for the other two, and a marketing joint venture between the BBC, Crown Castle and BSkyB to launch a wholly free-to-view package of services. The channel line-up would include Sky News and Sky Sports News and a new UK History service. The unsubsidized £100 set-top box would underpin the proposition. The target market would be those who would like wider channel choice but did not wish to pay a subscription – leaving BSkyB and cable a clear run in the pay TV field.

The main rival bid came from Carlton, Granada and Channel 4 in conjunction with a new company co-owned by David Chance, a non-executive director of Granada, and Ian West, both former BSkyB managers from Sam Chisholm's old team. Their proposal was to have a 'pay-lite' mix of free-to-view and pay TV services.

The other two bids – from SDN and from a company formed by the investment group Apax Partners – were more limited in scope. Their proposals were for what the ITC termed the 'platform operator model'.[39] They would manage the infrastructure for whatever broadcasting services were willing to sign up with them. Thus they were not in the service provider or service marketing business themselves and could not, on their own, offer a guarantee of making digital terrestrial a commercial success. The two serious bids were, therefore, the 'unholy alliance of the giants' (as its critics termed the BBC-Crown-BSkyB consortium) and 'the people who brought you ITV Digital' (as its critics termed the Carlton-Granada-Channel 4 team).

Informed by the results of the technical tests, all the bidders except Apax Partners opted for the technical solution which offered more robust coverage with fewer channels (in the industry's technical shorthand, '16QAM'), in preference to the 'greater channel capacity/smaller reception area' technical standard which had been in use since 1998 (termed '64QAM').

During the month of June a major political and public relations contest was waged. The BBC consortium was willing in principle to offer membership of its proposed marketing joint venture to ITV/Channel 4 and SDN as the other multiplex licensees, but did not expect them, at any rate at this stage, to accept. So there was no fudging of the choice. If the question was 'Whom do you trust to relaunch digital terrestrial television and make a success of it?', the answer tended to be the BBC consortium. However, if the question was 'Do you really want all possibility of pay TV to disappear from digital terrestrial TV, including Channel 4's FilmFour and E4?', doubts set in.

Politicians were said to want to see the retention of an element of pay, though, of course, it was not their job to decide. While the Government did not appear intent on abolishing the licence fee for the BBC's next Charter term, eliminating pay entirely from digital terrestrial could potentially entrench the licence fee forever, undermining any possible long-term strategy (stemming from the 1986 Peacock enquiry) of moving the BBC in stages towards subscription funding. The Treasury would not have wanted to have its longer term options restricted by being boxed in by the free-to-view strategy.

The BBC's public position was to oppose any element of pay TV on digital terrestrial television for the present while the platform was in crisis, without ruling out the possibility of its introduction at some later date. However, Greg Dyke subsequently acknowledged that the free-to-view bid was important to the BBC defensively: the more free-to-view receivers that went into the market with no conditional access capability for pay TV, the harder it would be to switch an all-digital BBC to an all-subscription BBC.[40]

The work of compiling our bid in late May and early June was intense. Greg Dyke led the team personally. On 4th July we came into the office at what seemed like the crack of dawn to await the ITC puff of smoke (the announcement had to be made before the Stock Exchange opened, apparently). We all stood around the fax machine in Greg Dyke's outer office waiting in suspense. I was sufficiently confident to have packed two bottles of champagne in my briefcase before leaving home. We opened them as the news came through that the ITC had selected our bid, 'based on the following factors:

- The opportunity provided by the consortium for a fresh start for DTT by offering a distinctive new proposition to consumers.
- The consortium's top level resolve to launching and sustaining a service for the duration of the licence.

- Their approach to addressing technical issues required to improve the performance of the platform.
- The ambitious and clearly developed marketing strategy for the whole DTT platform.
- The combination within the consortium of management strength-in-depth of its members and their ability and commitment to deliver the stated proposition and hence promote digital terrestrial television in the UK overall.'[41]

The launch of *Freeview*

Exhilaration on 4th July soon gave way to a sobering assessment of the work which lay ahead to relaunch digital terrestrial. Andy Duncan, the BBC's Director of Marketing and Communications, took the lead here, in conjunction with Crown Castle and BSkyB. Relations within the consortium strengthened rapidly under the pressures of practical collaboration but many of the difficulties were outside the partners' direct control.

Relations with ITV, Channel 4 and SDN were cool. The commercial terrestrial broadcasters remained wedded to the idea of a pay TV ingredient on one or both of their multiplexes. They now opposed changing the technical standard despite having advocated it in their own bids: it would reduce their capacity for potential new commercial services and the benefits from a more robust signal no longer seemed to them quite so significant or important. As a result, the ITC, which had previously said that it was 'minded' to select a common standard with fewer channels and better reception 'in order to achieve consistency',[42] decided, after consulting the interested parties, making measurements and talking to its lawyers, to allow each multiplex to choose its own standard.[43] So the relaunch had to be planned for a mixed economy of 16 and 64 QAM and receivers would need to be able to handle both modes.

Relations with the rump of ITV Digital were equally tricky. Based in ITV Digital's Marco Polo House was a network management system for displaying channel and programme information across all six multiplexes. However, terms for buying it could not be agreed so BBC Technology experts had to re-create it. Later on the ITV Digital liquidator demanded that the million or so ex-ITV Digital subscribers who still had their old ITV Digital boxes – the bulk of the digital terrestrial audience at the time – pay £39.99 for the privilege of keeping them.[44] However, this threat evaporated once Carlton and Granada took stock of the implications for their 'digital dividend' as well as for their public reputation.

The receiver manufacturers kept their pledges to put new free-to-view set-top boxes into the market, albeit in pretty modest volumes initially, and Netgem, Pioneer and others joined the early entrants. However, the idea of designing a new Electronic Programme Guide for the digital terrestrial platform had to be deferred. An agreement that would have had to include the BBC-Crown

Castle-BSkyB joint venture and ITV, Channel 4 and SDN, plus the receiver manufacturers, proved far too ambitious.

Meanwhile, Crown Castle had yet to complete negotiations for programme services to fill its two multiplexes and the deferred Government approval for BBC Three meant that this service would not be ready in time for the digital terrestrial relaunch.

Amid all these pressures, Andy Duncan and his Crown Castle and BSkyB colleagues were able to announce that the three ex-ITV Digital multiplexes would be relaunched by the end of October 2002.[45] Together with the three multiplexes which had remained on the air, they would constitute a 30-channel proposition, entirely free-to-view, for which receivers would cost under £100. The new service proposition would be branded *Freeview*, notwithstanding Stuart Prebble's idiosyncratic decision to set up his own company with the same name.[46]

The channel line-up would include:

BBC One	ITV 1
BBC Two	ITV 2
BBC Three (later)	Channel 4
BBC Four	S4C & S4C2 (in Wales)
BBC News 24	Five
BBC Parliament	ITV News
CBBC	CNN
Cbeebies	Sky News
BBCi (text and interactive features)	Sky Sports News
UK History (using BBC archives)	Sky Travel
BBC & commercial digital radio stations	The Community Channel

The marketing message was kept very simple. All these services were available (in place of the analogue choice of only five channels) for the simple purchase of a fit-it-yourself set-top box. These were new services from the broadcasters you already knew and trusted. There was no subscription. Those who wanted pay channels could go to satellite or cable. This was TV through the normal rooftop aerial for people who did not want pay TV.

As the research had predicted, the target market was very different from pay TV's. *Freeview* was pitched more at an older, more conservative section of the population – closer to the BBC's analogue heartland than to typical multichannel subscriber households. The BBC commissioned a massive on-air promotional campaign, to mention all three platforms, but essentially to establish nationwide awareness of *Freeview* and to underline that there was no subscription.

Customer support arrangements were put in place: an updated postcode database for checking digital terrestrial coverage, a *Freeview* website, and a *Freeview* call centre. BSkyB contributed extensively from its expertise in this area and took the lead in briefing retailers and providing them with point-of-sale display material. The limited change of technical standard and modest increases in transmitter power produced better reception, particularly for the Crown Castle multiplexes with the least good coverage.

Freeview was launched on 30th October 2002. Consumers responded enthusiastically to the simplicity of the proposition. An estimated 65,000 set-top boxes were sold in the first two weeks.[47] By Christmas it was clear that demand for receivers in the shops had outstripped supply. By the end of its first year *Freeview* was able to boast over 2 million customers – its boxes, it claimed,

> the fastest ever new consumer electronic product adopted by UK households.[48]

2002 proved a good year not only for the BBC but for BSkyB as well. In October Oftel rejected ITV's complaint that, at £17 million per annum, BSkyB had overcharged it for access to the satellite platform.[49] In December the OFT, overturning its earlier interim findings, cleared BSkyB of having breached competition law.[50]

In ITV, Michael Green of Carlton and Charles Allen of Granada both remained Chairmen of their respective companies, but Steve Morrison, Granada's chief executive, left.[51] When, a year later, Carlton and Granada were given approval to merge into a single ITV, Charles Allen became the chief executive, but the shareholders rejected a proposal that Michael Green become chairman.[52]

Gradually ITV, Channel 4 and SDN established a *modus vivendi* with *Freeview*, though David Chance still pursued his 'pay-lite' idea. It took until 2004, but he and Ian West were then able to launch *Top-Up TV* – a scheme to make E4, Sky One, UK Gold, Discovery and other channels available for around £8 a month. The BBC, anxious not to dilute the simple message of *Freeview*, made difficulties over the positioning of the pay services within the digital terrestrial list of channels but backed down after *Top-Up TV* appealed to Ofcom.[53] *Top-Up TV* required the consumer either to buy a *Freeview* set-top box which included conditional access or to add a conditional access module to an integrated digital TV set, but its whole business plan as an add-on, with minimal fixed costs, was based on riding on the back of *Freeview*'s marketing. It had no incentive to damage, or slow, *Freeview*'s growth.

After *Freeview*, 'Free-sat'?

The success of *Freeview* heightened awareness that, while licence fee payers everywhere were funding the BBC's digital services, digital terrestrial coverage was limited to just under 75 per cent of the population and would remain so, broadly, until implementation of digital switchover began. Satellite and cable were essentially marketed as subscription services, so households without digital terrestrial coverage who did not want to sign a contract with a pay TV company felt disenfranchised. The BBC asked itself whether the concept of an open market in unsubsidized receivers could be transplanted to satellite – breaking what was in practice largely a BSkyB monopoly of satellite reception.

The first step would be to end encryption of free-to-view services on satellite, the rationale for which lay in copyright protection outside the UK. Because the satellite footprint covered much more of Europe than just the UK, broadcasters who had purchased UK-only rights for films and sporting events had a duty to prevent their reception in other European markets. The widespread use of English on the continent made this a bigger issue for UK broadcasters than, for instance, for German broadcasters. In 2003 Astra offered the BBC the option to move to a new satellite with a smaller footprint, not strictly confined to the UK but with a much reduced overspill area. The BBC took it and told BSkyB, without any warning, that it would no longer encrypt its services.[54]

After a row, which the two organizations managed to insulate from their *Freeview* partnership, and after the threat of ITC intervention,[55] the BBC switched to broadcasting on satellite in the clear and BSkyB receivers continued to display its services in their established slots on the BSkyB electronic programme guide. ITV, Channel 4 and Channel Five remained encrypted for the present but were reluctant to take on any continuing cost for supplying free-to-view customers with decryption cards. In 2004, BSkyB launched a pre-emptive free-to-view option under which it installed a satellite dish and set-top box with a funded card for a single payment of £150.

While ITV ultimately decided in 2005 to join the BBC in broadcasting in the clear, creating the long-term possibility of an open market in satellite receivers, BSkyB's *de facto* monopoly of reception meanwhile continued and, the £150 scheme notwithstanding, digital satellite remained primarily a pay TV service. The dominant platform for free-to-view reception was undoubtedly digital terrestrial, with *Freeview* set-top boxes becoming a 'must have' Christmas present for several years in a row.

End of crisis

From the end of 2002 onwards digital terrestrial television ceased to be at the mercy of the pay TV business and BSkyB, now a partner in *Freeview*, no longer posed a threat to its existence. As a free-to-view proposition, it was now supported by a genuine, indeed burgeoning, market.

The success of *Freeview* rescued the public policy of digital switchover. As 2002 neared its end, Tessa Jowell felt able to observe having seen the resilience of the technology and the marketing, I remain confident that switchover by 2010 is still challenging but achievable.[56]

However, the credit did not rest wholly with the technology and the marketing, nor with the foresight and initiative of the BBC – critical though these factors all were.

It was the generous licence fee settlement in 2000 which had made possible the BBC's development of its full range of digital services. The former ITV Digital multiplexes were awarded to the BBC and to a transmission company which had formerly been the BBC's transmission department. BBC publicity (as distinct from Freeview consortium publicity) could not give special treatment to Freeview – satellite, cable and, as appropriate, telephony were included in order to ensure platform neutrality – but BBC television trails, funded by the licence fee, were what made Freeview a household name. The role of subscription for terrestrial services, initially banished, was still very marginal even after the launch of Top-Up TV, while advertising revenue alone could not have sustained digital terrestrial television as a purely commercial market. Without the BBC's licence fee funding, the crisis would not have been short-lived.

While there had been no political rescue, digital terrestrial television in the UK survived the collapse of ITV Digital only by becoming significantly more dependent on public funding.

Chapter Five

Charting a New Course

With industry confidence restored and underpinned by licence fee expenditure, the public policy of digital switchover became more credible. It remained, however, a distant abstract goal. In some quarters of Government there was still a fond hope that the market would somehow spontaneously deliver the policy. Under this thinking, there was no need to set a firm date for switchover: it was just a question of waiting until the magic number of 95 per cent take-up was reached, and then – lo and behold – the Government's criteria of availability and affordability would have been met, nearly everyone would in practice have switched, and it would just be a question of some policy initiative to assist the last 5 per cent.

What torpedoed this line of thought – and made it clear that, if the Government wanted a public policy of analogue switch-off, it would have to help make it happen – was the work done under the aegis of the Digital TV Action Plan by the UK Digital TV Project.

Implementing the Digital TV Action Plan

The origin of the Action Plan lay in the consolidated list of tasks which had been drawn up in 2001 after the brainstorming session convened by the DTI. In early 2002 the DTI and the DCMS had published a list of some 65 tasks and, after a period of consultation, a forum of industry stakeholders adopted them formally as the Digital TV Action Plan. A joint Government-industry Digital TV Project – involving civil servants, regulators, various industry figures and consumer representatives – then began to tackle the various tasks.

The Government looked after its own responsibilities within a Government Digital Television Group chaired by Andrew Ramsay (DCMS) and David Hendon (DTI). A Spectrum Planning Group was established to bring together the Radiocommunications Agency, the ITC and the industry's other frequency planning experts. Cross-industry groups were set up to address market preparation and technology/equipment.

An additional group, led by the ITC, was in charge of a pilot project, called *Go Digital*, designed to simulate digital switchover in about 300 households in the Tamworth area in the Midlands and research the reactions and implications. I represented the BBC on this.

The various groups were brought together in a project team jointly headed by Jane Humphreys of the DTI, a wise enthusiast who had previously worked on the 3G telecommunications auction, and the impressively bilingual Catherine Smadja, who was on secondment to the DCMS from the French Civil Service. The project manager, Michael Readman, was a secondee from the BBC. The project team was accountable to a Steering Board chaired by DTI and DCMS ministers and had a line of communication and explanation to an open forum of industry stakeholders.

The Government did not follow Stuart Prebble's advice and appoint a Digital Csar – but it was persuaded of the need for a public figurehead whose job would be to chair the stakeholders. Industry soundings were taken by my successor as chairman of the industry's Digital TV Group, Professor David Youlton, to find the best person for the job. Barry Cox, deputy chairman of Channel 4 and formerly a leading ITV pioneer of digital terrestrial television, was selected for the role, with Sheila Cassells of BSkyB as his deputy.

Barry Cox brought to the job enthusiasm, commitment and extremely effective diplomatic skills. When he started the role, ITV Digital was still in crisis and switchover a distant prospect. He was undaunted:

> The job is not a poisoned chalice. I may be a bit perverse in wanting to take this on, but I've been involved with digital for 10 years and I'm fascinated by the issues it provides. There are few things that have such a mix of industrial policy, technology, commerce, public interest and government with a potential for change.[1]

The Digital TV Project team did not start from scratch. It could look back to the 1998 study carried out by NERA and Smith System Engineering for the Radiocommunications Agency,[2] the February 2000 report of the ITC's Genesis Project[3] and a report by the Digital Television Group – the work of its technical director, Peter Marshall – on technical impediments to analogue switchover and how they might be overcome.[4]

Against this background – and with the ITV Digital drama still unfolding – the Digital TV Project began work. The Government issued a consultation -document inviting views on how much spectrum should be cleared for re-use. The DCMS issued some initial guidance on the implications of switchover for landlords.

The DTI carried out a consultation on the role of integrated digital TV sets (as distinct from set-top boxes) in assisting the switchover process. The crunch question was whether all TV sets manufactured after a certain date should be digital, which would kill off analogue set sales in the TV replacement market and drive digital take-up. However, because the receiver market was an international one, the UK Government could not mandate this manufacturing obligation without prior action by the European Union. Accordingly, the DTI asked the TV manufacturing industry whether it wanted to adopt such a policy on a collective voluntary basis.[5] The industry, unsurprisingly, was ambivalent and divided, so there was no collective will to mandate integrated digital TVs.

During the first half of 2002 it was easy to dismiss the Action Plan as a cumbersome bureaucratic structure for carrying out a multitude of somewhat academic tasks designed to prompt more discussion than decision – and to observe that, even if all its tasks were completed, the Plan would not actually deliver switchover. However, this was unfair: conducting a range of studies, consultations and research activities was exactly the right way to start. The work may have been largely 'backroom' but, against the unsettling background of the ITV Digital crisis, an undistracted Digital TV Project team started to understand – really, for the first time – the full ramifications of the switchover goal.

Change of gear

In the autumn of 2002, I took over as project manager, initially on a secondment and then under contract to the DTI as a consultant.

The world of Whitehall was not wholly new to me, in that I had often dealt with Government officials on broadcasting policy matters, but it was a significant change of accountability and of perspective. The nuances of the relationships were important. While my contract was with the DTI, the project was jointly directed by the DTI and the DCMS – and it was also a joint project between the Government and Barry Cox's industry stakeholders. So while I had some residual commitment to the BBC's interests, in that the BBC was a key stakeholder, so too were all the BBC's broadcasting rivals – and my primary loyalty was now to the Government. It was because of the possibility of a conflict of interest that both the BBC and I felt that a direct contractual arrangement with the DTI was preferable to an extended secondment.

It was clear to me that the Action Plan project needed to change gear and, from the end of 2002 onwards, with the digital terrestrial crisis over, could do so with confidence. While the UK was consulting on whether or not the TV manufacturers would agree voluntarily to make the manufacture of digital television sets mandatory, the United States had decided to impose such a requirement by law. By comparison, the UK's switchover policy was seen as lacking conviction. *The Guardian*'s New York business correspondent's verdict was that

> The Government's attitude to digital TV resembles its attitude to Britain joining the euro: it is too worried about upsetting voters to make any actual decision and is in danger of being left behind.[6]

While still at the BBC I had been visited by two consultants auditing the Digital TV Project for the Government and I had commented that the objective of the Action Plan was unclear. Was it trying to deliver switchover or was it trying to deliver Chris Smith's preconditions for a Government decision? When I arrived in Whitehall I found that this view was shared within the project and that civil servants were drafting the removal of this ambiguity. The carefully crafted words with which the Government decided to clarify the Action Plan's objective were:

> To ensure that the criteria set for switchover are met so that Ministers can, if they choose, take the decision to proceed to full switchover by ordering the switching off by 2010 of analogue terrestrial transmissions.[7]

This still did not feel entirely satisfactory to me. The 'criteria' were those laid down by Chris Smith in 1998 – availability and affordability – to which he had appended the take-up target of 95 per cent and a reference to 70 per cent as an important milestone. So was the Action Plan's aim to deliver some threshold percentage of take-up? If so, how did this relate to having 2010 as an option? By the end of 2002 just over 40 per cent of UK households had adopted digital television.[8] It was pretty doubtful whether 95 per cent take-up could be achieved at all while digital terrestrial coverage remained constrained by analogue.

Moreover, the take-up figure – which had been presented as an indicator of affordability – was only a measure of the digital conversion of main TV sets. The average household had two TVs and a video cassette recorder (VCR). VCRs contained analogue tuners and the removal of analogue signals would incapacitate all analogue tuners in the home, not just the main TV. The major consumer costs of a policy of compulsory switchover were likely to relate to second and third TV sets and VCRs. Switchover would almost certainly entail some aerial costs for some households as well. So 'affordability' was actually quite tricky to assess. It was unclear whether the Government fully appreciated this or had fully committed to requiring consumers to replace their analogue reception equipment on the scale involved.

So I added my own gloss to the Action Plan objective and, with the Steering Board's agreement, we stated that the Action Plan 'should

- enable Ministers to decide *whether* to proceed to switchover and, if so
- enable Ministers to decide *how and when* to do so, with 2010 an option,
- and then help prepare for a *successor project to do the job.*'[9]

Early on I arranged an 'Away-Day' for the project team, designed to help think through the whole switchover process from beginning to end. I wanted to move their focus from trying to encourage the spread of digital television to being able to imagine what would actually be involved in switching off analogue. I invented a simulation with childish toys, monopoly money and role playing – with team members cast as the Cabinet, the Treasury, the broadcasters, the receiver manufacturers, the consumers and a potential spectrum buyer – and a year going by every ten minutes to represent the passage of time from 2003 to 2011. The game was to see whether, by the end, the 'Government' role players could close down analogue television without viewer deprivation and without disproportionate public expenditure – and remain electable. They managed it – but that was not the point: the underlying purpose was to build a shared picture of the complexities and issues which would arise at each stage and stimulate creative thinking about how to tackle the main conundrums.

Fortunately, we had some less contrived sources of learning. The first was the *Go Digital* pilot. Under this scheme we had temporarily converted around 300 homes to digital television by supplying them with digital receivers for free and withdrawing their access to analogue reception. We interviewed the householders before, during and after the experience. Encouragingly, this taught us that viewers with little or no initial interest in digital television became much more positive once they were exposed to it.[10] However, it also demonstrated that trying to convert an analogue video-recorder with a digital set-top box (treating it as if it was just another analogue TV set) was very cumbersome. Indeed, in practical terms, it was almost unworkable – with too many separate pieces of equipment to be wired up and too many remote controls to operate.

The second source was Berlin, where the first analogue switch-off in the world was actually taking place. Germany had insufficient frequencies to be able to simulcast digital and analogue terrestrial television. The only possible way forward here was to switch off analogue at the same time as digital terrestrial was introduced. Because analogue terrestrial played such a small part in German broadcast transmission and reception compared with satellite and cable, this was quite feasible. In a population of around 4 million, Berlin had around 150,000 households who relied on analogue terrestrial transmission for their main TV and another 90,000 or so who used it for second or third TV sets. So in 2002 the Berlin city government and the broadcasters embarked on a plan to introduce digital terrestrial transmissions that autumn and to withdraw the analogue terrestrial broadcasts by summer 2003. Despite a temporary shortage of set-top boxes in the shops, the whole process was managed smoothly.

We had a further invaluable source of expertise and understanding – the wide range of project participants whom the DTI and the DCMS had drawn together from within the industry, through secondments, consultancy contracts and research commissions. Greg Bensberg of the ITC led the team of spectrum planners tackling the central question of what a post-switchover frequency plan might look like. Danny Churchill, with a senior management background at Dixons Stores Group, led a marketing group which brought in professional advertising advice. Henry Price, a former BBC colleague, led a series of technical investigations together with Ian Dixon of the DTI and the Digital TV Group. David Harby came from Nokia to investigate the potential of interactive services. Barry Cox, supported by Marcus Coleman from the Digital TV Group, convened stakeholder groups of broadcasting and manufacturer experts, while the TV manufacturers' association organized some workshops.

As meeting followed meeting, we began to understand the full implications of switchover. We visited Berlin – three times in my case. The *Go Digital* pilot concluded and reported early in 2003. The UK broadcasters told us that switchover could never be a single event: the task of converting the transmitters from analogue to digital was so complex and time-consuming that the process would need to be organized, transmitter by transmitter and region by region, over a period of around four years, with two years' planning beforehand. The manufacturers told us that, for digital terrestrial television, the consumer equipment required to make digital recording attractively simple depended on the broadcasters transmitting information about advance programmes with technology which had never been fully implemented.

Switchover was clearly going to be neither swift nor simple – and waiting to reach a take-up threshold of 95 per cent, or even 70 per cent, before committing was incompatible with completion by 2010. For a four-year process with two years' notice, only a commitment around the end of 2004 would deliver the option of completion by the end of 2010.

The next step was to outline a workable switchover strategy. I mapped this into four phases, the first two of which fell to the Action Plan, with the last two the responsibility of the successor project charged with actual implementation:

PHASE ONE: investigating and understanding the subject, leading up to a government decision on *whether* to commit to switchover, after which voluntary consumer switching should be boosted by that commitment.

PHASE TWO: working out *how* to achieve switchover – which the Action Plan team would need to do before the end of 2004 so that the Government could decide *when* on the basis of a range of timing options including completion by 2010.

PHASE THREE: the run-up period of two years (or more) after the Government had announced the timetable, and during which it might be necessary to offer some incentives (carrots and/or sticks).

PHASE FOUR: the switchover process, region by region, lasting four years.

The heart of this strategy was to spread the operation – to think of switchover as a process taking place over several years and not as a 'Big Bang'. Berlin had 250,000 homes to convert. The UK, from a 2003 perspective, had around 25 million (very few digital homes at that point were completely free from any dependence whatsoever on analogue terrestrial signals). I described the central idea as a 'managed migration'.

Until the Government commitment was certain, the process could not properly start. Admittedly, take-up was rising – over 1.8 million set-top boxes (for all platforms) were sold in 2002. However, the replacement market – with no policy of mandating digital TVs – was playing no real part at all. 2002 saw the sale of only around 100,000 integrated digital TV sets, compared with over 4.6 million analogue TVs (and over 3.3 million analogue VCRs).[11] So firming up and publicizing the political commitment was an important step – and it would need to be accompanied by a convincing explanation of the benefits of switchover (as distinct from the benefits of digital television). After that, anyone replacing their TV and/or recording equipment could buy with switchover in mind.

Then it would be important to give plenty of advance notice of the compulsory switchover timetable. This would be essential on the investors' side. Without a firm, reliable timetable neither broadcasters nor TV manufacturers would invest on the scale required. There was a perception that the investors' interest in this respect was at odds with the consumer interest in leaving the timing unsettled and subject to Chris Smith's availability and affordability criteria. However, from a practical standpoint, the consumers needed to understand that there would be a compulsory phase – and why – and, from their own financial point of view, they would be likely to value advance warning too.

The period of advance warning should be two or more years during which as many households as possible should complete their switch to digital reception. As well as making political sense, this was essential logistically: if every household in the country waited until the eve of switchover before buying and installing their digital equipment – even with the regional switching pattern spread over four years – neither manufacturing production lines, retailers, aerial installers, nor call centre agents would be able to cope.[12]

Answering the question 'whether'?

In the summer of 2003 the project team pressed the Government to decide whether it was ready to move from Phase One to Phase Two, making a firm commitment in principle (and leaving timing flexible at that point) with a clear appreciation that the consumer cost, for many households, would go well beyond the cost of a single set-top box.

In order to secure not just DCMS and DTI but also Treasury agreement to this, we needed to deliver the results of a formal Cost-Benefit Analysis. This work was undertaken by a group which I chaired. At its heart was a team of Government economists, with Michael Hodson and Michael Crosse of the DTI providing the main driving force, supported by economist colleagues from the DCMS and the Treasury, DTI and DCMS civil servants on the policy side, some ITC input, some commissioned consultancy work, and an independent economic auditor.

Cost-Benefit Analysis studies are notorious among policy-makers for being inexact and any answers that emerge need to be heavily qualified by sensitivity analysis. We had no illusions about the difficulty of estimating the costs and knew this to be an easier task than putting a value on the benefits.

Before we could do either we had to get the intellectual foundations right. The guidelines for this kind of analysis tell you to compare the costs and benefits of a hypothetical policy initiative against those of the *status quo*. So what was the *status quo*? We decided firmly that we were not assessing the costs and benefits of digital television and comparing them with those of analogue television. We were not looking back at the 'do nothing' option of the mid-1990s. Digital television was already here and growing steadily. Our aim was to assess the costs and benefits of *digital switchover* and compare them with a 'base case' of *no analogue switch-off*, i.e. digital television and analogue television coexisting, like AM and FM radio, as far ahead as the eye could see. This meant, for example, that we would not count as a switchover cost the expenditure which consumers would make on digital receivers in any event, only the compulsory costs resulting from the policy.

The main headings we used for costs were broadcasters' transmission investment (on different digital terrestrial coverage assumptions), consumers' compulsory equipment costs (based on modelling of projected voluntary take-up) and marketing and practical support costs (as best we could estimate them). Subsequently we encompassed energy costs too.

On the benefits side we put a value on providing digital terrestrial coverage to hitherto excluded parts of the country and, a much trickier exercise, on the consumer benefits from whatever new services might be developed after switchover using released spectrum. This involved making an assumption about the amount of spectrum available for reuse, about the nature of the new services which could be provided, and about their potential attractiveness to consumers (on the basis of answers to survey questions). A simpler benefit to estimate was the savings to broadcasters from no longer having to transmit both analogue and digital versions of their services.

Timing issues were critical. The costs arising from switchover arose in the main *before* the event, the benefits only came *afterwards*. The longer the post-switchover period we included in the assessment, the higher the cumulative benefits: we selected a period ending in 2026, when the licences for the digital multiplexes granted in 2002 would reach the end of their second period of twelve years. The compulsory cost diminished the later the compulsory policy was imposed – but so did the benefits. We modelled results for different assumptions about the timing of switchover between 2010 and 2015.

In the late summer of 2003 we were ready to give the Government some preliminary answers. Oversimplified, benefits overall looked of the order of £6 billion and costs broadly around £4 billion. The work continued all through 2004, developing and refining the assessment, but by September 2003 we were ready to make an initial judgment. We published a central case (around which sensitivity analysis was based) estimating that, in net present value terms, switchover would produce a net economic benefit to the UK of between £1.5 and £2 billion:

> This gives a clear message that switching off, rather than maintaining dual transmission systems, is in the economic interest of the UK. The model does

not show that there is a preferred year for completing switchover, though it indicates that sooner is better than later.[13]

On that basis, the Government was willing to make the commitment in principle to switchover. Lord McIntosh, the Broadcasting Minister, announced that the DCMS would set up an advisory Consumer Expert Group which would help review the switchover criteria.[14] Then, on 18th September 2003, at the Royal Television Society's Cambridge Convention, came the announcement:

> The advantages of digital are such that the question is not whether, but how and when we will achieve switchover.[15]

I sat in the audience, eagerly waiting for Tessa Jowell to say these words, but this was the occasion when she was trapped in traffic, so they were read out on her behalf by Lord McIntosh. In press terms the announcement was distinctly *sotto voce*. The Government wanted the broadcasters and the other Action Plan stakeholders to know that it was committed, but it was not yet ready to take the political risk of saying so, loud and clear, to the public. Nonetheless, for those of us working on the Action Plan, here was a firm political decision. We could move on to our next task – mapping out *how* switchover could be achieved.

The question 'how?' (a) transmission
On the transmission side, Greg Bensberg's spectrum planning team developed a post-switchover frequency plan and addressed the practicalities of getting from here to there. We faced three main questions:

- How much spectrum should be retained for transmitting the digital terrestrial services post-switchover and how much could be released for new purposes?
- What level of digital terrestrial coverage should be planned post-switchover – matching analogue with near-universal coverage using around 1100 transmitters, or relying exclusively on satellite to reach those parts of the country where reinvesting in terrestrial transmission would be uneconomic?
- What would actually be involved operationally at the transmitter sites in switching off analogue and switching over fully to digital?

The first question was answered early on by a Ministerial decision. On the basis of the work done by the Spectrum Planning Group and the responses to a consultation on the subject, two main options emerged. The plan could aim to maximize continuity with the current transmitter pattern, which would minimize both broadcaster investment in new masts and consumer expenditure on new aerials: this would allow the release of around fourteen frequency channels. Alternatively, a radical new plan could be designed to maximize the amount of released spectrum, with a different transmitter pattern, which could free around twenty channels but would increase both broadcasters' and consumers' costs.

The Cost-Benefit Analysis team appraised both options and recommended the consumer-friendly continuity option. In January 2003, the Government announced that this would be the way forward:

> We now have sufficient information from the cost benefit analysis to enable us to take a decision on the basis on which the next stage of the spectrum planning work should proceed.[16]

The cautious wording kept the other option theoretically open but, within the project, we never looked back.

The extra spectrum available post-switchover could potentially be used for local television, high-definition television, interactive television services, wireless broadband, mobile television, or various forms of mobile telecommunications. In reality, it was far too early to be confident that all the possibilities had even emerged and certainly too early to bank on any which involved changes to international agreements on frequency allocations, so the working assumption was reuse for broadcasting:

> At present the agreements that govern the use of the radio spectrum internationally permit the primary use of the UHF spectrum for broadcasting only. This may well change in time to allow for greater flexibility as technologies converge and evolve. However there is no guarantee that such flexibility will be realised in the short term...
>
> We expect this plan to release at least 14 frequency channels cleared nationwide for reuse in the future. These released channels will be split into two groups, one at the top end of the UHF band and one in the middle of the band. There will also be frequencies interleaved between the six digital multiplexes which can be used for additional broadcasting services. These services could be additional national multiplexes or could support regional or local services.[17]

The target digital terrestrial coverage, post-switchover, took much longer to resolve. The answer really only started to emerge in the autumn of 2004 with the involvement of the new regulatory body, Ofcom, created by the 2003 Communications Act to replace a number of agencies including the ITC, the Radiocommunications Agency and Oftel. By this time the question was focused on the national public services – the BBC's licence fee-funded services plus the other traditional analogue services – ITV, Channel 4 and Channel Five. Should they be obliged to match analogue's UK coverage of 98.5 per cent in their digital terrestrial transmissions?

On the face of it, investing in around 1100 digital terrestrial transmitters, now that digital satellite was available, would be technically and financially inefficient. Digital terrestrial was currently reaching nearly 75 per cent of households with only 80 transmitters. Once freed from the constraints of analogue, these 80 transmitters could boost this figure up to about 94 per cent.[18] To reach the last 4 or 5 per cent, however, more than 1000 additional transmitters would be needed! Moreover, Ofcom estimated that 398 of them would each serve fewer than 300 households.[19] Cable could not be a substitute since its coverage was essentially confined to urban areas but digital satellite potentially could.

However, there were some physical and planning restrictions on satellite reception. Moreover, satellite remained a *de facto* BSkyB monopoly in the UK, with the prospects for an open market in satellite receivers uncertain. Although the BBC's digital satellite services were now unencrypted, those of ITV, Channel 4 and Channel Five all had to be decoded with a BSkyB card (ITV did not decide to transmit in the clear until September 2005).

Free-to-view satellite reception on a BSkyB set-top box had had a somewhat patchy history since 1998. Although BSkyB, by now led by Rupert Murdoch's son James, introduced a free-to-view option for a one-off payment of £150 in the autumn of 2004, it was unclear whether this would last until, and through, switchover.

Furthermore, free-to-view digital satellite reception was currently a more expensive consumer option than conversion to digital terrestrial with a *Freeview* set-top box (assuming no aerial problems). If digital terrestrial coverage was only partial, under the Communications Act the public service broadcasters would be obliged, at switchover, to fund the extra cost of satellite for households for areas without terrestrial reception. Identifying with any precision which households would be within, and which outside, a digital terrestrial coverage pattern of, say, 94 per cent would be difficult. So, after a period of consultation, Ofcom plumped for full digital terrestrial coverage, matching analogue with around 1100 transmitters.

Ofcom also undertook a further consultation on the detailed technical standards before settling, in 2005, on 64 QAM (with higher transmitter power to compensate for the coverage which would otherwise have been lost by this option) and a transition to the more complex chip based on 8000 carriers (8k) which could potentially improve reception and would allow for the local use of the single frequency network technique for certain south coast transmitters where foreign interference was an issue.[20]

With a working assumption about coverage, the Digital TV Project could draw out the practicalities of the switchover operation. If the public services were obliged to have around 1100 transmitters, and the commercial services on digital terrestrial were free to remain well below this level, some rationalization of which services were carried on which multiplexes would be required. At the time the public services were spread across four multiplexes, two BBC, the ITV/Channel 4 one and SDN's (which included S4C and Channel Five). We pictured grouping all the public services on the BBC and ITV/Channel 4 multiplexes, allowing SDN's to become a purely commercial multiplex.

We knew from the broadcasters that we would need to design a regionally phased operation for switching different regions in different years. We decided that this would be easiest for the public to understand if we used the ITV Regions as the regional units. Technical experts among the broadcasting and transmission companies then produced a draft regional order, starting with Border and West Country, which Ofcom put into the public domain in 2005.[21]

With NTL's help, we also teased out the fact that, at any given transmitter, not all the switching would take place on one day. The process would probably start with the withdrawal of one analogue public service, and the others would follow after viewers had acclimatized to the first change.

Moreover, the digital multiplexes would need to be moved to different frequency channels, partly to achieve the best coverage and partly to release the channels designated for reuse. This had implications at the reception end, since viewers would normally have to rescan their digital receivers with each frequency change. I pressed the broadcasters and the receiver manufacturers to develop the technology required to allow receivers to rescan automatically, to help smooth switchover for technically challenged consumers (such as myself).

The question 'how?' (b) reception

Before the analogue transmitters could be turned off, households would have to purchase and install digital receivers – whether for satellite, cable, broadband or terrestrial reception – to replace or convert every TV set they wished to continue to use. The scale of production and sales implied was daunting, especially given the continuing high level of sales (over 4 million p.a. at the time) of analogue TVs. In 2004 Ofcom estimated that only 26 per cent of all sets were digital, leaving some 35 million TV sets yet to be converted or replaced.[22] Take-up, especially in the regions selected for switchover in the first year, would have to accelerate sharply.

Faced with the inability of the industry to agree collectively to mandate integrated digital TV sets, the DTI proposed a labelling and communications initiative instead. Early in 2003 Stephen Timms, the DTI Minister who co-chaired the Digital TV Project Steering Board, announced that

> The Government, with industry and stakeholders, is considering a number of measures, including:
> - clear labelling of TV sets setting out what equipment consumers will need to receive digital signals; and
> - a consumer information initiative…

The aim of any future information will be to set out clearly the choices for consumers, either to buy a digital adaptor or an integrated digital TV, in preparation for the digital switchover. It will inform consumers that analogue TVs will require a digital adaptor to receive TV broadcasts after the analogue signal is switched off.[23]

It sounded simple, sensible and obvious – but it took eighteen months to implement. Some of the arguments during this period were about timing. Was it too early? Shouldn't the marketing of BSkyB and *Freeview* be given longer to drive up voluntary take-up before the idea of switchover, with its connotations of compulsion, was introduced? The counter-argument, from the autumn of 2003 onwards, was that, having decided on switchover in principle, the Government had a duty to inform consumers to help them buy wisely. There were worries about the risks of damaging the market, whether for analogue TVs or for digital set-top boxes, which were best put to rest by ensuring that the scheme was well designed and tested. There were 'creative differences' among the marketing professionals within the industry about the design of a logo and whether or not to use the word 'digital' – which were only finally resolved after additional consumer research.

Then there was the issue of responsibility: who would manage the process, who would be responsible for ensuring that the consumer information was reliable, what powers did they have to prevent misinformation and, of course, who would pay? In the end, the DTI agreed to manage equipment labelling, at any rate at the start – registering the logo, licensing its use to manufacturers and retailers (initially for free), sub-contracting the administration, funding the start-up costs, but expecting those who displayed the logo to pay for their own marketing and publicity. The information would be put out initially in the name of the Digital TV Project.

If this all sounds frustratingly protracted, it was. However, beneath some of the arguments lay a conceptual issue which it was important to get right. Was the Digital TV Project trying to specify – in any technical sense – a digital TV receiver? If so, was that its job? If not, how could we reduce the risk of consumers spending their own money on digital receiver models which worked now but turned out not to work, for one technical reason or another, after switchover?

We concluded that it would be inappropriate to specify receivers but what we did need to do, in respect of digital terrestrial receivers, was to require

- the capability to deliver digital versions of all the analogue services being withdrawn, including teletext;
- 'ambidexterity' in respect of key technical standards (between 16 and 64 QAM and 2k and 8k).

In order to use the DTI-registered logo, manufacturers would have to confirm that their digital receivers were technically compliant and retailers would have to pledge that they had trained their staff to give accurate and reliable information about switchover. On this basis the DTI 'opened for business' in September 2004 and the DCMS produced a consumer information leaflet to be handed out in the shops.

Under the post-switchover frequency plan, we aimed to minimize the need for new aerials for households switching from analogue to digital terrestrial reception. Since we would be retaining the same transmitter sites and increasing the power of the digital signal when analogue was withdrawn, a rooftop aerial delivering good reception before switchover should be able to perform equally well after switchover. However, some homes would undoubtedly need a new aerial, for example, if their current reception was not good. Poor analogue reception meant fuzzy pictures but poor digital reception would mean no pictures! This made it very difficult to predict reception on set-top aerials – which was an issue mainly affecting second and additional TV sets.

The aerial industry was diverse and fragmented, with highly professional companies at one end of the range and 'cowboys' and DIY at the other. Our concern, on behalf of consumers, was to ensure that households were not misled into thinking they needed a new aerial if they did not, but that, if they did, the job was effectively done.

Working with the industry trade association, the Confederation of Aerial Industries, we encouraged a benchmarking scheme to set quality standards for aerials and cabling and we gave a fresh impetus to installer training. Indeed, without a major initiative on training, we doubted whether the industry could meet the demands of switchover, especially for the more highly skilled installations for communal housing. The DTI worked closely with the relevant industry training organizations to develop a pattern of formal qualifications.

We gave a lot of thought to recording issues, especially in the light of the *Go Digital* findings. The essential point – not widely understood at the time – was that VCRs, of which the nation had some 35 million in use, contain an analogue TV tuner, enabling the user to record one programme while watching another. These analogue tuners inside VCR machines will cease to work at switchover. For people who do not want this facility (and the facility to record from different channels on the timer in their absence), this might not matter. After switchover they could drive their VCR off the digital TV set (or set-top box) so that they could use the timer to record the channel to which their TV is tuned – but they could not record any other channel.

Research showed us that around half the households in the UK valued the functionality they would lose.[24] To record and view, or record more than one channel on the timer, they would need to buy a recorder which included a digital tuner, a point we made in our September 2004 consumer information leaflet.

Hard disc digital recorders (PVRs, or Personal Video Recorders) were potentially attractive to consumers, if recording could be made simple using the Electronic Programme Guide (EPG). BSkyB's Sky+ system was an impressive product and a market leader in the field.

Initially the production of PVRs for digital terrestrial television was held back by the inability of the terrestrial broadcasters to transmit full advance programme information for display by terrestrial EPGs. In the summer of 2004, after several months' work by a cross-industry team led by Keith Hayler of Crown Castle, the technical problems here were cracked. Twin-tuner set-top boxes with an in-built hard disc became an established feature of the digital terrestrial market. This had been a conspicuously missing piece of the jigsaw. Only at that point, mid-2004, did I feel that we knew how to achieve switchover and, even then, only on paper.

Consumer perspectives

The strongest message we gave the Government was the importance of explaining the switchover policy to the public well before any compulsory timetable started to bite. Perceived coercion – consumers obliged to spend their own money on equipment they would not otherwise have bought at the time (or, in some cases, at all) – was potentially very unpopular, especially if the reasons for the coercion were not understood and accepted.

A change of approach would be needed here. Hitherto the emphasis in both the Government's and the industry's communications had been on the attractions of digital television. However, the benefits of acquiring digital television were different from the benefits of switching off analogue from a fixed date. The former were direct and immediate, the latter – widening digital terrestrial reception and facilitating the reuse of released spectrum for new services – were more indirect or distant. They were social, not just private individual, benefits.

The recommendations made to us by consultants, Scientific Generics, on the strength of their consumer research were

- the Government should clearly communicate to viewers the rationale both for switchover and for the timescale within which it is being pursued
- the current state of public opinion cautions against a timetable announcement until there is greater awareness
- digital television is widely seen as technologically inevitable, but consumers need to understand
  (a) why analogue needs to be switched off
  (b) why the pace is not being left to (gradual) market forces.[25]

The advice we received from another set of consultants, Stimulating World, on how to handle this explanation included the observation

There is no way of 'spinning' the bad news as anything other than bad news. This is going to cost many people effort, time and money, if not for their main TV set then for their other TV sets.[26]

We were by now in a position to estimate what the cost implications on consumers might be. It was clearly not a case of 'one answer fits all'. The compulsory cost arising from imposition of a switchover timetable would vary according to

- how much digital equipment the household already had as a baseline;
- how much equipment, above this baseline, the household wanted to continue to use after switchover;
- the householder's platform, equipment and service choices;
- prices in the year(s) in which the household made its purchases.

We reckoned that a household which only had one TV set to convert, chose to buy a digital terrestrial set-top box, and did not need a new aerial, might pay £40–£80 at 2004 prices. A household wishing to adapt two TVs and replace a VCR, by buying a twin-tuner digital terrestrial PVR and an extra set-top box, with no aerial complications, might need to spend around £200. If the household opted for free-to-view satellite to convert one TV set only, then the set-top box and dish would cost £150.[27]

Around 5 million households were in multi-occupation rented housing – estimated at 40 per cent local authority, 20 per cent housing association and 40 per cent private landlord. A common arrangement is for the landlord to be responsible for the aerial and wiring into each flat and for the tenants to own their own TV and recording equipment. The cost of converting an existing aerial system for a landlord could be as low as £600 spread across all the tenants or, if a new integrated reception system, offering a choice of platforms with pay TV options, was to be installed, as high as £110–180 per flat.[28] At that stage fewer than 1 in 5 local authorities and registered social landlords had upgraded all their systems to digital and many were awaiting a clear decision from the Government on the timetable.[29]

Nor, of course, were all television receivers confined to houses and flats. In the private sector there were hotels, pubs, clubs and offices to consider; in the public sector, schools, colleges, homes for the elderly, hospitals, military barracks and prisons. The senior DCMS and DTI civil servants, Andrew Ramsay and David Hendon respectively, gave public sector bodies advance warning in June 2004, to help them plan ahead financially.[30]

More detailed communications, advice and practical support for consumers and others would be essential once the switchover timetable was announced and the implications came into sharper focus. We believed that for many consumers complexity would be a bigger issue than cost.

We envisaged the creation of a new organization to lead the operational implementation of switchover which might need to

- advertise to promote awareness
- publish advice
- provide a postcode database, so that households could check which platforms were available in their area both before and at switchover
- manage a website
- manage a call centre
- explain how to connect different pieces of equipment
- advise how to find installation help where appropriate
- explain how to rescan receivers when the frequency changes took place at switchover
- help ensure appropriate consistency of message from the various organizations engaged in switchover communications.

Additional support would almost certainly be needed on some selective basis for the most elderly and infirm, for some disabled groups, and for those in serious poverty, for example. How such groups might be defined and what assistance might be provided at public expense was very much a political issue outside our remit. However, DCMS work in this area began in parallel. The Government received a report from its Consumer Expert Group on a range of consumer concerns[31] and proposals for publicly funded practical support and financial assistance from Ofcom's Consumer Panel.[32]

The question at the heart of our work was: if a switchover plan was well designed, well explained and communicated, and accompanied by appropriate support for vulnerable groups, would the public respond and convert their equipment on time? Based on a March 2003 survey, Scientific Generics initially classified 13 per cent of households as 'Unlikely to get DTV and cannot be persuaded'. However, after doing further survey work in November/December 2003, they advised that *the announcement of a switchover timetable* would trigger many people who would not otherwise have converted to do so. On that basis

> Around 95% of households would have one or more digital set converted by the announced switchover date.[33]

The question 'when?'

Our job, in the Digital TV Project, was not to decide the timetable for the compulsory phase, it was to prepare the ground for a decision by the Government, keeping 2006–2010 as a feasible option. We found very different perspectives among the stakeholders on timing.

The first view, to be found among some receiver manufacturers and retailers, was that the Government should urgently set the timetable. Until that had been done, the Action Plan activity was all theoretical and an insufficient basis for investment, but, once the dates were firm, the market would start to deliver the products and services required.

It was easy to see why the TV receiver industry might feel this. Our research showed that manufacturers and retailers stood to gain a substantial increase in business once the compulsory switchover timetable was definite.[34] However, they also faced high risks. Actual switchover would probably kill the analogue TV market: after all, who would buy a TV set which would not work when you switched it on? So, before that point, they would need to invest in shifting their production lines to the manufacture of digital TVs.

Timing was critical for them. The analogue market was the industry's current bread and butter; TV set technology was beginning a transition from the cathode ray tube to LCD and plasma flat-screen sets, so high-volume production of cathode ray tube iDTVs could prove a costly mistake; and the industry had been caught out before, left with obsolete stock, first by the collapse of the UK satellite venture, BSB, and then by the collapse of ITV Digital. How could manufacturers be sure the Government would really go through with switchover? A clear public commitment by the Government to a firm timetable was critical to their business planning.

My project management response was that there was no point in anyone deciding *when* to switch until we knew *how*: so it was no good asking for decisions on timing during 2003 or early 2004. However, we would have resolved *how* before the end of 2004 in order for the 2006–2010 option to remain feasible, so a political decision should become possible after that.

A very different perspective, to be found among some consumer representatives, was that there was no urgency at all to announce dates, certainly not before take-up had reached 70 per cent, and meanwhile a number of consumer issues needed to be addressed. The Report of the Consumer Expert Group, completed in September 2004, highlighted concerns relating to coverage, affordability, consumer information, accessibility and consultation and stated:

> Put simply, consumers are far from ready for the analogue television signal to be switched off.[35]

However, the Report did recognize that

> There will inevitably be some element of compulsion in any decision about digital switchover, although the proportion of consumers affected depends greatly on the timing of any announcement, the date of switchover itself, and the extent to which a wide range of consumer concerns and needs are addressed before these take place.[36]

The terrestrial broadcasters favoured having a firm timetable. For them it was a precondition of the major investment they would have to make in digital transmission infrastructure. They were incurring costs from dual analogue and digital transmission which they needed to bring to an end before the analogue transmitter network either broke down or required major new investment. However, they were not in a hurry. Their audience shares in five-channel analogue homes were higher than in multi-channel digital homes. For ITV and Channel 4 the loss of share with the transition to digital would mean loss of advertising revenue (the position of Channel Five was slightly different in that digital switchover could give it fuller UK coverage).

The Government's initial view was that 2006–2010 – which we had advised was the earliest possible timetable but not necessarily the optimum – should remain the public position, qualified by the consumer criteria, until all the evidence had been assembled on which to take a firm decision. The UK wanted, if possible, to avoid the pattern in some other countries where ambitious switchover timetables had been announced only to be postponed: announcing a series of retreating dates would weaken the credibility of the policy. In weighing benefits and risks, Ministers had to balance the potential unpopularity of compulsion against the pressures from consumers in areas currently unserved by digital terrestrial who wanted to be able to receive terrestrially all the public service television services for which they had been paying their licence fee since 1998.

When the Government deferred key financial decisions on switchover until 2005, the 2010 option looked less and less credible. Resolution came through a process of Government and Ofcom consultation with the broadcasters about their preferred timetable. A switchover commitment would need to be incorporated in the BBC's new obligations once the Charter review process was complete and, more immediately, in new digital licences for ITV, Channel 4, Channel Five and Teletext, in accordance with the Communications Act. The Government asked the broadcasters what target date they wanted for the completion of switchover.

The answer was not crisply unanimous but in July 2004 Tessa Jowell and Lord McIntosh were able to make a written Ministerial Statement to Parliament reporting that

> While the broadcasters have not reached a full consensus on the optimum timetable, some – including the BBC – have suggested that 2012 may be the most appropriate date for the completion of switchover. This could mean beginning the switching sequence as early as 2007... OFCOM therefore plans to include reference to this timetable in the draft digital licences for Channels 3, 4, 5 and Teletext which they expect to publish for consultation later this summer.[37]

Following the Ofcom consultation in the autumn of 2004 a back-stop date of 2012, with an implied start-date at least four years ahead of that, became a strong working hypothesis for the whole industry. The Government position remained slightly guarded:

We continue to believe that an ordered process leading to the earliest practicable switchover remains desirable given the advantages to consumers, the broadcasting industry and the future growth of innovative new services. We believe that switchover should be broadcaster-led but that the final decision on timetable should balance these benefits against the need to ensure that the interests of the most vulnerable consumers are protected.[38]

The successor project

We were clear that, once the Action Plan had created the preconditions for the key political decisions, a new organization and project structure would be required to implement switchover. The Digital TV Project, suited though it was to feasibility study tasks, was too loose an alliance of diverse parties and had no legal foundation allowing it to enter into contracts. Nor would it be Ofcom's job to lead implementation, though its regulatory roles would be of central importance. So, having addressed the questions *whether*, *how* and *when*, we started, in the autumn of 2004, to map out the elements of a successor project with the legal and operational capability to implement.

We recommended that, so far as possible, implementation should be through normal business channels – with the Government and Ofcom setting the framework and broadcasters, manufacturers and retailers playing in position and collaborating as appropriate.[39]

Closely related to this principle was our assumption that funding responsibilities should also, so far as possible, follow normal business channels – with broadcasters paying for transmission investment through contracts with transmission companies; broadcasters funding their own communications about how to receive their services in future; retailers and aerial companies promoting and selling reception equipment; satellite and cable companies marketing their own equipment and services; and consumers buying with their own money (subject to any publicly funded assistance the Government might decide should be given to vulnerable groups).

However, for new operational tasks – 'front-line' marketing and communications and the provision of practical support to consumers – we advised that a new organization, which we dubbed 'Switchco', would be needed. Close coordination between the broadcasters on transmission investment and synchronization of switchover operations with the sale and installation of reception equipment would also be essential. There was clearly a question of how many organizations would contribute, on what basis and in what proportions, to the costs associated with any quasi-joint venture activity.

Led by Barry Cox, the terrestrial broadcasters set up a 'Switchco' Working Group to create a proper legal and financial basis for the organization. The BBC provided seedcorn funding, enabling Andy Townend from BBC Strategy and Distribution to head a small team of seconded staff, working in liaison with the Government and Ofcom.

The receiver manufacturers and retailers complained that a broadcaster-led 'Switchco' would not fully understand their business.[40] Specifically they were angry that BBC on-air promotion for BBC digital television drew attention to the availability of low-cost set-top boxes for *Freeview* but made no mention of the small number of integrated digital TVs on the market. Through the Digital TV Group they organized themselves into a 'supply chain' covering all aspects of reception and established two representatives on the 'Switchco' Working Group, after which relations improved.

The 'Switchco' Working Group was at the heart of the design of the successor project but it was not the only element in it.

Ofcom would continue to be responsible for licensing and regulation, technical standards, frequency planning (including the potential reuse of released spectrum), and the regulation of competition in the transmission industry (a role it had inherited from Oftel).

The Government had oversight of the BBC, Channel 4 and S4C, was the guardian of consumer interests, had to ensure the public sector's readiness for switchover, and was preparing a Regulatory Impact Assessment of the switchover policy. This assessment would have to spell out all the possible implications of switchover, including, for example, the net increase in energy consumption with all the additional set-top boxes required, and any waste disposal concerns arising from the sudden obsolescence of analogue TV sets. And, of course, the Government would have the ultimate say over the timetable provisionally fixed by Ofcom and the broadcasters.

So who would be in charge of implementing switchover? It is a golden rule of project management that there must always be someone in charge and the history of failed projects is full of examples of muddled responsibility. Our answer was the Government, even if it stood well back from the operational aspects. A board or committee chaired by Ministers (and supported by a programme manager) would be needed to ensure that Government, Ofcom, 'Switchco' and other stakeholder activity was appropriately coordinated. Under the Action Plan the two senior civil servants, Andrew Ramsay (DCMS) and David Hendon (DTI) had been, in Whitehall jargon, the named 'Senior Responsible Owners'; under the successor project they would retain this responsibility.

Risks and risk management

Throughout the Digital TV Project we had maintained a register of the risks associated with switchover and, as we neared the completion of our tasks, we subdivided this into risks related directly to the Action Plan tasks and the potential risks associated with actual implementation. We were now in a position to focus more sharply on the latter and to assign responsibilities for controlling them.

Barry Cox and I held a couple of Risk Management Workshops, the first specifically for organizations which would have to make a major financial investment and the second for a wider group of interested parties. The output was a list of 25 risks which

- identified each risk individually;
- assessed its probability and the potential consequences (scale of 1–3);
- assessed the potential impact of such consequences (scale of 1–3);
- gave it a score, probability x impact (scale of 1–9);
- identified the 'owner', responsible for controlling it;
- summarized the action already taken by the Digital TV Project;
- recommended further action.[41]

The full list included, for example, the risks of muddled responsibility, inadequate or mismanaged communications, reception equipment shortages, misinformation from retailers, inadequately trained aerial installers, unprepared public sector bodies, excessive increased energy usage, legal challenges to switchover, and international restrictions of the UK's freedom to use the cleared spectrum as it wished.

The risks would alter as implementation proceeded: some would be reduced or eliminated, others would need to be added. So this was essentially a risk analysis to be handed over to the successor project for ongoing management. As a snapshot at the end of 2004, it indicated a judgment that the level of risk of digital switchover was high. Of the 25 listed risks, 12 had scores of 6 (high probability x medium impact or medium probability x high impact). A further 2 had scores of 9 (high probability x high impact):

- consumer reluctance
- technical complexity for consumers[42]

The 'owner' of the former, responsible for reducing it to a minimum, was the Government; the 'owner' of the latter would be 'Switchco'.

Within the Digital TV Project we took some steps of our own to reduce the risk of technical complexity. Starting in 2004, we carried out a technical trial, primarily for digital terrestrial technology, among about 500 homes in two Welsh villages served by the Ferryside relay transmitter on the South Wales coast. It was small-scale: the transmitter mast resembled a telegraph pole! Our aim was to go beyond the scope of the *Go Digital* pilot by actually switching off the analogue transmitter permanently and, specifically, to test whether we had now solved the recording issue which the *Go Digital* pilot had highlighted.

The Ferryside trial was based on a Memorandum of Understanding between the DTI, the DCMS, the BBC, the ITV/Channel 4 multiplex and SDN, in close collaboration with the transmission companies. I chaired the steering group at the outset but we brought in Emyr Hughes, with a strong background in Welsh broadcasting, to manage the trial. The broadcasters and transmission companies managed the transmission side; David Harby did much of the work on the receiver side, in conjunction with an excellent local retailer; and Stella Mair Thomas managed the communications.

First, we had to explain the trial, including the intention to switch off analogue transmissions at the end, and establish that we had local support to proceed. Then we gave the community a digital terrestrial television service for the first time (a number of the homes already had BSkyB's satellite service). We offered households, for free, a modest kit of digital reception and recording equipment appropriate to their circumstances (if they wanted something more expensive, such as an integrated digital TV set or a continuing subscription to BSkyB or *Top-Up TV*, they could pay the extra themselves). Twin-tuner PVRs were normally prescribed to convert a linked analogue TV and VCR.

Next we allowed a period of three months for the community to become accustomed to using the new equipment and for resolving any difficulties, whether with receivers, recorders or aerials. Then, in March 2005, all the households were asked whether they wished to retain the digital services and equipment or revert to the analogue services only. Eighty-five per cent responded, of whom 98 per cent wished to retain the digital services.[43] This allowed the trial team to switch off the analogue transmissions. It was an historic step in the UK's digital switchover operation – and it worked smoothly!

It was, of course, somewhat artificial, in that the householders had not paid for their reception equipment. The standard equipment on offer had also been carefully chosen: David Harby, with George Fullam of the manufacturers' association, had investigated and demonstrated reliable combinations of receivers and recorders over the preceding months. But, in miniature, the trial was a rehearsal for UK-wide implementation, e.g. in the careful preparation of briefing and guidance material for the householders and, where appropriate, personal visits to assist the elderly and disabled.

All age groups in the community coped well, both with the initial equipment installation and with switchover itself. They found the twin-tuner PVRs workable for recording. They appreciated the new services their digital equipment brought them. Many of them would probably have appreciated automatic receiver rescanning, had it been possible by then, but, with guidance from the team, they managed. A detailed report followed in 2005, listing the many learning points, but meanwhile the headline for risk-conscious policy-makers was essentially reassuring: we now knew how to do switchover, not just on paper, but also in practice.[44]

Completion of the Action Plan

At the end of 2004 the Digital TV Project Team completed its work. Our findings and recommendations were gathered together into a report. Jane Humphreys (DTI) and Catherine Smadja (DCMS) coupled this with other related

Government work and put it forward to their Ministers. It was published, together with an updated version of the Cost-Benefit Analysis, in 2005.

We had undertaken a feasibility study for the practical implementation of switchover, concluded it was feasible, presented a blueprint for how it could be done, and mapped out the major risks to be managed. As Sheila Cassells of BSkyB summed it up:

> The Action Plan has prepared the ground for switch-off. The voyage – sometimes with stakeholders rowing in opposite directions or going round in circles – has taken us to the Christopher Columbus point. We will not fall off the edge of the world by switching off.[45]

Chapter Six

Politics and Responsibilities

On 15th September 2005, Tessa Jowell gave the Government's public blessing to the phased region-by-region timetable for switchover which had been developed in conjunction with Ofcom and the broadcasters. The pattern would be based on ITV Regions:

2008	Border
2009	West Country, HTV Wales, Granada
2010	HTV West, Grampian, Scottish Television
2011	Yorkshire, Anglia, Central
2012	Meridian, Carlton/LWT (London), Tyne-Tees, Ulster[1]

The preceding May the Labour Party had won a third term of office and its manifesto had included a commitment to this timetable, albeit in the small print. By now around 60 per cent of UK households had digital television and the market was continuing to drive both free-to-view and subscription take-up – so the election passed without this pledge prompting any significant political or press controversy.

Retaining her Government position as Secretary of State for Culture, Media and Sport, Tessa Jowell then had the triumph of London's successful bid to host the 2012 Olympics. So, before announcing the digital switchover dates, she made a swift check to ensure that the process would not disrupt either the nation's or the world's Olympic viewing – a new entry to the switchover Risk Register. Satisfied on this score, she was able to declare at the Royal Television Society's September Cambridge Convention:

> I am completely confident that our timetable is a sensible one... For Government, these dates are not simply a vision, they are a reality, and we intend to ensure they are achieved.[2]

Thus began Phase Three of our 'managed migration' strategy – forewarning the public, with plenty of notice, of the compulsory switchover timetable.

'Hard' dates

The September 2005 announcement completed the process of revising the original Labour approach, devised by Chris Smith. While the criteria of availability and affordability had remained paramount in theory, the Government now knew, through the work of the Digital TV Project, that

- switching off the analogue signals could not be a single event – it would need to be phased region-by-region and, even at the level of the individual transmitter, one service would probably be switched off ahead of the others;
- near-universal (i.e. comparable to analogue) digital terrestrial coverage could only be achieved at switch-off, as a result of the withdrawal of the analogue transmissions, and, until then, 95 per cent digital take-up was unlikely to be achieved;
- other indicators of affordability were readily available.

It was pretty obvious that industry investors – broadcasters purchasing new digital transmission networks and receiver manufacturers switching their TV production lines from analogue to digital – would be unlikely to commit seriously without a set of hard dates. By 'hard' they not only meant dates to which there was real political commitment and which were therefore unlikely to slip (unlike the 2006–2010 hypothesis). They also meant dates which could not be overridden by other criteria ('Oh, sorry, we can't switch the transmitters for Birmingham to digital next month, as originally planned – we've just had a new survey revealing that only 92 per cent of households within the defined area have so far converted one digital receiver, so the operation must be postponed until we receive survey results showing 95 per cent – sorry we can't say when that will be'). Since the Government's public policy of switchover was dependent on coordinated industry investment, this investor perspective, ultimately, was likely to prevail.

However, consumers too had an interest in a hard date for their own areas. If switchover was definitely going to happen, and would require expenditure on their part, consumers naturally wanted to know when and to have plenty of advance warning. Moreover, forecasts produced by Scientific Generics under the Action Plan clearly showed that a firm timetable would influence behaviour and that

> around 15% of households who had not previously converted first sets would do so before switchover started in their region once people were aware that firm regional dates have been confirmed.[3]

So the Government position changed – though only after the proposed timetable had been included in the Labour election manifesto. The stance now was that waiting until 95 per cent had switched before making the final commitment would involve delaying the start of switchover for seven years from 2008 to 2015 and carried four significant risks:

- deprivation of around 25% of households unable to receive digital terrestrial, although paying through the licence fee for the BBC's digital TV services

- delay in the release, and re-use, of 14 frequency channels which 'could have significant consequences for the economy and to UK industry'
- costs for the broadcasters of continuing simulcasting transmission, complicating financial and contractual planning
- damage to the UK's international credibility as a leader in the field of digital television, given that other countries were now starting to announce firm switchover dates of their own, with risks to the future of the TV receiver manufacturers' R&D activity in the UK.[4]

The corollary of committing to a set of hard dates, however, was the political imperative to make provision for potentially 'vulnerable' consumers who would need financial and/or practical assistance in order to cope.

Targeted assistance

Extensive research and consultation had taken place by the time the Government announced its outline proposals for targeted assistance in September 2005. Under the Digital TV Project, we had commissioned a series of studies by Scientific Generics which provided a rich bed of segmented data on take-up, practicalities and attitudes. There was evidence from the *Go Digital* pilot and the South Wales trial. There had been reports from the DCMS' Consumer Expert Group and from Ofcom's independent Consumer Panel. The DCMS had then consulted a number of relevant charities, including the Royal National Institute of the Blind, the Royal National Institute of the Deaf, Age Concern, Help the Aged and the Consumers' Association. It also consulted the BBC and the Department for Work and Pensions.

The analysis showed that what was required was not a simple handout of free or subsidized set-top boxes. The elderly and people with severe disabilities needed information and practical help.

Voluntary take-up of digital television among the elderly was relatively low: a 2004 report revealed that less than 20 per cent of those aged over 75 had switched and that only 26 per cent would regard themselves as voluntary adopters.[5] Satisfaction with the services they knew well, the comfort of having a TV set which was simple to operate, confusion about the meaning of digital television, concern about the complexity of installing and correctly connecting set-top boxes, unfamiliarity with on-screen menu options and navigation around digital services – as well as cost – all played a part. Economic analysis of the impact of switchover also concluded that

> In economic terms, it seems there is a possibility that costs may well outweigh real and perceived benefits for older people, particularly those over 75. This is partly because people aged 75 and over will be less attracted to and will benefit less from new television services developed in released spectrum.[6]

People with disabilities such as sight and hearing difficulties, often elderly, faced potential difficulties and additional costs in preparing for switchover. However, digital television could offer an audio-description service for those with impaired sight and subtitling, plus some signing, for people with impaired hearing. Announcing the outline scheme of targeted assistance, Tessa Jowell stated

> Many of those yet to go digital are exactly the people that the State has a duty to protect – the elderly, the disabled and the poorest. They have in many cases the most to gain from a fully digital world. And we have to make sure they aren't left behind.[7]

The Government therefore proposed that the necessary equipment for receiving digital television on one TV set, and the relevant support to install and use it, should be provided to

- all households with one person aged 75 or over;
- all households with one person with a significant disability (eligible for the Disability Living Allowance or Attendance Allowance).

This assistance would be free of charge to households in these categories which received Income Support, Job Seekers' Allowance or Pension Credit – but otherwise the household would pay a modest fee. Specific help would be given to the registered blind to ensure they acquired receivers capable of supporting the audio-description services.

A trial of the proposed targeted assistance scheme was carried out amongst the over-75 age group in the Hulton ward of Bolton, an area chosen because of its ethnic and socio-economic mix, as well as the availability there of satellite, cable and digital terrestrial options.

The funding for the targeted assistance scheme would come from the BBC licence fee – and the Government pledged to take this into account in assessing the level of public funding the BBC would require from April 2007 onwards.[8]

Launch of Digital UK

Accompanying the Government announcement of the switchover timetable and the targeted assistance scheme was the launch of a new body called Digital UK. Its job was to lead the implementation of switchover. This was the 'Switchco' we had recommended in the Digital TV Project and the result of the design developed by the 'Switchco' Working Party. It had quietly started the preceding April while it was still using the name 'Switchco'. It was formed by the main terrestrial broadcasters 'at the Government's request' as an impartial not-for-profit organization.[9] Its members were the BBC, ITV, Channel 4, Channel Five,

Teletext, S4C and the multiplex operators Crown Castle and SDN, who were all represented on the management board and contributed funding. Two further positions on the board were for representatives of the receiver manufacturers and retailers.

Barry Cox, who had chaired the stakeholders throughout the Digital TV Project and then chaired the 'Switchco' Working Group, now became its chairman. A new chief executive with a marketing background was brought in from outside the broadcasting industry – Ford Ennals, formerly managing director of Universal Music's direct marketing division, and prior to that Group marketing director for Lloyds-TSB. Andy Townend, the acting chief executive of the embryo 'Switchco', was appointed Director of Commercial and Business Affairs.

Over the spring and summer of 2005 they recruited colleagues and planned the new organization's public launch to coincide with Tessa Jowell's 15th September announcements at the Royal Television Society Convention. Large full-page advertisements on 16th September announced the arrival of the newly christened Digital UK and began the major task of explaining switchover to the public.

Digital UK had three roles

- to coordinate the technical roll-out of digital terrestrial television across the UK, region-by-region, in accordance with the timetable agreed with the Government;
- to communicate with the public about digital switchover to ensure everyone knows what is happening, what they need to do, and when;
- to liaise with TV equipment manufacturers, retailers, digital platform operators and consumer groups to ensure understanding of, and support for, the switchover programme.[10]

Digital UK would need to be platform-neutral and find appropriate mechanisms for encompassing satellite and cable, as well as the receiver industry, in its communications about the digital future. In terms of take-up, BSkyB – whose chief executive, James Murdoch, signalled his unease over the compulsory nature of switchover[11] – was still the principal provider of digital television to UK homes (and in 2006 would top 8 million customers). Satellite and cable operators would want to ensure that Digital UK's publicity was not skewed in favour of the terrestrial platform.

Digital UK announced that, as well as mounting a national public information campaign to raise awareness of switchover, it would communicate directly to people in every region three years before switchover is due to start, writing to every household twice during the switchover period and working closely with local councils, community groups and charities. It launched a new website and call centre service. It also publicized the DTI-registered digital logo, developed by the Digital TV Project, as a certification mark for information, goods and services designed to help consumers through switchover.[12] Ford Ennals emphasized Digital UK's role in assisting people:

> This is not about some glossy advertising campaign. This is about providing a service to viewers. There is a very strong public service dimension to what we are doing. This will reach every household in Britain and we need to provide special assistance to those who need it.[13]

Digital UK had a small start-up budget for its first year of operation and aimed to spend around £200 million over the full switchover period, most of which was envisaged as coming from the BBC. Although Digital UK had been created at the Government's request, it had no direct income from the Government.

Constitutionally and financially the relationship between Digital UK and the Government was therefore a subtle one, reflecting some careful political positioning by the Government.

The Government's stance

During our work on the Cost-Benefit Analysis, the Government took the view that it was not itself a direct beneficiary of digital switchover.

This was in marked contrast to the position, for example, in the United States where the financial proceeds from auctioning the spectrum released by switchover were seen as a major federal government benefit.

The UK Treasury pointed to the 'digital dividend' system, instituted to incentivize the commercial terrestrial broadcasters to develop digital TV, whereby they paid less for their analogue licences as their digital audiences grew. Under this arrangement the Government was in effect losing money during the run-up to switchover. In 2002 the Government had received a major report on spectrum management and pricing following a review led by Professor Martin Cave[14] and, in its response, had backed both pricing and spectrum auctions in principle.[15] Tessa Jowell subsequently confirmed that, following switchover, the Government favoured auctioning the released spectrum through Ofcom.[16] However, from its perspective of 2004, the Digital TV Project noted that

> the extent to which spectrum pricing and/or spectrum auctions will make a contribution to the Treasury is unclear.[17]

So the Government positioned itself as a facilitator of change in broadcasting transmission technology for the consumers' benefit. The long-term beneficiaries would be consumers of whatever new services were developed using the released spectrum; the more immediate beneficiaries would be viewers unable to receive digital terrestrial television while analogue remained; and the broadcasters themselves would benefit from savings when they ceased dual analogue and digital terrestrial transmissions.

In doing so the Government avoided a major political pitfall. Had its motive for making switchover compulsory been perceived as the pursuit of Treasury revenue, the policy would have been portrayed as, in effect, a tax. People compelled to spend on new reception equipment could easily have turned round and said, 'If the Government is receiving the financial benefit from this, then the Government can pay for my new equipment.' The UK Government was much more interested in avoiding financial and political risk than in pocketing revenue and stressed that Government financial benefit was not a policy driver.

The terrestrial broadcasters' starting assumptions about the Government's role were rather different. Remembering the £22.5 billion sum paid in the 3G telecommunications auction in 2000, they tended to assume that the Government would be a prime beneficiary and, as such, would take the lead in designing and funding both the public information campaign and the targeted assistance scheme.

The broadcasters were not particularly keen to have their brand images tarnished by close association with the compulsory digital switchover policy nor to have their call centre staff explaining Government policy to angry viewers. Indeed they had a slight tendency to forget that they were engaged in a technology-led modernization of their terrestrial transmitters and, in that sense, were merely doing what BSkyB had already done – without any Government involvement – when it switched its business and its customer base from analogue to digital satellite.

So, for much of the period preceding the September 2005 announcement of the timetable, the targeted assistance scheme and the formation of Digital UK, the linked questions of who would provide the funding and who would lead the public explanation for switchover received different answers in different quarters. The political dance between the Government and its broadcasting 'partners' had been characterized by a certain amount of 'After you... No, please, after you...'

This had started in 2003 when Government departments had to put in their financial bids to the Treasury for the public expenditure plans for 2005/6, 2006/7 and 2007/8. With an election in the offing in 2004 the Government was keen to maintain or increase public spending in certain key areas of voter concern – health, education, nurseries, railways – without further increasing taxes and, therefore, to make substantial economies in non-priority areas of public spending.

Chancellor of the Exchequer Gordon Brown's March 2004 budget set out the broad figures available for public expenditure. Commentators were quick to see the likely implications for different Ministers and departments:

> The lion's share of the extra resources will go to health and education, as they consume a rising proportion of the nation's income... And while Mr Brown has

promised that key departments including defence and transport will have their budgets protected from inflation, the real gains they see are likely to turn out to be quite small... The rest of Whitehall... will probably face real-term cuts.[18]

The Budget also included a commitment to make an efficiency saving of £20 billion by 2008 by cutting some 40,000 jobs in Whitehall.

Over the following three months, leading up to the announcement of public expenditure decisions in July, individual departmental spending aspirations were assessed in detail, in the light of their priorities. The Department for Culture, Media and Sport stated that its aims were to

- improve the quality of life for all through cultural and sporting activities;
- support the pursuit of excellence; and
- champion the tourism, creative and leisure industries.[19]

It was also presiding over London's bid to host the 2012 Olympics.

Direct public expenditure on digital switchover was explicitly ruled out, as a press leak informed the broadcasters. In one of a series of bilateral meetings in which several departments had their bids turned down, Tessa Jowell was reported as having clashed with Treasury Minister Paul Boateng:

> A week later it was the turn of Jowell, culture secretary and leading Blairite. Boateng and the four Treasury officials present gave her a rough ride. Jowell asked for funds to meet the cost of publicising the government's switchover to digital television... Boateng refused, and the minutes note: 'Jowell said that if the burden was shifted to broadcasters it would be much more difficult to be certain of timing... Broadcasters had received legal advice which stated that they should not fund the promotion of switchover.' Boateng replied: 'The discussion on digital switchover should provide the Department of Culture, Media and Sport with added resolve in negotiating with broadcasters'.[20]

The issue of 'who pays?' was linked to the politically delicate question of 'who tells the public about their compulsory expenditure?' During the voluntary phase of our 'managed migration' strategy, promoting digital television was relatively straightforward – the broadcasters publicized the attractions of their services and the retailers marketed the reception equipment. Once the prospect of announcing a compulsory timetable loomed, the whole subject of communications became much more sensitive. The Government was ultimately in charge of switchover as a public policy but that did not mean a kamikaze political stance where Ministers had to take all the flak of any public annoyance or frustration over switchover, right down to sorting out aerials and set-top box connections.

Evidence of potential public opposition to switchover was modest in 2004 and 2005. David Elstein, who had been hostile to digital terrestrial television from the outset and pessimistic about its future during the ITV Digital crisis of 2002, remained a public critic of the feasibility of an early switchover.[21] Chris Goodall, the consultant who had worked on Greg Dyke's scheme for funding switchover through spectrum auction proceeds back in the mid-1990s, dubbed switchover an illiberal policy with high costs.[22] However, these were voices which were heard mainly within the broadcasting industry.

In the political arena David Cox warned the 2004 Labour Party Conference in the *New Statesman* that including switchover in the party's election manifesto ran the risk of newspaper headlines like 'How Labour will trash your telly'.[23] After the 2005 election the GMB trade union, with 600,000 members, voiced its doubts about the proposed 2008 start-date and called for priority to be given to improving digital terrestrial reception.[24] Then, following Tessa Jowell's September 2005 announcement, *Times* columnist Mary Ann Sieghart struck a shriller note:

> You thought the poll tax was unpopular? Just wait till you hear this. The Government plans to force us all to switch to digital TV, at a cost, to some of us, of hundreds of pounds and incalculable technological anguish.[25]

It was an illustration of the political danger – and raised the question of who was seen to be doing the forcing. Was it the Government? Or, if the Government was neither funding the policy nor benefiting from it financially and was not setting the pace so much as endorsing a timetable which had originated with the broadcasters, could the responsibility be spread? The Government took the view that, while it was ultimately responsible for switchover and must explain Government policy, the terrestrial broadcasters should be responsible for funding and leading implementation and for publicity explaining to their viewers how to receive their TV services in the future.

To overcome any broadcaster reluctance to accept these unsought responsibilities, the political and legal tools available were the Government-managed process of reviewing the BBC's Charter and Ofcom's licensing system for the commercial terrestrial broadcasters.

Enlisting the BBC

BBC Charters, which are granted by the Crown, have conventionally, though not invariably, had a ten-year term. The previous one, the BBC's eighth, dated from 1st January 1997 and was due to expire on 31st December 2006. During the BBC's early history ahead of each Charter expiry date the Government would set up a Committee of Enquiry of 'the great and the good' to consult widely and then make recommendations on the terms for the next Charter. Major landmarks in the BBC's history were the Crawford Committee of 1925–26 which recommended the formation of the Corporation from the original British Broadcasting Company, the Ullswater Committee of 1935, the

Beveridge Committee of 1949–50, the Pilkington Committee of 1960–62 and the Annan Committee of 1974–77. However, most famously after Beveridge (which recommended against introducing commercial television) and again after Annan the government of the day chose to go against some major Committee recommendations. So, more recently, governments had varied the approach in order to consult but also to keep a rein on the process.

To prepare for a Charter expiry at the end of 2006 the Government initiated a BBC Charter Review procedure which would run through both 2004 and 2005. In the event the BBC and the Government had a major row in 2004 over a *Today* programme report on the preparation of the Government's intelligence dossier on Iraq's alleged weapons of mass destruction. Following the suicide of a BBC source, the resignation of the Prime Minister's official spokesman and publication of the Hutton report, this culminated in the resignations of the BBC's chairman, Gavyn Davies, and director-general, Greg Dyke (to say more on this would involve saying a lot more). Both the Government and the BBC were at pains to prevent the Charter Review process becoming infected by the crisis and, in particular, to safeguard the BBC's editorial independence for the future. The Government named Michael Grade as the new BBC chairman and the Board of Governors appointed Mark Thompson as the new director-general.

The Government had launched a public consultation on the BBC's future at the end of 2003, emphasizing the change in the broadcasting environment:

> This Charter review takes place against a vastly different backdrop to the last one in 1996. By the end of 2003, more than 50% of UK homes will have digital television in some form. In 1996 this figure was zero. In 2003, 50% of homes have access to the Internet. An estimated 4% had access in 1996. It is essential that as the digital communications revolution gathers pace the public has a chance to shape the BBC's role within it. The future switchover to digital broadcasting makes this all the more important.[26]

Over the course of 2004 and 2005 the Charter Review proceeded. The DCMS commissioned independent reviews of the BBC's Internet and digital services. In June 2004, the BBC published its own vision of its future – *Building Public Value – Renewing the BBC for a digital world*.[27] Tessa Jowell appointed an Independent Panel, chaired by Lord Burns, to marshal the evidence from the consultation and research, organize public seminars and review the main themes. Having received its report, the DCMS published a Green Paper on the BBC in March 2005. The BBC and other interested parties then published their responses over the next few months.

In parallel Ofcom undertook its statutory review of public service television broadcasting, embracing the wider range of broadcasters (ITV, Channel 4, Channel Five, S4C and Teletext) with public service obligations as well as the BBC, concluding in February 2005.

The major issues were the future of the BBC Board of Governors, the range and quality of BBC services, the future of the licence fee system and whether the BBC should continue to be the only recipient of licence fee income. In relation to digital switchover, especially to its funding, these questions around the licence fee were of central importance.

In 2003 Barry Cox had given a set of lectures in Oxford, looking ahead to an all-digital world, and called for an end to compulsory licence fee funding for television, dubbing the BBC a 'cultural tyranny – a largely benevolent one, admittedly, but a tyranny nonetheless' which ought in future 'to rely on our willingness to pay for it voluntarily.'[28] However, although the licence fee system was debated during the Charter Review process, Tessa Jowell had signalled the likely outcome in an October 2004 newspaper interview:

> If you asked me to bet on what I think will be the outcome of the charter review, I think you would be wiser to put £5 on the licence fee continuing than £5 on the licence fee not continuing for the next charter period.[29]

Much more unpredictable was whether the BBC would continue to have a monopoly of licence fee revenue or would be obliged to share it with other public service broadcasters.

During 2003, Charles Allen, Granada chairman at the time, had called for the Government to hand over a 10 per cent slice of the licence fee to ITV.[30] During 2004, Channel 4 aired its case for some public funding to complement its advertising revenue. Ofcom rejected this Channel 4 plea at this stage[31] but thickened the plot when its review of public service television broadcasting included a proposal for an entirely new additional publicly funded broadcaster. Its argument was that the existing public service obligations on the terrestrial commercial broadcasters would be weakened as they faced increased competition in an all-digital market. Leaving the BBC as the sole public service broadcaster was, it argued, undesirable. To encourage competition in public service broadcasting (PSB) it therefore suggested the creation, in the medium-term, of a new digital multimedia Public Service Publisher. Such a body might need a budget of around £300 million p.a., one possible source for which was the licence fee:

> Once the level of funding for the BBC has been determined, there is scope for an enhanced licence fee model to fund plurality of PSB supply, either in the automatic buoyancy that comes from an increasing number of households, or in an increase in the level of the licence fee.[32]

Then, in January 2005, Lord Burns submitted the Independent Panel's final report to the DCMS and reported a high degree of consensus on funding:

Although there are some reservations about the licence fee as a means of funding the BBC, for the time being the balance of the debate lies in its favour, at least until digital switchover is complete. However, over time sustaining the BBC will become increasingly difficult when conditional access is available. This may lead to a combination of funding methods, including a lower licence fee supplemented by subscription for some services. To encourage a plurality in PSB following digital switchover, there may be an element of competition for licence fee funds.[33]

As others circled threatening the revenue it had traditionally regarded as exclusively its own, the BBC allied itself firmly with the Government on digital switchover. First, it set out the ways in which its programme services created democratic value, cultural and creative value, educational value, social and community value and global value, seeing these as continuing purposes in the digital age. It also stressed its commitment to universality, fairness and equity and accountability. Then, on switchover, it added:

The UK has the opportunity to become a fully digital nation, in which the benefits of the new technologies are available to all. The BBC can help make it happen. Because of the appeal of its content and the trust the public have in its brand, the BBC can play a particularly powerful role in enabling the less affluent and digitally adept to make the most of the new technologies, ensuring no one gets left behind. It can lead a public information campaign with a special focus on the digital have nots. It can be a leader and co-ordinator across the industry.[34]

Specifically the BBC pledged to

take a special responsibility for bringing the final cohorts into the digital television universe.[35]

While this fell short of volunteering to fund any targeted assistance scheme, it certainly did not signal resistance to such an idea.

When the Government published its Green Paper on the BBC's future, it firmed up its expectations in this area.

The BBC needs to take a leading role in the organisation and funding of digital switchover, using the licence fee to bring the benefits of digital TV to all. The BBC should:

• Help to establish and manage the organisation that will co-ordinate the technical process of switchover – currently known as 'Switchco';

- Play the leading role in the public information campaign that will tell consumers when and how the switch will happen, what choices of equipment they have and how they can install that equipment;
- Help to establish and pay for schemes to help the most vulnerable consumers make the switch and pay for it.[36]

The BBC's obligations in respect of digital switchover would be included in the new Charter and agreement due to run from January 2007. The licence fee system would continue, subject to further reviews towards the end of the switchover process, and

> One of the conditions of the new licence fee settlement will be that the BBC should play a leading role in the process of switching Britain over fully from analogue to digital television.[37]

Barry Cox's verdict was that, in effect, the DCMS and the BBC had done a deal – a secure licence fee in return for leading digital switchover.[38]

However, getting the BBC into position was only part of the process of preparing for the September 2005 switchover announcement. As Stephen Carter, Ofcom's chief executive, observed:

> The Switchover project cannot happen without the BBC, equally it cannot happen from the BBC alone with the other actors simply dragged along in the slipstream.[39]

In parallel, the other analogue terrestrial broadcasters needed to be enlisted.

Ofcom and the commercial terrestrial broadcasters

The Government had direct oversight of S4C, on whose grant-in-aid it commissioned a review, and held some responsibilities in relation to Channel 4. However, the central role in bringing the other terrestrial broadcasters to accept digital switchover responsibilities alongside the BBC lay with Ofcom.

While the various ITV regional companies had now formed themselves into ITV plc, their licences, awarded by Ofcom's predecessor the ITC, reflected a lot of history. Back in the all-analogue days, Mrs Thatcher – reportedly after noting that London Weekend Television sent forty-odd staff in order to interview her[40] – had decided that, in the interests of greater efficiency, the ITV franchises should be auctioned in 1991. The winners would be judged on the size of their bid after meeting a 'quality threshold'. The results were bizarre: two incumbents discovered they had no opposition and won with bids of only £2000 a year, London Weekend assessed its competitor as weak and won with a bid of £7.58 million, while elsewhere another incumbent bid £59 million but failed to satisfy the ITC. Few disagreed with Greg Dyke's retrospective verdict:

It was a mad system and by the mid Nineties it was very hard to find a Conservative MP who admitted to having voted for it, let alone proposing it in the first place.[41]

So, when digital terrestrial television came along and the Communications Act was drafted, no one was keen to repeat the ITV licence auction process.

The concept of the licences for commercial terrestrial broadcasters was rooted in the analogue world and embodied the principles that

- analogue terrestrial spectrum was scarce and gave near-universal access to the UK population;
- commercial broadcasters awarded the use of it should therefore make financial payments to the Treasury;
- such broadcasters ought also to carry certain public service obligations (e.g. in the fields of news and regional programmes) distinguishing them from straight commercial broadcasters with no such regulatory obligations (e.g. BSkyB).

Ofcom had to adapt this framework to the new circumstances of an all-digital world in which spectrum would no longer be scarce and commercial competition would be tougher by reviewing the level of the commercial companies' public service obligations. As we have seen, ITV and Channel Five already enjoyed a 'digital dividend' under which their payments to the Treasury were reduced as their audiences shifted from analogue to digital. The Ofcom review of public service television broadcasting now proposed to reduce ITV's non-news regional programming commitment and Channel Five's news scheduling requirements during the transition to a fully digital system.[42] Indeed, it was, at least in part, to offset such reduced obligations that Ofcom favoured the creation of a new Public Service Publisher.

In designing a new set of licences for the commercial broadcasters, and reviewing their related payment obligations, Ofcom wanted to support the emerging timetable for digital switchover and deliver collaboration with the BBC and others in the industry on implementation. While the BBC was in principle keen on switchover since it would bring BBC digital services to virtually all licence fee payers, the commercial companies needed more persuasion. Although switchover would bring them savings on transmission and give Channel Five extra coverage, their share of advertising revenue would fall in a more competitive all-digital industry.

Under the Communications Act Ofcom was obliged, before the end of 2004, to offer all the current ITV analogue licence holders, Channel Five and Teletext 'digital replacement licences' to take the place of their analogue licences. Ofcom also drafted a digital replacement licence for Channel 4, although the process for granting it involved the Government. In September 2004, Ofcom therefore published draft digital replacement licences for consultation and digital switchover featured strongly in the proposed terms. Specifically there would be

- an obligation to achieve digital terrestrial coverage 'equivalent to, or substantially the same as, the analogue coverage' at switchover by converting to digital 'all 1154 current analogue transmitters'
- a duty to cooperate with everyone involved in the administration , organisation or implementation of digital switchover in the UK
- a duty to report implementation progress
- a duty to ensure that all analogue viewers are made fully aware of the switchover date 'at least two years in advance and are given all the necessary information as to how they can continue to receive the service after switchover'
- a switchover timetable, with a backstop date of December 31st 2012, and an obligation 'to ensure that this timetable is met'.[43]

The commercial broadcasters were given a deadline for commenting on the drafts before the licence terms were finalized. Then the broadcasters were required to decide before the end of the year whether to accept them. They were able to decline, in theory, but if they did so they would probably lose their current analogue licence the following year. Moreover, they would forego Ofcom's offer to review, almost certainly favourably, their financial terms. Ofcom's aim was, if possible, to make them an offer they could not refuse – and it succeeded. In mid-December 2004 Ofcom was able to announce a clean sweep of acceptances.[44] The new digital licences would run through switchover to the end of 2014.

The review of the financial terms took place in 2005. The baseline for the review was the *status quo* under which the ITV companies and Channel Five paid the Treasury £230 million in 2004, a reduction from the 2003 total of £270 million primarily as a result of the 'digital dividend'. In 2005, if there were no other change, their combined payment was predicted to be about £180 million.[45] In addition to the growing take-up of digital television, changes to recording technology, allowing viewers to bypass advertising breaks, and the development of on-demand services would also affect the market. With switchover now firmly timetabled, the commercial broadcasters faced the prospect of a continuing fall in their advertising revenue. They looked to Ofcom for some relief.

Assessing the future financial outlook for the commercial terrestrial broadcasters was a complex task. The methodology had been aired in a consultation during 2004 and then published.[46] ITV and Channel Five payments to the Treasury had two elements – an annual percentage of qualifying revenue (PQR), reflecting the contracting value of the analogue licence, and an annual cash sum which increased in line with inflation. Ofcom proposed to recover

95 per cent of the value of the licences through the PQR. As more households switched to digital, the PQR payments would continue to decline.

Ofcom explained that by law the fixed annual cash payment had to be based on the principle of a fresh licence bid. So, although no one wanted another auction and the intention was to exclude new competition and simply assess new financial terms for the incumbent, Ofcom would have to pretend that an auction was taking place. It had to estimate what the second-highest bidder in a hypothetical auction would have bid since

> the amount an incumbent would bid in a competitive auction would be the minimum required to beat the second-highest bidder.[47]

Following the application of its methodology to the market conditions it predicted during the run-up to switchover, Ofcom estimated that for 2005, instead of having to pay £180 million, ITV and Channel Five would only be charged about £90 million.[48] ITV told its shareholders that, at the point of switchover, it estimated that its annual payment would have fallen to a mere £4 million.[49] Since Channel 4 did not make payments to the Treasury, its financial outlook was not included in the scope of Ofcom's review, but the Government announced that

> In the light of the revision of financial terms for ITV by OFCOM and representations by Channel 4, the Government intends to look separately at the impact of digital switchover on Channel 4.[50]

All this, needless to say, was welcome news to the commercial broadcasters who were now emerging from their digital low point following the collapse of ITV Digital and recovering some enthusiasm for digital terrestrial television. ITV had launched ITV 3 in 2004. In 2005 it announced plans for an ITV 4 and a new children's channel,[51] though it closed down its rolling news channel.[52] It also bought Multiplex A from SDN for £134 million.[53] Channel 4 made E4, and later FilmFour, available via *Freeview* and, in October 2005, launched a new service, More 4. ITV and Channel 4 also formally joined *Freeview*. For the new chief executive of Channel 4, Andy Duncan, this was no *volte-face*, since he had previously played a central role in designing and launching *Freeview* at the BBC in 2002. However, ITV Chief Executive Charles Allen's announcement was evidence of a new mood:

> The rapid growth of the DTT platform and the success of *Freeview* offer a great opportunity for ITV as a content provider, channel owner and multiplex licence holder. There are real benefits for ITV in growing and developing *Freeview*, and the most effective way for us to do that is to be at the heart of the marketing effort.[54]

Then Channel Five expanded its digital channels and acquired *Top-Up TV*. As a group, therefore, the terrestrial broadcasters were much more closely aligned with one another by 2005–06 than they had been back in 2002.

The joint Digital Switchover Programme

In giving the terrestrial broadcasters the responsibility for implementing switchover, in conjunction with the wider industry, the Government and Ofcom thus aimed to provide them with the necessary financial resources. Switchover may not have been a priority in the Government's public expenditure plans, but it would nonetheless be financed by a hybrid public funding scheme – a combination of the BBC licence fee and foregone payments from commercial broadcasters to the Treasury.

While this enabled the Government to stand back from the operational leadership of switchover, and to depoliticize it to some degree, Ministers still retained ultimate responsibility, as Tessa Jowell made clear:

> When a new technology comes along, Governments have two choices. And only two. They can follow it, trying to make retrospective sense of how society is changing as a result. Or they can be ahead of the curve, shaping the future and ensuring that the fruits of that new technology are evenly spread. We have chosen the latter course.[55]

In terms of communications, the Government saw its job as explaining to the public the 'why' of digital switchover and Digital UK's job as explaining the 'how'. Moreover, the DCMS, the DTI and Ofcom all had continuing responsibilities for aspects of switchover which fell directly within their remits. As envisaged by the Digital TV Project, a wider programme of coordinated activity had to be managed alongside the work of Digital UK.

The DCMS and the DTI were responsible for briefing other Government departments and, through them, other public sector bodies on the need to prepare, financially and practically, for switchover themselves. Schools and colleges, hospitals, care homes, military barracks, prisons and public sector office buildings would all need to make provision.

A larger concern was communal housing with communal TV systems, which spanned both the private and the public sectors. The DCMS found that by early 2005

> A large proportion of social landlords have started to upgrade (around 60%) with only 20% having made no plans. Discussions with bodies representing private sector landlords suggest that progress by private landlords to update communal systems is slower, but this probably masks considerable variation between different regions and different types of landlords.[56]

The DCMS and the Chartered Institute of Housing published detailed guidance for housing professionals' use.[57]

The DTI continued to own the digital switchover logo, used to brand sources of reliable information on switchover and equipment which would work technically through switchover. This was a certification mark scheme and, although responsibility for administering it was transferred to Digital UK during 2005, the DTI was ultimately responsible for ensuring that displays of the logo in the marketplace complied with the certification mark requirements.

The DTI and the Environment Department (DEFRA) had environmental responsibilities. The Government acknowledged that, despite the savings on transmission,

> Digital switchover will increase energy use and will therefore contribute to climate change. Most of the additional energy usage is attributable to the rapid increase in the take-up of set-top boxes, particularly for second sets, which would not otherwise be converted until replaced.[58]

Improvements in reducing the power used by set-top boxes could be obtained by encouraging manufacturers to implement an EU Code of Conduct on the energy efficiency of digital television. The DTI also had to oversee the implementation of the EU Waste Electrical and Electronic Equipment Directive which made the producers of electrical goods financially responsible for their ultimate disposal. The working assumption was that switchover would accelerate the disposal of analogue TVs and VCRs.

Ofcom had a number of critically important responsibilities in relation to switchover, even after the technical foundations had been settled. It led the frequency planning and international frequency coordination work and was responsible for preparing for the European regional conference in 2006 which would plan spectrum use for the post-analogue terrestrial broadcasting era. It was already grappling with the issues surrounding spectrum pricing for non-broadcast users and would need to design the post-switchover pricing regime for broadcasters. It would be in charge of consulting on possible future uses for the broadcasting spectrum released by switchover and for organizing its auctioning. It had also inherited from one of its predecessors, Oftel, the role of regulating the transmission companies, both of whom now had new owners and new names (Crown Castle transmission became National Grid Wireless and NTL became Arqiva).

In November 2005 Ofcom also revisited the question of compulsory consumer costs, including the impact of switchover on energy consumption, partly to deal with some of the wilder figures appearing in the press. It published a report which put an indicative cost of £132 on converting a household with two TVs and a VCR and estimated that digital equipment would account for between £2 and £8 of average annual household electricity bills.[59]

So it was essential to design some mechanism for coordinating the switchover roles of Digital UK, the Government and Ofcom. Neither the Government nor Ofcom wished to be held legally responsible if Digital UK failed to do its job – or vice versa – so the carefully devised solution was to have a joint Digital Switchover Programme without having a joint venture:

> The joint Digital Switchover Programme has been formed with the aim of coordinating the work of DCMS, DTI, OFCOM and Digital UK. Representatives of these bodies form the Switchover Steering Group, which has collective responsibility for the monitoring and governance of the programme. Oversight of the programme is by the Ministerial Group on Digital Switchover, which enables DCMS/DTI Ministers and representatives of key stakeholders to receive and comment on the progress reports, and to raise issues that could impact the successful achievement of the programme.[60]

Parliament, the BBC White Paper and the licence fee

Given the implications of digital switchover for virtually every household in the UK, Parliament's involvement in assessing and debating the policy during its period of formulation had been modest. Essentially the decisions on timing and funding had been forged by the Government, Ofcom and the terrestrial broadcasters, albeit with a lot of consultation with other interests. Ministerial statements had kept the record straight, Parliamentary questions had been asked and answered, but, hitherto, there had been no major Parliamentary occasion when the nation's democratic attention was caught by a mainstream political debate on the policy of a managed migration to a compulsory switch-off of analogue TV.

A Conservative Government had initiated the policy (enshrining the framework for digital terrestrial TV in the 1996 Broadcasting Act), a Labour Government had developed it, and the Liberal Democrats were not opposed to it. No single piece of legislation symbolized analogue switch-off: while it featured in the Communications Act and in the BBC's post-2006 Charter, both of these involved wider issues. In their constituencies, individual MPs heard demands for *Freeview* to become universally available, on the one hand, and concerns about the costs and practicalities of switchover for the poor and the elderly, on the other. The politically safe course was to sound broadly supportive of switchover in principle, to express caution about the practical difficulties of implementing it, and to stand well back from carrying full responsibility.

However, in 2005–06, as Government decisions were made to firm up the implementation, MPs were drawn more fully into the subject. The House of Lords appointed a Select Committee on the BBC's Charter Review which looked at digital switchover in 2005. The Committee did not question the principle of switchover but, keen to keep the licence fee level low, opposed the Government's proposal to use the licence fee to fund it:

> We see no reason why the licence fee payer should fund analogue switch-off. Licence fee payers already face covering the costs of replacing their analogue television sets and recorders and possibly updating their aerials. In addition the Government are set to benefit financially from analogue switch-off. It is estimated that the benefit to the UK economy will be between £1.1 and £2.2 billion. The Government will be in direct receipt of substantial proceeds from any sale of the analogue spectrum. In these circumstances it should be Government and not the licence fee payer who fund switchover.[61]

When Tessa Jowell rejected their recommendation, the Lords Committee returned to the subject in a further report in early 2006, focussing especially on the intention to fund the targeted help scheme through the licence fee and concluding:

> We therefore urge the Government to consider again covering the costs of providing targeted help with digital switchover from general taxation.[62]

In March 2006 the Government published its White Paper on the BBC's new Charter, generally reinforcing the proposals in its earlier Green Paper. Specifically on digital switchover, it reaffirmed the BBC's central role in providing leadership and funding and named 'Building digital Britain' as one of the BBC's six core purposes to be incorporated into its next Royal Charter. The BBC's key switchover responsibilities would be

- extending the digital transmission network;
- informing the public, both directly and through Digital UK;
- helping the most vulnerable TV viewers.[63]

The degree to which the Government was using the BBC as a switchover policy instrument was evident from two specific provisions in the White Paper. First, the Government proposed to 'retain the flexibility, under defined circumstances, to ask the BBC' to make some of its digital terrestrial multiplex capacity available to other broadcasters.[64] This was envisaged as a mechanism for moving Channel Five and S4C out of the former SDN multiplex and gathering all the public services onto the three multiplexes which would have full (1100+ transmitters) coverage. Second, referring to the process for reviewing Channel 4's financial prospects in the light of switchover, the Government indicated that

As part of final decisions on the licence fee settlement, we will consider forms of assistance such as asking the BBC to provide Channel 4 with financial help towards meeting its capital switchover costs and Channel 4's desire to secure a limited amount of digital terrestrial capacity from the BBC.[65]

Hard on the heels of the Government White Paper on the BBC, but ahead of any decision on the level of the licence fee for the future, came the publication of a Commons Select Committee report. This was the work of the House of Commons Culture, Media and Sport Committee, specifically tackling analogue switch-off.

The Commons Committee received testimony from BSkyB which challenged the principle of compulsory switchover. BSkyB opposed the decision to extend digital terrestrial transmission for the public services throughout the UK, which it saw as a device for protecting the terrestrial broadcasters' audience share, and was critical of the Cost-Benefit Analysis. It also expressed a broader judgment:

As a business, Sky has always been a strong advocate of consumer choice. We have been uncomfortable with a programme involving a forced migration to switchover imposed – with its associated costs – on a substantial percentage of people who have no wish and no need to move to digital.

…The Government's case for compulsory switchover by 2012 has not been made. There is no pressing national interest which merits compulsion or demands that switchover must be accomplished by that date; the costs of switchover have been understated; and – because of the way in which switchover is to be accomplished – the main benefits will accrue to public service broadcasters, and in some cases their shareholders, rather than to consumers or the nation.[66]

However, the Committee, chaired by Conservative MP John Whittingdale, noted this view, pinned the political responsibility for compulsion on the Labour Government, and then turned its attention to implementation:

No-one would dispute that it would be wasteful to go on indefinitely using large amounts of valuable spectrum for analogue television when the number of viewers is steadily shrinking. However, the case for forcing the pace by starting the switch-off process when a sizeable number are still choosing to stay with analogue is more controversial and potentially risky. The Government should therefore be commended for a bold decision to proceed with complete analogue switch-off by 2012. All attention must now focus on ensuring that switchover takes place with the minimum cost and disruption. We must also ensure that the opportunities that it will present for a whole new range of digital services are exploited to the full.[67]

Among the 34 recommendations the Committee made were identifying a single Government Minister within the DCMS as the visible and accountable champion of switchover – and a rethink on using the licence fee to fund the targeted assistance scheme:

> While transmitter upgrading is clearly a broadcasting cost the provision of television and other receiving equipment is a social cost in recognition of the need to provide compensation to vulnerable groups. We believe that the use of Exchequer funds to meet this cost is more progressive and justified given the value of the spectrum released. It also places responsibility properly on a Minister's desk. We recommend that the Government should reconsider this option.[68]

How did the BBC feel about the idea of licence fee funding for the targeted assistance scheme? In contrast to its former director-general, Greg Dyke, who opposed it,[69] the BBC was willing to agree, but with reservations. BBC Chairman Michael Grade had told the House of Lords Select Committee that there was 'a large measure of conditionality in terms of our support'.[70]

Caroline Thomson, who had become the BBC's Director of Strategy, spelled out the BBC's conditions to the Commons Committee:

> We are content to go along with that on the basis of four criteria; that the licence fee is not being used as a substitute for social security payments, which clearly would be totally inappropriate; that any scheme meets all the state aid requirements and is platform neutral; that it does not in the end, partly because of the flat-rate nature of the licence fee, put an unreasonable burden on the licence fee payers that would put the long-term future of the licence fee at risk; and that it is not at the expense of our core services. With those provisos, we have been content to agree with the Government's request that in principle we should do this.[71]

It was a statement which fell short of committed enthusiasm. Research subsequently published suggested that the public was also ambivalent about the idea, with 53 per cent in favour and 47 per cent against.[72]

The BBC at this stage had seen the licence fee system preserved, certainly through to the completion of digital switchover. The key question now was the level at which the fee was set. The BBC had announced earlier a major programme of savings, involving the abolition of 3784 posts, a 19 per cent reduction in its UK public service workforce.[73] Against this background, it set out its own view of the licence fee funding it believed it required, excluding at this stage any provision for the targeted assistance scheme. It argued that, taking into account various self-help initiatives, and simply to achieve its own broadcasting objectives, it would require an increase of 1.8 per cent p.a. above inflation. Taking account of 'additional industry costs related to switchover, such as the marketing costs of Digital UK' and making provision for the possibility of a new charge for spectrum, it said it needed increases of inflation plus 2.3 per cent.[74] Funding for the targeted assistance scheme would be extra.

The initial public response was negative. A *Times* leader, headed 'Greedy Auntie', labelled it as absurd, even allowing for the 'element of trade union politics at work here' and warned that

> The much-heralded process of 'going digital' is the perfect cover for a blank cheque from the public. It is also an exaggerated element of BBC accounting.[75]

The response from ITV and other BBC competitors was also hostile. The Government arranged a seminar chaired by Lord Burns to debate what was widely regarded as purely an opening bid and published a report by consultants PKF on the BBC's value for money and efficiency which suggested there was further scope for making efficiency savings.[76] Ofcom announced that the imposition of a spectrum charge would not arise before 2014.[77] So during 2006 the assumptions behind the BBC bid continued to be challenged, while the funding for the targeted assistance scheme had not been included in the BBC calculations in the first place.

The Government stood firm on its decision to fund targeted assistance from the licence fee and worked closely with the BBC on the practicalities of implementing the scheme, including a requirement for legislation to allow the use of social security and licence fee databases to help identify the households which would qualify for help. Estimates were made of the likely take-up and the cost was estimated at around £600 million. Provision for this became a ring-fenced element of the final licence fee settlement.[78]

While the funding arrangement for the targeted assistance scheme gave rise to a new round of questions about responsibility and managerial accountability, it was consistent with the central role played by the BBC and the licence fee in UK digital switchover policy throughout:

- the BBC had been instrumental in launching digital terrestrial television in the 1990s, retaining the proceeds from the privatisation of its transmission arm in 1996 and receiving modest above-inflation licence fee increases in 1998/99 and 1999/2000;

- the BBC had been in a position to rescue the digital terrestrial platform in 2002 following the Labour Government's decision in 2000 to reverse the below-inflation increases due to follow and to grant increases of 1.5% p.a. above inflation for the period up to the end of 2006/07;
- the BBC was providing the bulk of the funding for Digital UK.

The UK recipe for digital switchover was a very distinctive blend of public policy and the market.

Chapter Seven

Consumers are Voters

Switchover was never going to be a popular policy. The political challenge at the heart of the strategy was to ensure that unwilling consumers did not become vocal hostile voters in any significant strength.

As we have seen, throughout the period of switchover policy formulation, political discussion of the central issue of principle remained relatively muted and this in turn helped keep the subject low-key among the public at large. Yet switchover could not in the end be implemented without public support. Everyone had to buy, or have already bought, a digital receiver in order to continue to receive television: there could be no question of smuggling in the policy in semi-secrecy. The only way to avoid a poll-tax-style rebellion was through persuasion to ensure that, ultimately, the great majority of the public accepted the case for making the switch and were prepared to regard some compulsion as a regrettable necessity in the wider public interest.

Softly, softly

Over the years the task of persuasion was undertaken on a 'softly, softly' basis. Information was made public, usually without much fanfare, steadily and gradually, avoiding so far as possible any sudden move which might frighten the horses.

To use the word 'stealth' would be to imply greater premeditation than was often the case. One of the main reasons for a gradual approach was that the political intention only crystallized gradually. At the outset, the Conservative Government had presented analogue switch-off as a long-term aspiration which would be further considered after five years or, if this proved sooner, when digital take-up reached 50 per cent. Then, under Labour, Chris Smith set the criteria of availability and affordability. The message to the public, rightly at the time, was 'no need to worry yet'.

During the prolonged phase of voluntary take-up under the strategy of managed migration, it made sense for the communications drive to come primarily from the consumer marketing messages of broadcasters, retailers and the receiver industry.

The Government positioned itself carefully in relation to the voting public. Switchover was far from being a major plank in Labour's election platform and, in political terms, it carried far more danger than advantage. The Government stance, as we saw in the preceding chapter, was that switchover was a product of technological change in the broadcasting industry, with leadership coming from the broadcasting and TV receiver industry: it was the Government's job to facilitate smooth change and to stand up for the consumer.

As the consumer's friend, the Government therefore led much of the work of consulting consumer representatives. When setting out the criteria for switchover in 1999, Chris Smith had also created a Viewers' Panel to

> assess the evidence provided by industry, broadcasters and government at each review stage both to perform a reality-check on it and offer independent advice to government on the issues which matter most to the public. I would envisage membership of the panel being drawn from all parts of the UK, and including some members drawn from names submitted by The Voice of the Listener and Viewer, the Consumers' Association, the National Consumer Council, and organisations representing pensioners.[1]

The Viewers' Panel met on four occasions, gathered opinions from a range of representative bodies, commissioned a report from the research agency MORI and produced a report at the end of 2001 recommending that analogue broadcasts should not be switched off until virtually everyone had switched to digital.[2]

While the Panel was then abolished, the UK Digital TV Project involved consumer representation from the outset, both among the Stakeholder Group and at Steering Board level. Additionally the DCMS commissioned further MORI research on take-up and attitudes, including an investigation of the impact of digital television on deaf and hard-of-hearing and on blind and partially sighted consumers.[3] The DTI commissioned a series of in-depth studies from Scientific Generics on the usability of digital TV reception equipment,[4] on attitudes towards digital television[5] and on the impact of switchover on adoption intentions.[6]

In 2003, as it became clear that at some point the Government would need to name a definite timetable, the DCMS created a new Consumer Expert Group to advise it both on the clarification and development of its switchover criteria and to advise and assist in the process of wider public consultation. The Expert Group reported in September 2004, recommending that before announcing switchover, and after launching a public information campaign,

> Government should carry out a formal public consultation exercise on a regional and sub-regional basis about the policy, timetable and process for analogue switchover.[7]

The Government, however, while publishing plenty of information on its website, concluded that it was inappropriate to carry out a large-scale public consultation across the whole range of switchover issues. What areas of decision were really open to the public to influence at this stage? On timing the broadcasters were being consulted and the Government wished to base the decision, so far as possible, on their joint view; while on the regional order, the broadcasters and Ofcom advised that this should be based essentially on technical considerations relating to frequencies and the interdependence of certain transmitters.

The next round of consumer representative consultation was therefore focussed on the much narrower area, where the Government clearly did have the lead responsibility, of designing the targeted assistance scheme. Advice was taken from Ofcom's independent Consumer Panel, who reported in November 2004,[8] and from a range of charitable organizations.

Meanwhile further evidence came in from pilots and trials – first from the 2002–03 *Go Digital* pilot,[9] next from the Ferryside technical trial in 2004–05,[10] and then from the Bolton trial in 2005–06 which was specifically focussed on the needs of vulnerable groups to assist the design of the targeted assistance scheme.[11]

The public policy process leading up to the announcement of the switchover timetable thus involved a great deal of consumer consultation and research, without ever widening into any high-profile public debate on whether compulsory analogue switch-off should be happening at all.

The benefit of this approach from a political standpoint was that, up to the time when Digital UK was formed and ready to take over a major part of the communications role, the Government avoided any major storm of adverse publicity of the kind that might have triggered a popular press 'feeding frenzy'.

The corollary, however, was the public's lack of knowledge. The policy moves and the related website publications happened so gradually that you could only see the various steps towards switchover if, like the consumer organizations most actively participating, you were watching all the time. If your attention was mainly elsewhere, you could, if you looked occasionally, see that switchover now seemed a bit closer than last time you looked, but, rather as in the children's game 'Grandmother's Footsteps', you never really perceived the movement. The result was that, during the period of policy formulation, awareness among the wider consumer public remained relatively low.

A survey by Ofcom's Consumer Panel, based on 2004 survey data, showed that fewer than one in three adults had heard of the term 'digital switchover' and only one in five could correctly describe what it meant. Summarizing the position, their report observed

> Understanding of digital switchover is low generally, and lower still amongst older people aged 65 and over and those in low income households. It does appear that understanding digital switchover leads to more positive perceptions, but a significant proportion of residential consumers don't know enough to have an opinion either way.[12]

Given that this snapshot of awareness was taken well ahead of the September 2005 Government announcement of the region-by-region timetable and the targeted assistance commitment, the findings were perhaps no surprise. After all, not only had the Government been proceeding in a series of small steps, but the broadcasters' and retailers' marketing had focussed on the consumer attractions of the digital proposition. They were interested in attracting the potentially interested households, rather than persuading absolutely everyone – in gathering the apples almost ready to fall, as it were, leaving the unripe ones alone, so a low level of awareness of switchover was to be expected at that point.

Within the UK Digital TV Project the question of whether a Government-led switchover information campaign was needed sparked heated debates. One school of thought held that the task of persuasion was best accomplished by industry engaging with the public as consumers, without the Government complicating commercial marketing with political arguments. The counter-argument was that the Government should give consumers intending to replace their analogue TV sets or video recorders as much information about switchover as possible – but, then, until some of the switchover thinking was more advanced, any public information would be incomplete and, in some respects vague (what exactly was the message about replacing your video recorder?) A premature switchover information campaign risked causing public confusion.

These were largely issues of timing. The principle of concentrating first on the public as consumers was without doubt right but public opinion needed to be prepared, through the communication of the public policy arguments (why switch? why must it be compulsory? what are the compulsory cost implications?) when the timetable for analogue switch-off was set.

Consequently, the scale of the communications task awaiting Digital UK, in conjunction with the Government and the industry, during the period from 2005 and 2006 onwards, was formidable.

Diagnosis of the needs

The Government's low-profile consultation and research activities did at least mean that, by the time Digital UK started its work, consumer-related issues were understood in depth. The picture of the households which would need persuasion during the timetabled compulsory phase of switchover was not of stereotyped 'refuseniks', some blurred amalgam of the slow, the vulnerable and the resistant. The Government-commissioned research enabled different strands of reluctant adopters to be identified and segmented, and their respective needs to be separately diagnosed.

Scientific Generics divided consumers who had not adopted digital television into 'Could be's' and 'Won't be's' and pictured a set of thought processes which people followed in making their decision. In order to become an adopter the consumer needed to move, in order, through three different issues which can be characterized by the questions

- what do digital TV platforms stand for in my value system?
- what content does digital television offer me, given my usage and viewing tastes?
- what is necessary to make digital TV a reality in my household?[13]

The first issue could be a sticking point and would prevent 'Won't be's' from turning into 'Could be's', because at heart they did not regard digital television (DTV) as better television (as distinct from better technology).

> Such an assessment draws on people's value systems, their views of TV *in general*, and on their knowledge of DTV platforms and operators. For example, they may ask, 'is it a good thing for society that there are hundreds of channels and that people may watch more TV as a result?' If they think that multi-channel TV is a 'Bad Thing', they will tend to oppose DTV.[14]

The response to this group could perhaps best come from broadcasters with a reputation for quality services – explaining, for example, that BBC Four broadcasts many Proms concerts and transmits foreign films in their original languages and thus brings to digital television cultural ingredients which were much rarer on the BBC's traditional two analogue channels. Given the level of concern about the potential increase in children's exposure to non-stop cartoons, emphasizing the quality of digital television's public service children's channels was another argument which could be deployed. However, expanding what this sceptical set of viewers might consider good television would not necessarily overcome their objections to the proliferation of what they regarded as poor quality channels across digital television as a whole.[15]

For those who crossed the first attitudinal barrier and started to consider what digital television could offer them in content terms, however, the broader range of digital channels was definitely a plus. Different groups of the audience were attracted by different features – whether news on tap, richer sports coverage, music channels, a greater choice of feature films, or the documentary range provided by nature or history channels. Scientific Generics noted that

> Those people that reject or do not adopt DTV in this level fall into two groups. The first group comprises people who reject DTV '*incorrectly*' because they would find it useful if they had it. For this group, the solution is through better information or personal experience. The other group rejects DTV '*correctly*' because for them, there is nothing that DTV offers that they value over and above that offered by existing analogue services. For this group the solution would have to be a change in the digital offer.[16]

The good news, which could be traced back to the *Go Digital* pilot, was that 'a significant proportion of the "digitally disinterested" can be won over when they understand the benefits of digital TV'.[17] The main route to persuasion here therefore lay through broadcasters' and retailers' marketing and information communications, coupled with the evolution of the mix of channels within both the *Freeview* and the pay TV offerings. BBC trails for the BBC's new channels, available via a choice of platforms, made a substantial impact, together with the 'come and see my new digital TV' effect as more neighbours, friends and relatives became digital households.

The other important finding relating to the 'Could Be's' was that the announcement of a definite switchover timetable would, of itself, trigger an increase in digital take-up. The proportion of households who might have voluntarily switched their main sets to digital by 2010, if no switchover date were announced, was estimated at between 70 and 80 per cent; while the impact of an announcement could be to boost main TV set conversion by 15 per cent, with the implication that

> Even if no television was previously scheduled to be converted, in all but 5% of households at least one television is likely to be converted before switchover.[18]

Thus, during the run-up to the various regional switchover dates, the great majority of the population could be expected to move to the final question in the decision-making process – 'what is necessary to make digital TV a reality in my household?' – and most could be expected, if fully informed, to take action on the strength of the answer. Some of this action, unavoidably, would be 'last minute', in areas where households had to wait for the implementation of analogue switch-off before digital terrestrial reception became feasible locally.

Practical difficulties

The analysis showed, however, that, while the great majority could be expected to cope, an important minority would face serious difficulty at the point of analogue switch-off:

> 5% of households say they will never convert. The cost and complexity of conversion appears to be a large barrier for these people.[19]

Some of the concern expressed over cost in the research survey was based on misinformation. Reflecting the history of digital TV as pay TV, many in this group assumed there would be both a start-up cost and a monthly charge. While 52 per cent considered that *Freeview* was the cheapest option, only 18 per cent knew that it involved no monthly charge.[20] So, clearly, fuller communication of this point, and information about the free-to-view satellite option, could allay some concerns. However, a residual cost issue would remain for households with low incomes.

Another potential barrier for some consumers related to practicalities. While setting up and using a digital TV set-top box was straightforward for many people, it would be daunting for some. The issues included:

- connectivity with existing equipment (TV and VCR, for example), which could be old and for which the instructions may have been lost;
- less than perfect installation instructions with the new set-top box;
- physical difficulties of reaching the back of the TV set;
- technophobic inhibitions about the back of the TV set;
- confusion over the roles of multiple remote controls;
- inexperience with using on-screen menus and uncertainty, for example, over use of the OK or Select buttons on the remote control;
- unfamiliar features like the interactive services, where the on-screen menu needs to be related to the use of four coloured buttons on the remote control.

The report on the usability of digital equipment noted that

> Understanding how to interact with digital TV is undoubtedly more complex for the user than with analogue TV. For example, in general more control steps are needed to achieve the same result, such as watching a TV programme. This is one of several factors which indicate that a different mental model is involved in interacting with digital TV. The mental model for analogue TV is simple, intuitive and even ingrained in most people, but that for Digital TV has moved from the traditional TV interaction paradigms towards a model much closer to that of the personal computer.[21]

Detailed research tested the practical difficulties likely to confront those with visual, hearing, dexterity or cognitive impairments. These are not, of course, wholly separate groups: with advancing age many of us qualify under two or more of these headings. Among the over-75 age group, it was estimated, that

- 23.7% were 'excluded' from being able to buy a set-top box
- 48.1% were 'excluded' from being able to install it
- and 24.8% were 'excluded' from being able to start using it.[22]

The clear implication of these findings was that the needs of those at risk of being cut off from television by analogue switch-off were by no means simply financial. Installation assistance, for which some could afford to pay and others not, would be needed on a significant scale.

Evidence from the Ferryside and Bolton trials

The research studies on the needs of those who would need most information, persuasion and help was augmented by data from the Ferryside trial, which switched the nation's first transmitter fully to digital (albeit affecting only some 500 homes), and the Bolton trial, which was focussed on helping design the targeted assistance scheme.

The Ferryside experience was that, while most householders could install and use digital equipment without help, a minority needed advice via a telephone helpline, and a small minority, mostly the very elderly and disabled, needed a lot of help, including personal visits. Age, however, was not a barrier to enjoying digital television.[23]

A specific piece of research commissioned by the DCMS into the needs of elderly and disabled viewers in Ferryside made recommendations for the future including

- personal training sessions, e.g. by an installer, with plenty of practice, a personalized 'Getting Started' guide, a follow-up phone call and, if necessary, a follow-up visit;
- the use of large buttons, with more space and larger labels, on remote controls, and a 'home' button to get out of sub-menus and return to the opening screen, 'to give the elderly more confidence to investigate functions by pressing buttons without the fear of being unable to get back to "normal" television channels.'[24]

The Bolton trial did not encompass switching off analogue television; it was based around the concept of identifying vulnerable households, supplying them with digital equipment for one TV and researching what was involved in assisting installation and use. The aim was to investigate the level of support which vulnerable groups would need, to test communications and practical arrangements and to help inform assumptions about the costs of targeted assistance.

The trial report noted that not all elderly people needed outside help – two-thirds of the sample had either managed or relied on friends and family – but elderly people needed time to adapt to using digital TV, so support was not necessarily a single event. Other learning points for the designers and providers of the targeted assistance scheme included

- concerns which needed to be covered in communications (e.g. you don't need a new TV set but you might need a new aerial)
- the need for suitable equipment (large, clearly marked remote control buttons, easily accessed sub-titles for the hard-of-hearing, audio-description for those with impaired vision)
- the potential help which local authorities and charities could provide, though the level of support was likely to vary considerably

- the practicalities of delivering equipment ('Many elderly and/or disabled people can take a long time to answer… and they may not be able to come to the door at all. There is limited value in leaving a card with small print and a phone number to ring back, especially if the delivery company's phone is answered by a machine.')
- the value of a telephone helpline answered by a person, ideally with a familiar accent
- the organizational challenge of bringing together central control of marketing and information, regional co-ordination of technical resources for aerial and installation work, and local co-ordination of 'user support' resources
- the need for targeted assistance costs to cover not only an information campaign and call centre resources but also liaison with other agencies and training, for engineers and volunteers.[25]

The other point increasingly obvious to both the Government and to Digital UK was that, while eligibility for targeted assistance might be tightly defined, the boundaries in real life were less tidy. Some 74-year-olds would require more help than many 76-year-olds, while the benefits of easy-to-use remote controls could be widely appreciated.

Acting on the research findings

The research undertaken under the Government's leadership into the needs of consumers who would not have migrated to digital TV voluntarily ahead of switchover was thorough. Comparison with the preparations made in Germany and Sweden before switching individual regions suggests that it was exceptionally so. The twin requirements for communication and direct support, and the different subsets within each of these two headings, were well understood. The next step was to translate the understanding into effective action.

This was central to winning public support for, or at least grudging public compliance with, the compulsory analogue switch-off. The great majority of the population, the research indicated, would be able to cope with switchover themselves by the time it happened, if they had not already switched long before. They were unlikely to rebel on their own account if

- they were given full information and explanation of the reasons for switchover and of what they needed to do by when;
- they knew where to turn for reliable help if they needed it.

So staged consumer communications to every household – creating awareness and giving early warning first, then explaining the local switchover plan in detail – plus back-up sources of advice on particular issues such as retuning or recording were fundamental to the task of public persuasion.

Then a sharp focus was needed on those who would experience difficulty in installing or using digital equipment. This was vital for the people concerned and, in addition, the knowledge that the elderly and the disabled would be looked after, would help convince the wider community to accept the policy of compulsion.

The UK would gain little benefit from having the best researched understanding of switchover in the world unless it acted on the findings.

Consumer communications

The Government had gently started some direct communication with consumers back in 2004, ahead of the September 2005 announcement of the switchover timetable and ahead of the creation of Digital UK. At that stage the DCMS put publicity effort behind the launch (undertaken jointly with the DTI and the receiver industry) of the 'digital tick' logo to identify digital equipment which would work through switchover. Labels with the logo were printed, training materials for retail staff compiled, and leaflets made available for distribution through retailers and other outlets such as libraries. The focus here was on guiding people who were intending to replace their viewing equipment to buy wisely with as much knowledge of switchover as could be given at that point.

This initiative was accompanied by press briefings on Government policy statements, for those who wanted policy detail, and by a soft awareness-raising for the wider public over the 2004 Christmas season of consumer electronics purchasing. The *Daily Mirror* carried a 'Twelve Days of Christmas' competition, with industry-donated prizes including digital TV sets which could be won by answering questions like 'How many turtle doves did my true love give to me (a) 4 (b) 2 or (c) 3?' Terms like 'switchover' or 'switch-off' were certainly not used, but the opportunity was taken to introduce the 'digital tick' to a wider public and to refer readers wanting more information to the Government website where they could, in fact, find a full archive of switchover policy papers.[26]

When in 2006, following the timetable announcement and the creation of Digital UK, the Commons Select Committee recommended that far more public explanation of switchover was needed, the Government responded:

> In October 2004, the Government began a public information campaign to raise awareness of the switch to digital television and why it is happening. The campaign consisted of a mixture of public relations activity at both a national and regional level (a total of £350,000 has been spent on this activity) and the creation and distribution of information leaflets and other materials. Over one million leaflets have already been distributed through retailers, libraries and Citizens Advice Bureaux. The Government will continue to take responsibility for communicating its policy on digital switchover.
>
> The responsibility for ensuring that everyone receives all the information they need about the switchover process is primarily one for Digital UK.[27]

Digital UK made a publicity splash at the time of its formation in 2005. Full-page ads in the national press trumpeted, 'a programme that will change British television forever' and explained the rationale, the timing and the ways of obtaining further information.[28]

Digital UK then set about appointing its media agencies and preparing its communication strategy for 2006 onwards. Extensive consultation took place with the broadcasters, involving all platforms, and with the receiver industry. The Digital TV Group had played a valuable role in bringing together the supply chain of TV and aerial manufacturers, retailers and installers – and this side of the industry was represented on Digital UK's board. It took a close interest in both the content and the timing of all marketing communications.

In May 2006 Digital UK launched its major national advertising campaign, based around television slots on both BBC and commercial television channels, introducing a friendly robot character named 'Digit Al' in animations voiced by Matt Lucas of *Little Britain* fame. Short television spots, popping up during the ad breaks on commercial channels or during trail slots on the BBC, aimed to raise public awareness of digital switchover, to publicize the 'digital tick' and to introduce Digital UK as a source of information and help.

Consumers now had mass exposure to the subject of switchover. The public information campaign ran during the run-up to the football World Cup, coinciding therefore with a peak in receiver industry promotions and sales as well as a period of high TV audiences. Digital UK's chief executive, Ford Ennals, announced that

> There are six different adverts in the first phase and 91 per cent of the population will see them seven times.[29]

Television features were accompanied by radio and press advertising. Regional publicity was focussed on the first three regions due to switch – Border, West Country and Wales.[30]

Within the Border region, which would be first, communications were much more intensive. Digital UK appointed a regional manager and an advisory group, with membership drawn from local government, consumer groups, retailers and voluntary organizations, to coordinate local communication and activity. A major three-day event was organized in Carlisle, with a Digital UK exhibition, a visit from Shaun Woodward, newly appointed as the Broadcasting Minister at the DCMS, and speeches from the local MP and a local government chief. Border's regional organization and communications, making their initial impact two years ahead of the region's analogue switch-off date, would serve both as a model and a learning exercise for other regions thereafter.

The wider support operations provided by Digital UK nationally included a call centre and a website, explaining when switchover was happening, how to get digital TV via the different platform options, what it might cost, how recording would be affected and where to seek help. Specialized advice was also available for landlords with responsibility for converting communal housing.

Digital UK also explained straightforwardly why switchover was happening:

- fairness: 'so long as the old TV signal is running, around one in four UK households will not be able to receive all the available digital TV services through their aerial and one in five can't receive channel Five'
- better TV, with extra channels, on-screen TV listings, interactivity, Digital Teletext and 'some digital boxes have special access features such as subtitling, signing and audio description for those with hearing or sight problems'
- new services and technology after freeing up the airwaves: 'this could include high definition television and video and TV clips through your mobile phone'.[31]

In 2006, Ofcom's Consumer Panel was able to report a significant increase in awareness and understanding of digital switchover since its previous report,[32] and Digital UK, of course, now had its own mechanisms in place for tracking awareness and assessing the effectiveness of its communications investment.

A telephone survey investigating readiness in the Border region, commissioned by the DTI and undertaken early in 2006, found 72 per cent awareness of the 2008 digital switchover date and wide diversity in degrees of readiness within the organizations contacted in sectors such as social housing, care housing, day care centres, hospitals, schools and hotels:

> Half the organisations have not yet started preparing or drawing up firm plans for the switchover… A quarter of these feel that there is 'plenty of time'; for a further fifth the reason given was that 'the decision would be taken elsewhere'. Nevertheless, the majority are confident that they will be ready in time, although a third are unsure.[33]

In July 2006 Ofcom and Digital UK published the first results of their joint quarterly tracker surveys, showing that, in the preceding quarter, awareness nationally was at 66 per cent and awareness within the Border region had increased to 82 per cent.[34]

Receiver design

Implementing some of the findings of the research into the needs of consumers who would find switchover most difficult depended critically on design decisions by the TV receiver industry – raising the issue of whether there should, or could, be any public policy intervention in the commercial decisions of the reception supply chain.

The foundations for some very broad-brush governmental involvement in receiver specification had already been laid through the 'digital tick' scheme. As we saw in Chapter Five, this had required the DTI to take a view about the criteria receivers and recorders would have to satisfy if they were to be certified as products and services designed to work through switchover. Behind the commitment by Government and, later, by Digital UK to publicize the 'digital tick' to consumers lay a set of administrative and contractual arrangements to ensure that manufacturers only displayed the logo on equipment which would genuinely work through switchover. Manufacturers had to apply for, and be granted, a licence to use the switchover certification mark.

Alongside this scheme for licensing the display of the logo on equipment was a complementary scheme for retailers wishing to promote the mark and to inform and educate consumers about digital switchover. Digital UK worked closely with the industry in offering companies assistance with staff training and introduced an accreditation scheme for Approved Digital Advisers, backed by compliance monitoring including mystery shopping, to help ensure that training did actually take place.

Also in position by 2006, having been spearheaded by the DTI, was a Registered Digital Installers scheme enabling aerial and TV installers to display the 'digital tick' if they had gained a Level 2 (or above) NVQ (National Vocational Qualification) in electrical and electronic servicing, had undertaken criminal records disclosure and obtained public liability insurance.

These certification schemes, dating back to the Action Plan, were essentially designed to protect consumers against poor service and/or misleadingly marketed products. They involved setting minimum conformance criteria and avoided any detailed external intervention in specifying any but the most fundamental product features. In order to display the 'digital tick' on a digital TV set or set-top box, a manufacturer had to confirm that the product could

- access the digital replacements of all the analogue services being withdrawn
- handle widescreen and 4:3 picture changes
- receive and handle Service Information (for channel information and navigation)

and, in addition, digital terrestrial receivers had to be capable of handling 16 and 64 QAM and 2k and 8k signals and to perform satisfactorily against a set of recognized tests available from the Digital TV Group for a range of functions including interactivity.

There were no great issues here for satellite and cable and, once the market for *Freeview* reception had matured, these criteria were straightforward and uncontroversial for most manufacturers of digital terrestrial receivers.

However, the Scientific Generics research and other work, notably by the ITC and Ofcom, had shown that for some viewers, especially the elderly, detailed design features such as remote controls and their relationship to on-screen displays could be a barrier to switchover. The universality of analogue switch-off, the political need for the voluntary acceptance of compulsion, and the planned targeted assistance scheme for elderly and disabled viewers, now raised receiver design as potentially a matter of public policy.

Ofcom had a statutory duty under the Communications Act to promote the development and availability of easy-to-use consumer equipment. This gave it a legitimate role in the industry's eyes as a champion of the interests of the elderly and the disabled. This role stopped short of intervention, however: it could publicize good practice but not mandate it.

In March 2006 Ofcom published a summary of the extensive programme of research which had been undertaken in this field. Its report included two 'prototype checklists' which had been developed through a process of user and expert evaluation. While this work encompassed all platforms, Ofcom felt it would be of most use in the digital terrestrial receiver industry, where practice varied so widely among the different manufacturers. The first checklist was for receiver design and covered remote control handset and buttons, on-screen text and navigation processes. The second checklist was for easy-to-use installation and set-up instructions and diagrams for digital terrestrial television receivers. In presentation Ofcom was anxious not to overstep its role. The purpose of these checklists, it stated, reassuringly,

> is to provide an informed starting point for equipment manufacturers to refine and develop their own good practice guidelines.[35]

The DTI went further. It commissioned further work to identify receiver designs which might best meet the various needs of the elderly and the disabled, to assess how widely such designs might appeal across other consumer groups, and to understand the technical and commercial practicalities of bringing such specially designed products into the market.

A report, commissioned from i2 media research, explored a range of possible services and products which could offer solutions for viewers likely to have most difficulty with switchover. For installing and setting up reception equipment, it suggested establishing certified digital television equipment installation services and relying, where possible, on integrated digital TVs, or TVs and recorders, which removed the problems of connecting different hardware boxes.

Other ideas in the report included the concept of a 'transparent adapter' which gave easy access to digital versions of the familiar analogue channels and a separate setting for those who wanted the full range of services. Audio-description services met the needs of those with impaired vision and an audio setting to reduce background noise would appeal to those with impaired hearing. While these suggestions were essentially designed for vulnerable groups, they could also appeal, for example, to viewers with low confidence in using technology.[36]

A further Scientific Generics report studied both equipment options and a 'realisation strategy'. While some products for relatively small groups of severely disabled users could only reach the market with some charity support, two potential products were identified as commercially viable.[37]

The first was the provision of an alternative simple remote control with buttons for the main channels and five extra 'favourites', bypassing menus and in effect creating a reduced functionality option on set-top boxes. The market for this was estimated at over 2 million. The second product, for which the market might be over 5 million, simply involved adopting ease-of-use best practice, while retaining full functionality. So the features might include:

- one remote control for both TV and set-top box with well-spaced buttons;
- a flip-lid or cover on the remote control to hide the more complex functions;
- a 'home' button which 'gets you home to safe ground';
- the use of large text for on-screen menus;
- simple operations, with step-by-step guidance.

The DTI also commissioned Ricability, the Research Institute for Consumer Affairs, founded by *Which?*, to produce test reports on a wide range of digital TV products to help inform consumers and encourage best practice. Its first report was on indoor aerials.[38]

The range of needs and potential solutions identified in both Ofcom's and the Government's work cautioned against any 'one-size-fits-all' approach. The public policy aim was to encourage the market to produce solutions which would meet the targeted assistance scheme's, and other complementary, needs. However, envisaging that the companies sub-contracted to implement the targeted assistance scheme would need to place orders for consumer equipment, the Government, with advice from the BBC, published, and consulted upon, a set of Core Receiver Requirements relevant to older and disabled people, for use in this context.

Energy costs

Meanwhile another issue with the potential to spark a consumer revolt against switchover surfaced. A July 2006 a *Daily Telegraph* headline read

Analogue switch-off blamed for energy crisis.[39]

The energy implications of switchover had first been addressed in the Cost-Benefit Analysis we undertook within the Digital TV Project and, following further work, an exposition of the subject was included in the *Regulatory and Environmental Impact Assessment* published by the Government in

September 2005.[40] The substitution of digital terrestrial for analogue terrestrial television would produce major energy savings at the transmitters. However, on the consumer side, energy consumption would rise, reflecting the number of new set-top boxes requiring power and the tendency to leave the equipment on standby, when not in use. One reason for the growing use of the standby function was linked to timer recording and therefore not a consequence of digital switchover at all. Another driver, however, was associated specifically with digital television on all platforms – the delivery of software updates.

Without switchover, the voluntary take-up of digital TV was adding, year by year, to electricity consumption. Even if consumers were willing to pay the costs, this was still an issue against the political background of environmental concerns over global warming and Kyoto treaty commitments to limit greenhouse gas emissions. However, the compulsory element of switchover brought an extra level of concern – the Government could be said to be compelling people who did not want extra television not only to buy new reception equipment but to consume additional energy on a continuing basis as well.

Government economists modelled the environmental impact of the increased use of set-top boxes due to switchover. Since different assumptions could sway the results significantly, their analysis was presented in the form of low and high increased usage scenarios. Electricity consumption, measured in gigawatt-hours per annum, was estimated as rising by between 966 GWh (low scenario) and 2816 GWh (high scenario) above the level predicted in the absence of a compulsory switchover timetable:

> The increase is equivalent to a 0.37% increase in domestic electricity consumption. The increase also represents a cost to consumers of between £68 million and £197 million per annum and a total cost (including net carbon cost) of £75 million and £218 million per annum. It should be noted that the extra energy costs of a single terrestrial STB (set-top box) might be in the region of £2–£3 per year and consumers will probably take this into account when purchasing or using equipment.[41]

Ofcom subsequently published a report confirming that switchover would in most cases require new equipment which would increase the amount of power consumed by a household. The implications at household level 'will be small but… still noteworthy' and, looking wider than just the cost of a single terrestrial set-top box, it estimated the increased electricity costs to householders at between £2 and £8 per year.[42]

Improved technical design, the gradual replacement of set-top box arrangements by integrated digital TV sets as main TV sets were replaced and the spread of new recording technology could all be expected to reduce the impact. The Government also encouraged manufacturers to sign up and adhere to an EU Code of Conduct which included tight limits on the amount of power equipment consumed when in standby mode. The Code set a maximum standby consumption of 2–3 watts for many consumer electronics products but had not proved effective in practice and terrestrial set-top boxes could be found in the market with standby consumption of 9 or 10 watts.

In 2006 public opinion became more sensitive to energy concerns. Several factors contributed to the changing mood. Higher costs of oil and gas were clearly reflected in household bills and led many households to consider what action they could take to control utility costs. More broadly, political fears about the UK's dependence on foreign suppliers of energy, controversy about the case for a new round of investment in nuclear energy and increasingly obvious evidence of the impact of global warming in the Arctic led even people who could afford a few extra pounds on their bills to challenge increased energy consumption on principle.

The Energy Savings Trust, an organization funded by both Government and the private sector to promote reductions in carbon dioxide emissions, proposed to extend its 'energy saving recommended' labelling scheme to set-top boxes with the aim of strengthening the effectiveness of the EU Code on standby power.[43] In its 2006 Energy Review, the Government also pledged to lead a drive to raise basic standards of energy efficiency generally and in particular

> Working with other governments, manufacturers and retailers, we will seek to… limit the amount of stand-by energy wasted on televisions, stereos and other consumer electronics.[44]

So, while UK public policy stopped short of imposing mandatory energy consumption limits on receiver manufacturers, the Government was proactive in recognizing that the consumer-voter had both direct financial and wider environmental concerns here.

Preparing for practical implementation

In the end, of course, implementing switchover in the UK requires more than explaining the policy to the public, urging householders to equip themselves and assisting those who would have most difficulty. It involves a complex technical operation requiring transmitter engineers to climb masts, install new transmission equipment, turn off the analogue terrestrial signals and begin high-power digital terrestrial transmissions on the correct new frequencies. This task is to be undertaken region by region, transmitter by transmitter and programme channel by programme channel. The operational responsibility lies with the transmission companies under contract to the terrestrial broadcasters.

The final stages of the communication strategy, after all the early warning and exhortation, need to be closely synchronized with this work, explaining to householders exactly what will happen where and when and offering sources of help – via Digital UK's website and call centre and/or via the targeted assistance scheme – as appropriate. The aim is to ensure, so far as possible, that no one loses their access to television for more than the minimum amount of time needed for the technical work.

While the Government carries the ultimate responsibility for initiating and explaining the rationale of analogue switch-off, no one ever suggested that politicians should spearhead the practical operations. That job needs to be done by broadcasters, multiplex licensees and transmission companies, together with the reception supply chain, linked to the targeted assistance scheme and supported by coordinated communication planning.

Smooth and successful practical implementation requires not only advance planning and communications but also leadership, clarity of responsibilities, a wide range of relevant professional skills, effective coordination of diverse activities, sufficient resources and the ability to respond flexibly to feedback.

It is always possible, however thorough the preparation and awareness-building, to have a crisis during the practical final phase of switchover implementation. This could arise through a mismatch between the timetables for transmission switching and those for receiver production and distribution. There could be management failings or contractual disputes affecting the logistics or quality of the help and advice services. Communal housing managers or hospital managers could be tardy. Costs could simply have been underestimated. The risks at this stage are high, since the consumers most affected are being compelled to spend their own money on equipment they do not really want or even perhaps fully understand. Their tolerance of any poor administration is therefore likely to be low. Any major problem has the potential to be magnified by adverse press coverage which could give the whole switchover process a bad name.

It is one thing to design an operational plan on paper, quite another to make it work smoothly in practice. A steep learning curve at the beginning is highly likely. With this in mind, the Government announced that analogue switch-off would be implemented in Whitehaven, a Cumbrian town of about 25,000, in the autumn of 2007, ahead of the rest of the Border region.[45]

Only in 2013 will we know how successful UK-wide implementation proves. While poor performance will be punished by adverse publicity, success will be rewarded by an absence of fuss or complaint, with everyone able to watch television the day after, having experienced the minimum of inconvenience or confusion. As with the Y2K campaigns to avert the much feared millennium computer bug, the absence of crisis would be no small achievement. The art is to make switchover, for the consumer-voter, almost a 'non-event'.

The Government rejected the Commons Select Committee recommendation for a single Minister, within the DCMS, to be the unambiguous leader of the UK's digital switchover implementation:

We believe that the success of the development of the policy through the Digital Television Action Plan and the subsequent development of the switchover programme is testimony to the value of joint leadership by the Department of Trade and Industry and the Department for Culture, Media and Sport. Having worked together as joint lead departments since 1999, we see no reason now to change the current arrangements.[46]

If implementation were to go seriously wrong, leading to widespread public disenchantment and the risk of a significant postponement of the timetable, the post-mortem investigation would no doubt include the observation that the chain of command was less than completely clear. If, however, it proves a success, credit will quite fairly be claimed by the DCMS, the DTI, Ofcom, Digital UK and the BBC, as well as by the wider broadcasting and receiver industries, and each will say that no one organization could have managed it alone.

Chapter Eight

International Perspective

In total the UK's planning and preparation for digital switchover took five years, from early 2002 through to late 2006. Not surprisingly, during this period other countries started catching up and, in some cases, overtaking.

Jointly with colleagues from Oxford's Programme in Comparative Media Law and Policy, I submitted evidence to the Commons Select Committee on the development of digital television and the progress towards digital switchover in other countries.[1] We surveyed the three main digital TV markets – the United States, Japan and Western Europe – and found both the differences and the similarities illuminating.

The United States

On September 11th, 2001, to the horror of a global live television audience, the twin towers of the World Trade Center in New York crumpled to the ground following the direct hits on them by passenger aircraft hijacked by Al-Qaeda suicide terrorists. In the aftermath of the trauma the United States Government set up a special 9/11 Commission to investigate what, if anything, could have been done to prevent the attack and what could be learned from the way the response had been handled. Among the principal lessons were shortcomings and practical difficulties in communications to, and among, the front-line rescuers in and around the towers. Improvements in radio equipment, contingency planning and training were highlighted but so too was the need for an increased assignment of spectrum for such public safety operations.[2]

Five years earlier, in September 1996, a Public Safety Wireless Advisory Committee had recommended a new allocation from the band of spectrum where TV was located – and the following year the Federal Communications Commission (FCC) had proposed that its policy of switching to digital TV could free this spectrum.[3] Following the 9/11 Commission report, the strong practical incentive to clear broadcasting spectrum for the emergency services created political momentum and public support for digital switchover which was unique to the United States.

Leap to digital HDTV?

Back at the beginning, however, the digital television agenda in the United States was not about enhancing public safety but about high-definition television (HDTV). Indeed American terrestrial broadcasters first became interested in this subject as a ploy to head off pressure to share underutilized spectrum with both public and commercial mobile radio users.[4] At the time the only HDTV in the world was the *analogue* Hi-Vision system developed by the Japanese national broadcaster NHK in conjunction with Japanese receiver manufacturers.

In 1986 Japan put forward this analogue high-definition system as the basis for a global standard. Had this been agreed, it would have placed the Japanese consumer electronics industry, already a powerful force in an increasingly global market, in pole position for the next generation of technology. With over 100 million homes and over two TVs per household, the American market was prime territory for selling new television products. American companies reacted by lobbying within the USA for a concerted R&D effort to develop an American version of HDTV.

So in 1987 the FCC set up an Advisory Committee on Advanced Television Service (ACATS), chaired by former FCC Chairman Richard E. Wiley, with membership overlapping substantially with the broadcasting technical standards coordinating body, the Advanced Television Systems Committee (ATSC). A key member was General Instrument who, in 1990, dropped a bombshell on the industry by announcing that it had designed an *all-digital* HDTV system. Within a few months, three rival all-digital systems were also put forward. American digital HDTV would certainly trump Japan's analogue system.

The FCC Advisory Committee rallied behind the all-digital concept and the proponents of the rival digital HDTV systems formed what they called the Grand Alliance. They set out to design the best combination.[5] As the different components emerged from their tests, the ATSC documented the specifications for what was to become known as the ATSC Digital Television Standard. The picture format would be widescreen. Following pressure from the computer industry, the question of whether the picture should be based on the traditional broadcasting interlaced scanning system or on the computer industry's progressive scanning technique was left open.[6] Broadcasters would be free to choose and TV sets would need to be able to handle both.

Technical specifications were set for standard definition digital television as well as for HDTV and, in 1995, when testing procedures were complete, the Advisory Committee recommended adoption of the ATSC standard. After a period of consultation, the FCC adopted it in 1996 – and held to it in later years when there was a brief flurry of interest in the rival digital technology emerging in Europe. The ATSC standard was for digital terrestrial television: cable had its own standard setting body and digital satellite used proprietary technology.

To deliver HDTV in practice was a job for the market – guided by the regulatory hand of the FCC.

Regulating the terrestrial broadcasters

The United States has around 1700 terrestrial broadcasters, divided broadly into three categories: commercial stations affiliated to the major networks (NBC, CBS, ABC and Fox), independent commercial stations and public broadcasting stations. Around 60 per cent of American homes have cable and around 20 per cent (and growing) subscribe to direct broadcast satellite – so terrestrial television accounts for less than 20 per cent of reception. When digital television appeared as a possible new development, terrestrial broadcasters saw it as an opportunity for technological survival.

The FCC's initial approach to digital terrestrial television was to loan all the existing terrestrial broadcasters an additional frequency (sufficient for an HD channel), require them to invest in HDTV production and transmission, oblige them to simulcast their analogue service in digital HDTV for perhaps fifteen years, then shut down all analogue transmission and take back the extra frequency. The 'carrot' for terrestrial broadcasters lay in free new spectrum and the absence of any new competition.

However, this plan involved plenty of broadcaster expenditure but it did not deliver any obvious source of additional revenue – simulcast advertising carried on the HD channel would initially be to tiny audiences. HDTV sets were likely to be very expensive. The commercial flaws in the FCC's original vision were apparent to Reed Hundt, who became the chairman in 1993 and later wrote:

> I never met anyone who truly believed that the broadcasters would give back the analog channels. In the foreseeable future, Americans were not about to throw away their 200 million analog televisions, so broadcasters would not stop sending signals to them… We had inherited a crazy policy…[7]

Many broadcasters wanted to be able to introduce extra channels in standard definition to attract extra revenue and, by the time the legal foundations for launching digital terrestrial television were laid down in the 1996 Telecommunications Act, HD had become optional. The terrestrial broadcasters would be loaned the extra spectrum but whether they used it for HD was left to their discretion and commercial judgment. Their obligation was simply to

> provide a free digital video programming service the resolution of which is comparable to or better than that of today's service and aired during the same time periods that their analog channel is broadcasting.[8]

The requirement to simulcast the analogue service did not have to start immediately nor be 100 per cent until the analogue switch-off date was imminent (and later the simulcast requirement was dropped entirely).

In return for commercial flexibility, the broadcasters were required to achieve digital switchover on an accelerated timetable. The political focus had shifted via the wider agenda of the Information Society to the more specific benefit of auctioning released spectrum to reduce the federal budget deficit.

TV stations affiliated to the major networks were required to invest first: those in the ten largest local markets had to build their digital facilities by May 1999 and others in the top 30 markets by November 1999. All commercial broadcasters would have to complete construction by May 2002 and public TV stations by May 2003.[9] Digital frequency allocations would be concentrated in a defined section of the current broadcasting band, allowing spectrum to be cleared systematically. The FCC's target was to terminate analogue broadcasting by 31st December 2006.

However, the broadcasters lobbied for a softer switchover date and found ready allies in Congress. As one congressman subsequently put it,

> If on New Year's Day 2007, consumers turn on their TVs and see only snow, that could be the end of our congressional careers.[10]

The Balanced Budget Act of 1997 therefore introduced an escape clause whereby analogue broadcasts could continue after 2006 if

- a major network affiliate was not broadcasting a digital signal in its local market,
- receiver converters were not generally available, or
- fewer than 85 per cent of households in its area were equipped to receive digital television, whether terrestrially, by satellite or by cable.

Yet Congress remained keen to secure the financial benefit and expected significant portions of the spectrum due to be released to be auctioned in advance of analogue switch-off.

This plan soon hit problems. In 2001 the National Association of Broadcasters warned the FCC that about a third of its members would fail to meet the May 2002 deadline for beginning digital transmissions.[11] Many faced planning or financial hurdles relating to transmission masts. Meanwhile digital TV receiver sales were slow, as consumers waited for more digital content and lower receiver prices: around the end of 2000, HDTV sets cost between $1,000 and $14,000 while analogue sets were mainly priced between $100 and $700.[12] Shops continued to sell around 25 million analogue TVs a year. The digital market was dragging its feet. No date for 85 per cent take-up could be confidently forecast.

In the light of all this, and in the aftermath of the 9/11 terrorist strikes, the FCC was forced to rethink, with three main results. First, it publicly admitted that 2006 was no longer credible. Second, it accepted the need to assess case by case the arguments by broadcasters unable to launch on time, accommodating deserving cases and penalizing undeserving ones. Third, and most importantly, it broadened the regulatory framework from terrestrial broadcasters to encompass (a) the receiver industry and (b) the cable and satellite companies (between them accounting for over 80 per cent of households).

Regulating receiver manufacturers

In 2002, under the leadership of Chairman Michael Powell, the FCC proposed voluntary action by all sections of the industry to speed up the full transition to digital, including a commitment from receiver manufacturers to include, on a phased basis, digital terrestrial tuners in all new TV sets. The suggestion was to start with the largest screen sizes, since they were the highest priced and the additional cost would therefore be least visible here.

The Consumer Electronics Association (CEA), representing receiver manufacturers, firmly rejected the idea, mainly on the grounds that it would unnecessarily increase the price of TV sets for the great majority of households served by cable and satellite who did not require a terrestrial tuner in order to receive TV.[13] The CEA also felt that government intervention in the retail market was inappropriate in principle.

Frustrated and concerned that each new sale of an analogue TV potentially added to the difficulties of completing digital switchover, the FCC decided in 2002 to make the inclusion of digital tuners in new TV sets mandatory.[14] It proposed to use powers it had been granted under the All-Channel Receiver Act of 1962 when TV stations on the UHF band were being introduced alongside the established stations on the VHF band and manufacturers had to be compelled to make receivers capable of receiving both. The CEA took the FCC to court. The Court of Appeals backed the FCC.

So in 2003 the mandatory policy went ahead on the following timetable:

For screen sizes of 36" and above
50 per cent by July 2004; 100 per cent by July 2005
For screen sizes 25" to 35"
50 per cent by July 2005; 100 per cent by July 2006 (later modified to March 2006)
For screen sizes 13" to 24" and for VCRs, DVD recorders with tuners
100 per cent by July 2007.[15]

Essentially this was a political message to the industry. Policing these regulations, especially the 50 per cent requirements, was never going to be easy. However, the message proved effective, the receiver industry began to shift its analogue:digital production ratio, and, after further consultation, the FCC subsequently brought the July 2007 deadline forward to March 2007 and extended the policy to smaller screen sizes too on the same timetable.[16] The TV set replacement market was now yoked to digital switchover.

Regulating cable and satellite

Another fundamental issue was what role cable and satellite, the carriers of broadcast TV services to around 80 per cent of US households, would play in the policy of turning off analogue terrestrial transmission.

In 2003 the FCC blessed an agreement between the TV set manufacturers and the cable companies on a standardized interface between the digital cable input and a digital TV set, making it possible to 'plug and play' one-way digital cable services without the need for a set-top box (though a cable card would be needed for conditional access).[17] This meant that digital TV sets with a tuner for cable and an ATSC digital terrestrial tuner could be sold as 'digital cable-ready' in an open market.

Cable companies were already obliged, under 'must carry' rules, to relay the local broadcast services. Satellite operators were not obliged to carry local broadcast services but, if they chose to do so for a particular market (which, in general, was an attractive business proposition), they had to carry all the relevant local services.

The next big issue was how these 'must carry' rules, those for cable and those for satellite, should be applied during the period leading up to analogue switch-off. Did the 'must carry' obligation cover the new digital as well as the analogue broadcast service ('dual carriage')? And if the new digital frequency channel was being used to broadcast several standard definition services, did they all have to be carried ('multi-casting')? The FCC's answer to both questions was 'No',[18] but for broadcasting industry lobbyists this remained disputed territory.

Finally, the ground rules needed to be laid for the post-switchover era in which terrestrial and satellite television transmissions would be all-digital but much of the cable industry was likely still to be analogue. The broadcasters wanted cable companies to be obliged to carry their digital signals for HD and digital viewers. Digital cable, although growing, still accounted for less than half of total cable homes in mid-2005. Cable operators wanted to be able to 'down-convert' the digital signal at the headend for continuing analogue distribution to continuing analogue TV viewers. Both lobbied Congress. The National Cable and Telecommunications Association held out the prospect of no fuss from cable viewers when analogue terrestrial ended:

> If you adopt our down-conversion proposal, you can guarantee that 66 million cable households will have access to the same programming the day after the transition as the day before.[19]

Industry pressures

By 2005 industry pressures were mounting to jettison the 85 per cent digital penetration threshold and fix a hard date for full digital switchover. In testimony to the Senate, communications equipment provider Motorola reiterated the case for granting new spectrum for public safety users and pointed to the potential the cleared spectrum would also have for advanced wireless broadband.[20]

In April 2005 leading electronics companies, including Microsoft and Intel, came together to form the High Tech DTV Coalition to push for the opening of new business opportunities. Coalition members emphasized the suitability of the released spectrum not only for public safety organizations' use but also for wireless broadband. Aloha Partners, a potential buyer of new spectrum licences, underlined the social value wireless broadband could bring to rural areas where, it argued, the consumer beneficiaries could outnumber those affected by the withdrawal of analogue television.[21] Electronics industry companies estimated the potential spectrum auction proceeds at between $10 billion and $30 billion.

The Consumer Electronics Association (CEA) similarly pressed Congress to act, dubbing the spectrum due to be cleared 'beachfront property':

> The analog TV broadcast spectrum is ideal for advanced wireless broadband applications. A hard date will spur innovators to come up with a broad range of new wireless services. New technologies will give unprecedented access to rural and underserved areas, while driving down prices for all wireless consumers… But the rationale for a hard date goes deeper than promoting new technologies… The gravest threat to our safety is another national calamity like we suffered on September 11th 2001… The stakes are too high to delay the setting of a hard deadline.[22]

The Consumer Electronics Retailers Coalition added its voice to the call for a hard date. Its interest lay in any such date being completely reliable. Given this, it would be willing to put labels on analogue TV sets in the shops explaining the implications of analogue switch-off to potential buyers.[23] Both the CEA and the retailers criticized the broadcasters for not doing more to publicize and explain digital television.

Consumer representations

While politicians, regulators and industry senior managers vigorously debated the ground rules and the timing for digital switchover, most consumers had little or no knowledge of what was in store for them. A 2002 report found that 85 per cent of survey respondents had never heard of, or were only somewhat aware of, their government's digital transition policy.[24]

Consumers were represented in the political arena by the Consumers Union, the Consumer Federation of America and American Association of Retired Persons. Significantly, none of these bodies opposed digital switchover in principle. The Consumers Union, for example, could see some consumer advantage if the released spectrum were used not only for public safety but also for broadband. Their demands were for a 'consumer-friendly' implementation, with financial protection for those compelled to switch.

The Government Accounting Office estimated in 2005 that about 21 million households (or 19 per cent) relied wholly on terrestrial television. It noted that these households were disproportionately non-white and Hispanic and disproportionately poor.[25] In addition, switchover would affect millions of cable and satellite homes who had second and third TV sets (e.g. in bedrooms or kitchens) with terrestrial reception.

Estimating how many sets in how many households could potentially go black on a hard analogue switch-off date was contentious. The Consumer Electronics Association reckoned that in 2005 32.7 million of America's 285 million TV sets were used for over-the-air reception.[26] At the other end of the range, the Consumers Union and Consumer Federation testified that

> About four in ten American households, or about 42 million households, continue to rely on about 80 million over-the-air televisions for some or all of their television viewing. Given very low sales of digital-ready televisions in recent years, virtually all of these sets are likely to be capable of receiving only analog signals.[27]

With such needs in mind, the terrestrial broadcasters invited the receiver manufacturing industry to design cheap converter boxes which could keep analogue TV sets functioning once they only received a digital signal.[28] The Consumers Union argued that all affected households should be compensated for the full costs of such converter boxes.[29] The Consumers Union website told its readers, 'You may not know it, but your TV could soon go dark…' and urged them to petition Congress for financial support.

Gearing up for full switchover

I visited the United States to do my main research on digital switchover there in September 2005. This was in the wake of the traumatic disaster of Hurricane Katrina, which wreaked terrible damage on New Orleans and much of Louisiana, Mississippi and Alabama and shattered Americans' confidence in their ability to mount effective emergency rescue operations. The immediate practical impact in Congress was to postpone virtually all other business, including possible legislation on digital switchover.

However, Hurricane Katrina kept digital switchover on the political agenda. A bi-partisan quartet of two senators and two members of the House of Representatives wrote to *The Washington Post* to urge implementation of the 9/11 Commission's recommendation on additional spectrum for public safety services.[30] Budgetary pressures reinforced the case. In the light of President Bush's 'open-wallet' approach to post-Katrina reconstruction, Congress would not wish to forego a multi-billion dollar federal budget contribution from auctioning the cleared analogue spectrum.

So, in the autumn of 2005, a strategy for completing digital switchover by a fixed date started to emerge. The favoured timing was early 2009, after the 2008 presidential and congressional elections and while the newly elected politicians could still pin the responsibility on their predecessors. The priority was to bring in the spectrum auction revenue. The political decision was made early in 2006 with the passage of the Deficit Reduction Act. Switchover should be complete by the end of 17th February 2009. A $1.5 billion subsidy fund was created: eligible households could have up to two $40 coupons with which to buy converter boxes. Management of the subsidy scheme was entrusted to the National Telecommunications and Information Administration (NTIA).

The list of unfinished regulatory business was still significant but the ingredients for a high-level plan were ready. The FCC had a timetable for finalizing the post-switchover frequency plan well in advance of 2009. It had ruled out doing a phased switch-off, region by region, because of the complexity of frequency boundary issues. Broadcasters who failed to start digital broadcasting could have their digital licences rescinded and all the analogue licences would end at the switch-off date. Spectrum could be auctioned in advance of clearance.

The cable companies would have time to reengineer their cable headends. A major consumer education drive, building on a retailers' 'Tip Sheet' and on agreed industry templates, would be required, involving the FCC, the NTIA, broadcasters and receiver manufacturers as well as retailers. The diminishing number of analogue TV sets still on sale in the shops could be required to carry explanatory labels. Cheap converter boxes would be manufactured in high volume to be in the market by the time the coupons were made available.

Nonetheless, implementation would be challenging. While Congress and the president had decided the switch-off date, neither would necessarily lead the public explanation nor be responsible for ensuring that the transition worked smoothly. The logistics of so much technical change at a single point in time would be formidable with a potentially huge spike in the demand for technical advice and assistance that would need to be resourced. While this was primarily a task for the market, not for government, some coordinating mechanisms would be required across a diverse industry of broadcasters, cable and satellite companies, and receiver manufacturers and retailers who had spent much of the preceding period lobbying against one another.

Japan

Partnership between government and industry, and collaboration between competing industrial enterprises, developed much more readily in Japan. It did not need to be specially invented for implementing digital switchover. Defying the ideological polarization of the cold war, Japan had constructed its own mix of planned capitalism and political-industrial collaboration. As Michael Tracey described it:

> To the outside observer there is a stark, almost cold and awesome, rationality to Japanese culture and society. The crispness of organisation, the sense of order, the need – emotional perhaps but rational in its manifestations – for clearly defined goals and purposes on which everyone agrees, have

underpinned the quite extraordinary development of this society since the defeat of 1945. Nowhere have these elements of Japanese social order been more manifest than in the development of new communications policies.[31]

False start

In the 1980s the clearly defined goal jointly pursued by the government, the consumer electronics companies and Japan's national public service broadcaster, NHK – was the development of high-definition satellite television. Like other countries, including the UK, Japan had been allocated a geo-stationary satellite slot in the sky for the purpose of direct-to-home satellite broadcasting. The attraction of satellite to NHK was its ability to reach outlying areas of Japan where terrestrial reception was impractical; the attraction of high-definition picture quality to the consumer electronics manufacturers was its appeal when viewed on the large flat-screen TV sets they were developing. Developing high-definition satellite broadcasting would give Japan world leadership in the television technology of the future.

As with so many of Japan's consensual strategic goals, this one was achieved – in *analogue*. By 1989 NHK was broadcasting two new 24-hour analogue satellite television channels, one of which carried an hour a day's experimental high-definition programmes using the Japanese Hi-Vision system.

Although it also included a commercial pay TV service, with the brash name of WOWOW, Japan's first venture into satellite television was essentially a public sector strategic investment for the wider benefit of Japanese industry. The satellite operation was run by a new Telecommunications Satellite Corporation, 50 per cent owned by the Japanese government and 50 per cent shared between NHK and Japan's yet-to-be-privatized telecommunications industry. Satellite households paid a supplementary licence fee.

Japan tried hard to sell the Americans its analogue Hi-Vision system, modified for terrestrial transmission, in preference to the fledgling digital prototypes they were testing. NHK's chairman toured Washington, extolling the virtues of Hi-Vision to government, regulators and broadcasters, and offering generous terms for a commercial deal;[32] but to no avail – the United States opted for digital high definition and Europe developed its DVB digital standards.

For the Japanese the global consumer electronics market suddenly seemed like a nightmarish game of snakes & ladders. Having climbed up to a position of potential world leadership in the 1980s, they now slithered down a snake. Their massive investment in analogue Hi-Vision had proved a false start.

Globally, analogue high definition was a cul-de-sac. Japanese receiver manufacturers, with their multinational global businesses, swiftly positioned themselves to manufacture digital receivers for the US and European markets. The Japanese government and industry had to swallow their pride and start catching up in the new global business of digital television.

Starting digital television

Under government leadership, broadcasters and manufacturers adopted their own set of digital television technical standards, distinct from the American ATSC and the European DVB systems, though with some similarities especially with DVB. Working through a joint body called the Association of Radio Industries and Businesses, they developed a system they called Integrated Services Digital Broadcasting (ISDB) designed to embrace digital satellite, digital cable, digital terrestrial, data-casting, multi-media and mobile services. In framing the standards for digital satellite (ISDB-S) and digital terrestrial (ISDB-T) television, they aimed to maximize technical compatibility, e.g. in the hardware-software interface, to facilitate the manufacture of high-definition TV sets which could handle both digital satellite and digital terrestrial reception. The free-to-view broadcasters – NHK and the advertising-financed commercial TV companies – also collaborated on developing and managing a common conditional access system to restrict copying for rights management purposes.

The digital terrestrial technical standards and spectrum allocation policy were designed to support mobile television, with reception on hand-held mini-TVs or on mobile telephones. If the Japanese could not be first-to-market in digital television, they aspired instead to be the most far-sighted.

In practice Japan's first digital broadcasts started outside of this government-regulated framework. Rather as Sky had done in the UK, multinational commercial companies entered the Japanese satellite television market using international communications satellites to offer multi-channel subscription services for reception either via their own proprietary satellite set-top boxes or via cable. Sky PerfecTV, as it came to be called after a subsequent merger, launched in 1996 and DirecTV followed in 1997. While the latter ceased operations in 2000, Sky PerfecTV built up over 3 million digital satellite subscribers.

Government-regulated digital satellite television, based on Japan's allocated direct-to-home satellite slots, began four years later in 2000. The government licensed NHK to provide three satellite channels – the first two essentially simulcasts of its analogue satellite services and the third wholly high definition (digital Hi-Vision). Two pay TV organizations were licensed – WOWOW and a new pay TV service, Star. Licences were also awarded to five services, financed by advertising, provided by sister companies of the main terrestrial commercial broadcasters. An open market in digital satellite receivers developed, with tuners either built into, or sold to accompany, large flat-screen TVs.

However, by the time these government-licensed digital satellite services were launched in 2000, NHK had built up over 10 million supplementary licence fee-paying households on analogue satellite.[33] Policy strategists knew that Japan had to switch to digital to be in the mainstream of television technology, and electronics manufacturers were keen to sell expensive new HD digital satellite TVs. Consumers who had bought their own analogue satellite receivers in the

1990s had a different perspective and, especially as the licence fee in Japan was purely voluntary, NHK could not alienate this constituency of 'legacy' households.

So a swift transition to exclusively digital satellite television was out of the question. The plan is to end high-definition programming on analogue satellite in 2007 but that will still leave millions watching standard definition output. Analogue satellite services are therefore due to continue until 2011.[34]

Committing to digital switchover

Through no coincidence 2011 is also the year in which analogue terrestrial television is due to end. The Japanese government boldly announced the analogue terrestrial switch-off date before digital terrestrial television in Japan was even launched. Indeed, for licensing reasons, a precise date was set – Japan is to switch fully to digital TV on 24th July 2011.

The prime mover here was the cumbersomely named Ministry of Public Management, Home Affairs, Posts and Telecommunications. There is no ambiguity in Japan about who is responsible for deciding the digital switchover date. The motives, as in other countries, are to remain abreast of changing television and telecommunications technology and to seize the opportunity to release, and re-use, scarce spectrum. In this high-technology economy, spectrum is seen as under increasingly heavy demands. Some of the surrendered frequencies are due to be used for digital radio and, while plans have yet to be finalized, the needs of telecommunications, including mobile communications, for more spectrum are seen as a driving force for switchover. The underlying vision – shared between government, broadcasters and manufacturers – is the creation of a modern digital communications-based society in which Japanese businesses can thrive.

The commitment to accomplish digital switchover by 24th July 2011 is ambitious. Japan is a populous country, with some 48 million TV households possessing over 100 million TV sets. Moreover, the population is densely crowded, with a high level of communal reception. Cable systems and master-antenna relay systems account for around 50 per cent of households. The cable companies are mostly small and local – there are over 600 – and many lack the capital to fund a major investment in digital infrastructure and digital cable receivers. The government is encouraging them to switch on the same 2011 timetable but has not required them to do so by law.

However, perhaps the greatest challenge comes from Japan's mountainous topography. This requires Japanese terrestrial television to rely on huge numbers of small relay transmitters: in total Japan has around 15,000 transmitting devices mounted on around 8000 transmission masts (compared to the UK's 1100+ masts). A further consequence of this is that spectrum is intensively used and vacant frequencies correspondingly scarce. Whereas in the UK it proved possible to find new frequencies for digital terrestrial television, at any rate covering around 75 per cent of the population, in between the frequencies used for analogue, this was impractical in Japan.

Accordingly, following the work of a Joint Study Committee Concerning Digital Terrestrial Broadcasting in 1999 and 2000, the Japanese government decided to spend 180 billion yen (about £900 million) reorganizing the analogue terrestrial frequencies in order to make space for digital terrestrial television.[35]

For the broadcasters this analogue adjustment programme constitutes a complex technical project beset with risk: early technical difficulties included unexpected sources of interference with communal systems which could only be rectified at additional cost. For viewers the downside in the short term is disruption: over 4 million homes need to be visited for TV retuning. The advantage of the scheme, however, is that, for the main transmitters, the digital terrestrial services can be launched on their correct long-term frequencies, thus avoiding the complex four-year region-by-region digital frequency changes which digital switchover involves in the UK.

Digital terrestrial services and receivers

The Japanese government awarded digital terrestrial licences to NHK and to the current terrestrial commercial broadcasters (of whom there are around 170), who, while spared the costs of the analogue adjustment programme, are both expected to make large investments in digital production and transmission infrastructure. NHK's investment over the period to 2011 has been estimated at 400 billion yen, i.e. around £2 billion, and the commercial sector's at 800 billion yen, or about £4 billion.[36] Eighty-five per cent of their output has to be a simulcast of their analogue terrestrial services and 50 per cent has to be in high definition. The latter is a key attraction for receiver manufacturers; it also has the incidental effect of requiring so much spectrum that, ahead of switchover, no new broadcasters can enter the market (a point which has perhaps helped soften the costs of switchover to the broadcasters).

New data-cast services would be part of the digital broadcasts and a segment within the spectrum allocated to each broadcaster was set aside for transmission to hand-held mobile receivers. Initially the content for mobiles would simply be the main terrestrial output but new regulations after 2008 might permit programming specifically designed for mobile reception.

Digital terrestrial transmissions to the Tokyo, Osaka and Nagoya regions – the main centres of high population – began in 2003. Digital terrestrial coverage was extended to the rest of the country in 2006 and transmissions for mobile reception also began then.

Because the consumer proposition is based on high-definition, mainly free-to-view, services, reception is designed to be on new integrated high-definition digital TV sets. These are normally flat-screen (as distinct from cathode ray tube) and are capable of receiving both digital satellite and digital terrestrial services (assuming the appropriate aerial). They were initially introduced at the top end of the market, with large screen sizes and prices in excess of £1000. There is as yet no substantial set-top box market, comparable to the UK's, although stand-alone tuners are sold to work with HD-ready TV monitors or with analogue Hi-Vision sets.

In 2004 analogue receivers outsold digital receivers in a ratio of 3:1;[37] by 2005 the ratio was closer to 2:1; but for digital TVs to start outselling analogue sets on a major scale, digital tuners need to be included in small screen-size models.

Collaborative Action Planning

In 2001 the Ministry, NHK and the terrestrial commercial broadcasters formed the National *Council* for the Promotion of Terrestrial Digital Broadcasting. Its focus is activity centred on the broadcasters: it has produced a 'road-map' giving dates and target coverage figures for the roll-out of digital terrestrial transmissions. It also monitors practical progress on the analogue adjustment programme.

In 2003 the Ministry convened a wider body, called the National *Conference* for the Promotion of Terrestrial Digital Broadcasting, which, in addition to the broadcasters, included the receiver manufacturers, the cable companies, local government bodies and other stakeholders. Its job is to make the switch to digital a national movement and it issues annual Action Plans in which target goals for various organizations are endorsed. Central to its work is receiver take-up. The end goal is the conversion to digital terrestrial (or to wired relays of digital terrestrial) of 48 million homes and 100 million receivers by 2011. Key milestones were set to coincide with the 2006 football World Cup in Germany and the 2008 Beijing Olympics.[38]

In order to carry out much of the promotional work outlined in the Action Plan, the broadcasters and the receiver manufacturers formed a non-profit joint organization to which they contribute funds and second staff. Formally called the Association for the Promotion of Digital Broadcasting, it is commonly known by the somewhat opaque abbreviation 'D-pa'. It runs an outsourced call centre, financed by a government grant, publishes explanatory leaflets, provides media briefings and urges the broadcasters to use their own airwaves for promotion.

One of D-pa's early initiatives was to propose a system for labelling receivers in shops – a 'positive' label branding digital TVs which will work after switchover and a yellow warning sticker, prominently displaying the date 2011, for display on analogue TVs. Publicity about switchover remained relatively low key, however, pending the achievement of nationwide coverage for digital terrestrial, the full implementation of the 50 per cent HD quota, and the arrival on the market of cheaper small screen-size digital TVs. Research undertaken by the Ministry in March 2005 showed that, while 66.4 per cent of respondents had heard about switchover as a long-term goal, only 9.2 per cent were aware of the 2011 deadline.[39]

When I visited Japan in 2005 a cumulative total of over 6 million digital terrestrial-capable receivers and cable set-top boxes had been sold (figures to the end of September),[40] leaving a dauntingly steep graph of projected sales required for 2011 to be workable. On this basis digital household penetration was quoted as around 13 per cent, though the methodology for measuring it was still under review.

Convergence of broadcasting and telecommunications

If some doubts remain as to whether 100 million digital receivers will really have been sold by 2011, they are offset by expectations of significant growth in Internet Protocol TV (IPTV) via broadband. Broadband reception of broadcast TV services in Japan is no longer confined to personal computers. A company called Softbank Broadband, for example, offers a basic subscription package of 34 channels and a video-on-demand service with 1000 titles for set-top box reception. The convergence of broadcasting and communications is seen as ushering in a world in which consumers arrange their own schedules for viewing at their own convenience. NHK's vision of the ultimate 'Integrated Services Television' receiver is one which includes a home server combining broadcasts and communications – an 'Anytime TV' for which a prototype is under development for a possible launch in 2007.

While, by UK standards, Japan's progress towards digital switchover has been modest after a late start, the Japanese government is unlikely to waver in pursuing this vision. A 2004 White Paper on Information and Communications strategy, subtitled *A Ubiquitous Network Society That Spreads Throughout The World*, noted that by the end of 2003 78.2 per cent of Japanese households had a personal computer; 61.7 per cent used always-on Internet connections; and 93.9 per cent had mobile phones, of which 56.5 per cent were Internet compatible.[41] This is the electronic environment to which digital television is now being added:

> These developments in the use of broadband, mobile phones and networks, digital broadcasting and information terminals are… leading towards the realisation of ubiquitous networks that enable anyone to access and exchange information of any kind freely at any time from anywhere, and from any appliance.[42]

Europe

In the 1980s Europe too had reacted to Japan's *analogue* HDTV initiative by developing its own rival *analogue* satellite system, including high definition, called MAC. Embodied in a European Directive, it proved technically over-ambitious and commercially disastrous. In the UK, as recounted in Chapter Two, British Satellite Broadcasting, using MAC, had failed, where Sky, using simpler low-cost technology, succeeded.

In the 1990s, therefore, European broadcasters and receiver manufacturers reacted against politically driven high-technology strategies and vowed to implement what the market would support. Many European countries, with a history of broadcasting dominated by the state or by public service, had relatively few TV channels. The market was ripe for multi-channel choice which new standard definition digital TV could supply. Unlike the USA and Japan, Europe therefore opted primarily for standard definition digital television. While there is now a growing interest in the UK and elsewhere in Europe in HDTV, no European country's switchover policy is based on it.

From the beginning, due to the failure surrounding the MAC initiative and the liberalizing trend in telecommunications regulation, the European Union favoured a market-driven approach to the transition from analogue to digital broadcasting. It endorsed the commercially based and collectively developed DVB (Digital Video Broadcasting) standards and, by deciding not be prescriptive in detail, it allowed considerable technical diversity, particularly in respect of Electronic Programme Guides, the hardware-software interface for interactive applications and conditional access.

Under EU rules integrated digital TV sets had to have a common interface into which different conditional access systems could be plugged, but no such requirement applied to set-top boxes, nor was there any obligation on pay TV companies to ensure that their proprietary conditional access systems would work via the common interface. The net result was that different set-top boxes were developed for different platforms in different national markets.

There were three main practical constraints on EU member states. First, they were not free individually to mandate digital TV sets:

> Free movement of goods within the internal market requires that national authorities do not impose administrative constraints for commercialising digital broadcasting equipment and compulsory technical requirements without previously informing the European Commission. Where such requirements would be necessary, they should be introduced Community wide and be based on European standards.[43]

Second, a multi-platform approach and competition between platforms was in principle desirable, which implied political platform-neutrality and 'a regulatory level playing field.'[44]

Third, while national governments could promote a specific digital television technology if this was justified by 'well-defined general interests', e.g. to achieve a fast and efficient switchover, policy interventions should be transparent, justified, proportionate and timely to minimise the risks of market distortion.[45]

Within this framework digital television policy decisions and timing issues were left largely to member states. No attempt was made at European level to map out a common switchover strategy or impose a common date for analogue switch-off. The result has been a very varied set of experiences in different European countries, reflecting different market sizes, the balance between platforms, the pattern of competition, the availability of terrestrial frequencies, the strength of the desire to safeguard public broadcasting and/or to foster broadcasting pluralism, and the degree of focus on re-using released analogue spectrum for other purposes.

It is not possible, therefore, to describe the European market in general terms in the way that the United States and Japanese markets can be characterized.

Two observations can be made:

- Western Europe is much further advanced than Eastern Europe
- smaller countries and/or countries in which cable and satellite predominate (and where terrestrial reception is therefore relatively unimportant) are likely to find it much easier to switch off analogue terrestrial at an early date than others.

For comparative analysis beyond this, it is necessary to look at some of the main national experiences.

Sweden

Sweden was an early pioneer of digital terrestrial television, launching in 1999. In the Swedish market of around 4 million households, two-thirds of households subscribed to cable or satellite, but analogue terrestrial viewers had only three national channels (two public service and one commercial).

The state-owned terrestrial transmission provider, Teracom, constructed the network and operated the transmitters. Three multiplexes were launched. Senda, a new technical organization affiliated to Teracom, provided an Electronic Programme Guide and conditional access. Programme services were a mixture of pay TV and free-to-view (including analogue simulcasts) but all were encrypted and customers had to pay for a decryption card even to view the digital simulcasts. Another Teracom affiliate, Boxer, was responsible for marketing and subscription management, including the sale or renting out of set-top boxes.

The structure was cumbersome, several of the services failed to launch, and the market stalled. A relaunch took place in 2000 with a fourth multiplex; Senda and Boxer merged; the public services ceased to be encrypted; and, although a major commercial broadcaster pulled out, a fifth multiplex was added. A hybrid free-pay market for multi-channel digital terrestrial TV developed, with take-up reaching over a quarter of analogue terrestrial homes by the end of 2004[46] (though the European Commission decided to investigate allegations of inappropriate state aid to Teracom).

The successful relaunch made switchover feasible. In 2004 the government established a Switchover Commission to work with the broadcasters and Teracom to plan the regional phasing for analogue terrestrial switch-off with an accompanying public information campaign. No consumer subsidies were planned but charitable organizations were mobilized to assist the elderly and the disabled. Starting in 2005, switch-off was accomplished in Gotland, Gävle and Motala. These first steps were completed smoothly and national switchover is due for completion by 2008.

Finland

Finland was also a pioneer of digital terrestrial television, again in a small market, 2.4 million households, with around 1.4 million terrestrial homes and 1 million on cable (satellite's role is relatively minor). Free-to-view digital terrestrial television was launched in 2000/2001 based on simulcasts, limited new content, and a heavy emphasis on interactive services provided via MHP (Multi-media Home Platform). Analogue switch-off was targeted for 2006. However, MHP-equipped set-top boxes were, first, hard to find and, second, expensive. Take-up was low.

Here too a re-think was necessary. MHP was sidelined. New funding was injected – charges to commercial broadcasters for analogue licences were halved and there was no charge for digital terrestrial spectrum. The Finnish national broadcaster, YLE, was given licence fee increases of 1 per cent p.a. above inflation. The digital service offering was strengthened by the introduction of a selection of pay TV channels provided by Canal Plus. Combined with the completion of near-universal coverage, these changes encouraged the majority of terrestrial households to switch to digital voluntarily.[47] In 2004 analogue switch-off was firmly scheduled for August 2007.

The Ministry of Transport and Communications undertook to lead a coordinated public communications campaign, working closely with the broadcasters who provided on-air trails. The Ministry also established a project group called TV2007, charged with coordinating preparations, liaising with the receiver industry, briefing public sector bodies and, in particular, training charity volunteers to provide a free set-top box installation service for the elderly and disabled. By the summer of 2006 around two-thirds of terrestrial households had adopted digital television. However, Finland had also committed to converting all cable households to digital by August 2007. The cable networks were ready but, in Finland, cable customers buy their own set-top boxes and, by mid-2006, only slightly more than a third had bought digital receivers, leaving the switchover team pondering how best to incentivize them before the final point of compulsion.

Spain

Spain was the other early entrant to digital terrestrial television. Terrestrial reception dominates the Spanish market, accounting for over three-quarters of the 13.7 million households.

The original business model was similar to the UK's initial pattern in that the dominant player was a pay TV company, Quiero. All the existing national and regional broadcasters were given spectrum to enable them to simulcast their analogue services and two additional national digital terrestrial channels, Net TV and Veo TV, were licensed as well. Switchover was targeted for 2012. However, the policy was hitched to Quiero's commercial performance since the receiver market depended on Quiero's provision of set-top boxes to its subscribers.

Quiero launched enthusiastically in 2000, in competition with pay TV on satellite and cable and invested heavily in soccer rights. It also marketed its ability to offer Internet access. Rather like ITV Digital, it ran into a combination of financial and technical problems and in May 2002 it ceased trading. This left the simulcasting broadcasters, who had only just launched, and Net TV and Veo TV, who followed, high and dry, broadcasting to a stagnant market.[48]

A period of frustrating inaction followed but finally the government redesigned the regulatory framework and the technical plan to facilitate a relaunch based on a *Freeview*-style offering. The state broadcaster, RTVE, was allocated two multiplexes and expected to provide a range of free-to-view services, ultimately covering 98 per cent of the country. The commercial channels based on advertising revenue were augmented by the conversion of a Canal Plus analogue pay TV channel to free-to-view and the creation of another new analogue terrestrial channel, both of which would be simulcast on digital. Regional digital terrestrial services were also strengthened.

The analogue switch-off target was brought forward from 2012 to 2010 and on 30th November 2005 Spain officially relaunched digital terrestrial television with no pay TV element at all.

Germany

The German television market is dominated by cable and satellite (much of the latter free-to-view) and of the 36 million households only 2.6 million rely on terrestrial reception.[49] The number of people who would be directly affected by analogue terrestrial switch-off was therefore relatively small and, as mentioned in Chapter Five, Germany started by completing the first digital switchover in the world in its capital city, Berlin, in 2003.

The switchover process was designed to happen on a regional basis, in 'islands' formed by large conurbations, under the regulatory authority of the

Lander who have responsibility for media regulation. Terrestrial frequencies are scarce and there was no possibility of having a lengthy period of digital and analogue simulcasting. The plan was therefore to launch digital terrestrial only a brief time before the closure of analogue terrestrial and market it on the basis that analogue transmissions would shortly cease.

It is significant that digital terrestrial was chosen to facilitate switchover. The alternative would have been to attempt to convert everyone to cable or satellite, with satellite as the non-subscription option. This, however, would have been more disruptive and expensive for consumers, satellite signals in urban environments are subject to high-building shadows, and many cable operations take their feed from terrestrial transmissions. Terrestrial is also valued by some consumers for portability and set-top reception, often for second or third sets (and Germany's technical planning takes this into account). The potential of digital terrestrial for mobile reception was also a factor.

Starting in the capital was brave, but, with a population of around 4 million, Berlin had only around 150,000 households who relied on analogue terrestrial transmission for their main TV and another 90,000 or so who used it for second or third TV sets. In February 2002 the Berlin administration and the broadcasters signed a Memorandum of Understanding mapping out a plan for the introduction of digital terrestrial television, with both new services and simulcasts of the existing ones, and for the withdrawal thereafter of the analogue services in two stages. The commercial broadcasters would have about 30 per cent of their transmission costs subsidised for five years. The agreed arrangements also covered funding and organizing communications and consumer support service to underpin the swap.

The level of transmitter power would be so high that all existing terrestrial aerials, including set-top aerials, were expected to work satisfactorily for digital, so consumers would only need to invest in set-top box adapters for their TVs. Receiver design would be simple – it certainly would not include MHP – and agreement was reached with the manufacturers to produce the required volumes below a target retail price. Households on social security would be given a voucher enabling them to be given a low price set-top box free. A rent-to-buy scheme was introduced for students. The publicity began in earnest, mainly on the analogue TV channels, and anyone with questions or difficulties could ring a call centre. If necessary a home visit could be arranged. The reduced functionality of video recorders with analogue tuners was not rated as a serious problem.

So in October 2002 Berlin launched digital terrestrial television. By the end of the year receiver supplies had dried up, partly because the manufacturers had not fully believed that the Berlin administration and the broadcasters were really serious. However, the shortage was temporary, the analogue services of the commercial broadcasters were withdrawn in spring 2003 and the analogue public services followed in the summer. By the time of the major international consumer electronics trade fair at the end of August, Berlin's analogue switch-off was an impressive success story.

Germany's strategy was for other major conurbations to follow, as North Rhine Westphalia, northern Germany and Bavaria duly did. By the end of 2005 analogue terrestrial switch-off had been achieved in nine regions, accounting for around 50 per cent of the population.

In 2005 the European Commission ruled that Berlin's the digital terrestrial transmission subsidy to commercial broadcasters had violated EU state aid rules and should therefore be paid back. However, in the wake of the successful switchover in Berlin, digital terrestrial was seen as less in need of subsidy and other regions have not offered a Berlin-style scheme for low income households.

Digital terrestrial roll-out should be complete by 2008. The public broadcasters have committed to bring digital terrestrial television to 90 per cent of the population, taking the signal beyond the major conurbations. However, coverage is not planned to be universal: the only free-to-view option envisaged for some rural areas is satellite and the implications for commercial broadcasters of switching off analogue terrestrial TV here could prove controversial. Nonetheless, full analogue terrestrial switch-off is expected before 2010.

The Netherlands

The Netherlands warrants a special mention as the first country to switch off analogue terrestrial television. Terrestrial reception has long been of very minor importance to the Dutch. In a market of 6.7 million households the vast majority, 92 per cent, subscribe to cable. Only the three public service channels, and regional services, were carried on analogue terrestrial and by 2006 only 74,000 households relied on it for their main TV set.

A digital terrestrial service called *Digitenne* was launched in 2003, based on set-top box reception, charging only a small subscription and offering around 25 TV channels plus radio. Its principal selling proposition was portable reception, especially for second TVs.[50]

Given this, switching off analogue terrestrial television in the Netherlands was relatively simple by comparison with the challenge in other countries. The public and regional services were made available free-to-view, with 98 per cent coverage, on *Digitenne* (which was promised access to the released spectrum in order to extend its pay TV offering). The Dutch Ministry of Economic Affairs informed the households still using analogue terrestrial of their platform options for the future, including the limited free-to-view service they could retain by buying a digital terrestrial set-top box. With plenty of targeted advice and a helpline, but no consumer subsidy, the Netherlands switched off analogue terrestrial television in December 2006. Much of the cable infrastructure remained analogue, however.

Italy

The Italian market is dominated by free-to-view multichannel analogue terrestrial services. In a country with 21.5 million households, cable penetration is low and satellite services, though they dominate the pay market, have limited penetration compared to other countries. TV via broadband is growing rapidly, through a service called Fastweb. Overall, however, as in Spain, terrestrial remains the dominant means of television viewing and digital terrestrial is seen as critically important to analogue switch-off.[51]

There are eleven analogue terrestrial channels, essentially constituting a duopoly since RAI, the public service broadcaster, and Mediaset, the dominant commercial broadcaster, own three channels each and between them account for approximately 90 per cent of the audience. Italian regulators attempted to introduce more competition, but in 2003 the so-called Gasparri Law overturned an earlier court ruling that would have forced Mediaset (in which Silvio Berlusconi, then prime minister, had ownership interests) to give up one of its three analogue terrestrial channels. The duopoly therefore remained strong when digital television was introduced and Mediaset and RAI have a strong joint grip on Italy's digital terrestrial television.

Mediaset was first to launch in December 2003 with a multiplex of five channels. RAI followed one month later with two national multiplexes. By 2004 there were two other multiplexes, one run by Telecom Italia and TV International and the other by a company called D-Free. Approximately 25 national channels and 40 local ones, including the simulcast of the existing national terrestrial channels, are available in total, with a mixture of free-to-view and event-based pay TV services. The business model for digital terrestrial was originally all free-to-view, based on advertising revenue. However, led by Mediaset, the broadcasters decided to challenge Sky Italia's satellite premium services and now offer pay TV events through pre-pay rechargeable cards.

Italy has had a rapid take-up: by mid-2004, approximately 500,000 digital terrestrial set-top boxes had been sold, the cheapest ones costing around 100 euros. Growth was kick-started by the Italian government's decision to offer subsidies of 70 euros to licence fee-paying consumers purchasing set-top boxes capable of providing interactive links to websites with the potential to support e-government development. Digital terrestrial set-top boxes containing MHP (Multi-media Home Platform) technology and Fastweb boxes both qualify, but satellite receivers do not. Few e-government services are yet available and few receivers have a return path but trials are underway. In response to complaints, the European Commission began investigating this subsidy.

RAI and Mediaset accompanied the subsidized receiver purchase scheme with a strong marketing campaign, and both are leading members of the Association for the Development of the Digital Terrestrial TV, which collaborates with the government in planning the full transition to digital.

The long-term aim is for digital terrestrial coverage of 90 per cent, with satellite perhaps used for coverage in the remaining unserved areas. Analogue switch-off is to be organized on a region-by-region basis. The local governments of Sardinia and Val d'Aoste volunteered to go first, once terms had been agreed with the government. Switch-off was officially planned for the end of 2006 but in practice this became a target for starting, not for completing, the withdrawal of analogue terrestrial.

France

The French TV market is characterized by a large variety of pay TV operators offering multichannel television. Canal Plus had long been providing analogue terrestrial pay TV when digital satellite became a possibility. It launched Canal Satellite and was subsequently challenged by a rival satellite platform, TPS (though the rivalry may not prove permanent). Satellite and cable penetration is limited, however, accounting on a combined basis for around a third of the country's 23.5 million households in 2005. Neuf Telecom, Free and France Telecom, among others, provide TV by broadband which is growing very rapidly – putting France ahead of other European countries in the spread of this technology. As in Spain and Italy, however, terrestrial remains the dominant means of television viewing and the existing terrestrial broadcasters remain major players.[52]

France was a relatively late entrant to digital terrestrial TV, following strong initial opposition from commercial broadcasters and lengthy debates about the regulatory framework. Finding frequencies was not easy and involved some analogue frequency changes.

Digital terrestrial was finally launched in 2005 when *Télévision Numérique Terrestre* (TNT) began on a free-to-view basis, with pay TV services following in 2006. Digital transmission obligations are based around providing about 85 per cent coverage by 2007.

While all other European digital terrestrial television, including the French free-to-view services, had hitherto used the well-established MPEG-2 coding system, France decided to introduce a new advanced compression system, MPEG-4, for digital terrestrial pay TV. MPEG-4 can achieve greater compression and is likely to be used in due course for high-definition digital terrestrial television, for which France is planning provision.

Analogue switch-off is envisaged around five years after the launch of digital terrestrial, provided digital receiver penetration proves high enough.

European coordination

In 2005, with a Radiocommunications Conference for Europe, the Middle East and Africa in prospect the following year, the European Commission had a fresh look at the case for coordinating and, to a degree, harmonizing the approach of the different EU member states. The Radiocommunications Conference agenda was focussed on adapting the old analogue frequency plan to take account of the transition to digital. If several European countries were trying to improve spectrum efficiency and alter the purposes for which particular spectrum bands were used, with spillover and interference issues for one another, harmonization could, at least in theory, produce a better result all round.[53]

In May 2005 the European Commission proposed that

> a deadline of the beginning of 2012 be set for completing analogue switch-off in all EU Member States.[54]

However, by then the Commission's original policy of encouraging a market-led approach and urging each country to follow its own switchover path had done its work. Digital switchover policies within the European Union were so disparate that a common switchover deadline was unworkable and unenforceable. The scope for achieving standardized frequency use across Europe was clearly limited, so complex multilateral and bilateral discussions would be required as different countries planned the re-use of released analogue spectrum in different ways on different timescales. The European Commission's main practical aims in advance of the 2006 Radiocommunications Conference were therefore to urge Member States to accelerate switchover and encourage them to be flexible in the uses they proposed for reusing released analogue spectrum, allowing for telecommunications and hybrid uses as well as broadcasting possibilities. From the UK's standpoint, the outcome of the conference provided a satisfactory foundation for reaching agreement with its neighbours.[55]

Across the globe

While not surveyed in detail here, mention should be made of digital switchover plans in several other European countries, including Austria, Norway and Switzerland (where one region completed analogue terrestrial switch-off in 2006 and national switchover is in prospect).

Digital television initiatives elsewhere in the world include Canada (which uses the same technical standards as the USA), Brazil (which is interested in the Japanese system), China (which has announced its own technology standards and formulated a national plan), Taiwan, Singapore, South Korea, New Zealand and Australia (where early hopes of high-definition TV take-up were disappointed and the switchover date was postponed amid a re-think). Other countries too are designing blueprints, undertaking pilots and introducing digital services.

The global outlook, ten years after our *Trooping the Colour* broadcast to the two 'refrigerators', is of digital television taking off in virtually all of the world's advanced economies, with analogue terrestrial switch-off as a strategic goal.

Chapter Nine

The Bigger Picture

In this chapter, we stand back to consider, first, the emerging purposes for which the spectrum due to be released in the UK might be used and, second, the relationship between digital switchover and the Information Society. Coupled with comparisons drawn from the rich variety of experience in other countries, this gives us a broader view of the UK's switchover policy.

Reaping the spectrum benefits

In the UK the responsibility for managing the re-use of the spectrum cleared by digital switchover lies with Ofcom. With the development of spectrum pricing and spectrum trading in areas outside broadcasting, Ofcom's broad approach is to let market forces play an increasing role in determining how spectrum is used. However, that does not necessarily mean an 'open house' in which anyone can bid for spectrum for any purpose: a regulatory framework is clearly essential in areas where international planning and coordination are involved.

Specifically in relation to the spectrum cleared by digital switchover, during 2005–06 Ofcom conducted what it termed a 'Digital Dividend Review' (a different use of the term 'digital dividend', not to be confused with its use related to the financial regulation of the commercial broadcasters). The aim was to consider the best way of packaging the frequencies available for use and to begin work on auction design.[1]

As Ofcom reviewed the possibilities, plenty of candidates from the broadcasting, telecommunications and computer industries began jostling in anticipation of an injection of additional spectrum into the economy – holding out promises for enhancing broadcasting, communications and, in some respects, the UK economy, society and democracy.

(i) HDTV

As we have seen, high-definition television formed part of the rationale for the introduction of digital television and the planning of digital switchover from the outset in the United States and Japan. Given the size and strength of these two economies, HDTV is bound to have an impact on the rest of the world's TV markets sooner or later, with the flat-screen TV, capable of working with either a standard digital or an HD set-top box, likely to become a global product. Moreover, increasingly, programme-makers in other countries wishing to sell programmes to the US or Japanese markets will be expected to produce them in HD. This would normally be a prerequisite for American co-production funding for a major drama or documentary series.

For Europe, HDTV was not judged to be the right answer in the late 1990s, when multi-channel television was still in its infancy and presented the main commercial opportunity. The UK's achievement of the highest digital penetration anywhere in the world over the early years of the twenty-first century is clear evidence that the market signals were read correctly. By contrast, Australia launched digital terrestrial with HDTV as part of its strategy in 2001, obliging the major broadcasters to simulcast 20 per cent of their schedules in high definition, but HD receiver sales were disappointingly low.

However, by 2005–06 HDTV was beginning to kindle serious consumer interest. Viewing DVDs in home cinema settings helped create a growing interest in improved picture – and sound – quality. In the UK around two-thirds of households had converted to digital TV by then and, for the early adopters, HDTV was expected to be the 'next big thing'. In the UK, BSkyB launched a digital satellite HD service in 2006. The BBC committed to producing all its home-made programmes in high definition by 2010 and meanwhile undertook experimental transmissions in conjunction with other broadcasters.

High-definition technology involves increasing the number of lines used to display the TV picture, producing a higher 'resolution'. Different HD formats have developed, with options for using 720 or 1080 lines and for interlace or progressive scanning, and with different compression systems, MPEG-2, MPEG-4 or VC-1. Sophisticated modern receiver technology, fortunately, can cope with a range of options. Anxious to avoid market confusion, the European industry, backed by the European Commission, defined the characteristics of receivers which could be marketed using an approved 'HD-ready' logo.

The arrival of HDTV in the UK ahead of digital switchover has a bearing on consumers' receiver equipment choice. HD reception will involve plugging an HD set-top box into an HD-ready TV screen. Viewers who think they might wish to take up this option before, during or soon after switchover might therefore be unwise to invest in a new digital TV set capable of standard definition reception only. It could be more sensible to buy an HD-ready one to which either a standard definition or an HD set-top box could then be added. This thought needs to form part of the already complex advice on offer to households not yet ready for switchover.

Capacity for HDTV is available on satellite and, potentially, on cable and broadband without regard to digital switchover. However, until analogue spectrum is released at switchover there is insufficient digital terrestrial spectrum in the UK for HD services to be accommodated alongside the *Freeview* range of standard definition services. Depending on the compression technology used, only two or perhaps three HD programme services could be accommodated in one digital terrestrial multiplex. So HD terrestrial transmission is a contender for the use of spectrum released by switchover – and a hungry contender too.

As broadcasting technology becomes cleverer and the converged communications revolution advances, it faces plenty of competition from other contenders.

(ii) Mobile television

When we first assessed digital terrestrial television within the BBC's Digital Television Project in the pioneering mid-1990s, one of its key advantages over satellite and cable, we concluded, was that it could be portable. We had in mind the widespread use of small TVs with 'rabbit's ears' set-top aerials in bedrooms, flats, student lodgings, holiday homes and caravans. As digital switchover came into sharp focus, however, the transmission planners became extremely wary about making any promises for digital set-top aerial reception: while good analogue terrestrial reception should be replaced by better digital terrestrial reception, borderline analogue reception could well be replaced by nothing at all.

However, as interest in portable digital television receded or remained modest, developments in the wider telecommunications field started to kindle excitement in the possibility of mobile television. First conceived as a service in buses, trains and taxis – or in the back seats of the family car – viewed on purposed-designed receivers, mobile television as a possible broadcast development then bumped into mobile telephony.

The mobile telephone has had a rapid growth in the UK and all over the globe. Initially developed for voice, mobile phones somewhat unexpectedly grew a text-messaging market, especially among the young, and then became capable of downloading music and taking digital photographs. The third-generation, '3G', phones, launched after the famous £22.5 billion spectrum auction in 2000, gave Internet access and could support video downloads, videophone calls, radio and – up to a point – TV reception.

The logical next step was some hybrid form of mobile broadcast television receivable on a purpose-designed mobile telephone, as the Japanese had been quick to spot. From 2004–05 onwards technical trials and experimental pilots were mounted in several countries. Technically, different options and variants emerged. The main contenders included two solutions derived from digital audio broadcasting (DAB) – Digital Multimedia Broadcasting (DMB), which had been adopted in South Korea, and DAB-IP, using Internet Protocol techniques. Then there was DVB-H, the set of digital television standards developed for hand-held reception by the DVB (Digital Video Broadcasting project) and widely piloted within Europe. One of the principal purposes of the trials, of course, was to test technical performance and related financial and commercial considerations.

Trials brought together in new relationships players from both the broadcasting and telecommunications industries, with the transmission company Crown Castle and the handset manufacturer Nokia undertaking an early United States trial in Pittsburgh, for example. In total over twenty countries conducted DVB-H trials in 2005–06, with Italy, the United States, Germany and Finland in the lead with plans to implement on a commercial basis.[2]

In the UK a DVB-H trial was mounted in Oxford by the mobile telecommunications company O2 and Arqiva (formerly NTL's transmission broadcast company), using a Nokia 'smartphone' with a TV screen. Sixteen TV services, including BBC, ITV, Channel 4, Five and BSkyB channels, were broadcast from nine transmitters to a sample of 375 O2 customers. Viewing took place during commuter travel, outdoors, at work and in the home. One early finding was that a significant share of viewing had taken place within the home,[3] suggesting that part of the appeal might be the personal nature of the receiver as much as its mobility. Meanwhile BT and Virgin Mobile conducted a trial in London using DAB-IP technology to offer both radio and five TV channels and committed to launching a service in 2006. Cambridge was also a site of pilot activity for more than one technical trial.

Ideas for mobile TV content extend from opportunities to view the previous night's TV programmes during a long commute to work, at one end of the range, through to short 'gobbets' designed to provide amusement or quick updates during enforced moments of idleness. However, before mobile television can become a significant part of the UK's pattern of broadcasting and telecommunications, technology choices need to be made and transmission networks planned and constructed. Relationships between broadcast content providers, broadcast transmission companies, mobile telecommunications providers and mobile handset manufacturers also need to shake down.

The principal connection between mobile television and digital switchover lies in spectrum planning, particularly if a requirement for additional frequencies for mobile television broadcasting could be met through the release of spectrum currently used for analogue television.

(iii) Broadband

The term 'broadband' is widely used to refer to a source of 'Always On' Internet and e-mail services, as distinct from the dial-up method based on the traditional domestic telephone. Broadband denotes a high-capacity communications pipe supporting high-speed connections, with an increasingly wide range of applications.

In relation to the delivery of video signals, the main challenge for the telecommunications industry was always 'the last mile', the connection to the individual home. The development of ADSL (Asymmetric Digital Subscriber Line) technology opened up opportunities for delivering digital TV and video-on-demand services like *HomeChoice* in London, as well as transforming ease of access to streamed video programming via the Internet.

The early years of the twenty-first century saw the emergence of Internet Protocol Television (IPTV) delivered via broadband. Essentially this technology converts television signals into 'packets' which are only sent to the user when requested. They can be viewed on a computer screen, on an IPTV set-top box, or via an in-home media centre. Potentially IPTV could become very important and, in significant respects, reshape broadcasting:

- it is technically very efficient, in that the complete range of service options does not need to be sent to every household all the time as it does in terrestrial, satellite and cable transmission;
- it offers increased scope for interactivity and an interface with other Internet services;
- it can support an enormous number of channels (for those who want scheduled channels) and programmes;
- it can provide video-on-demand, enabling viewers to become their own schedulers from a vast programme library.

As with other emerging new technologies, the first phase has been characterized by a wide range of experiments and pilots in a number of countries. In 2005, Robin Foster, formerly of the BBC and Ofcom before becoming an independent consultant, surveyed IPTV developments on four continents, including plans in Hong Kong for high-definition IPTV. He concluded:

> No one has a clear idea of how the market will develop. But a few common themes seem to be emerging. First, IPTV can and should be more than just conventional TV. It allows a much richer on-demand and interactive experience, and can provide access to a wider range of content than ever before.
>
> Second, a walled-garden approach, which restricts users of any service to a pre-selected choice of content, looks unlikely to succeed with a generation of consumers used to web surfing, with all the opportunities that brings.
>
> Third, the boundaries between the TV experience on the one hand, and the PC (personal computer) screen on the other, will become increasingly blurred as software programmes like Windows Media Player evolve to allow a rich, TV-like experience when users consume content from the web.
>
> And fourth, a complete free-for-all, in which consumers are left alone to find their way around the available content is also likely to fail. The challenge for the market is to find a new approach to packaging, sorting and branding content, which looks less like traditional television, with all its constraints, but which helps consumers with different needs and interests find their way to content they will find useful and enjoy.[4]

While Internet Television remained at an early stage in 2005–06, access to the Internet by broadband had become increasingly common. The number of broadband homes in the UK surpassed 7 million during 2005, with broadband subscribers exceeding the number of dial-up Internet subscribers.[5]

The growth of video services available by broadband has been complemented by the increasing sophistication of downloading and recording technology, allowing material to be stored and viewed at the user's convenience. In 2005 the BBC mounted a trial of an integrated Media Player designed to enable users to download television and radio programmes to their computers and enjoy them during the seven days after transmission. A digital rights management system deleted the material at the end of that period and prevented the user from e-mailing them to others.[6] Meanwhile, major movie companies, having observed the experiences of the music industry, began to work on schemes for legitimately downloading feature films.

In the United States, in particular, providing near-universal access to the Internet is increasingly regarded as a political responsibility, akin to the provision of water, gas, electricity and the telephone in the twentieth century. Wired communications technology, however, is not necessarily the most economic or practical method for achieving this. Interest developed therefore in the potential of wireless broadband technology. Philadelphia has announced its intention to give Web access to all its citizens by providing wireless broadband throughout the city, from small transmitters attached to lamp posts and traffic lights, and charging low-income residents only $10 a month for access.[7] Other American cities have considered similar wireless initiatives, amid concerns about legal objections from cable and telecommunications companies who had invested heavily in wired distribution.

Wireless broadband, however, requires spectrum. Here, too, in the UK as in the USA, is another contender for spectrum released through switching off analogue television.

(iv) Local TV

Another candidate bidding for additional spectrum post-switchover in the UK is local television. In the twentieth century the UK never developed a pattern of local and city TV in the way that nearly all other advanced economies with large markets did, not just in North America but in many Western European countries too, often based on cable. Germany, France, and Italy, for example, each had over 100 local channels, and Spain many more. Provision for local television was therefore built into their designs of digital terrestrial TV.

In the UK, under what were termed 'Restrictive Service Licences', analogue terrestrial frequencies had been allocated on a temporary basis to a motley group of local TV providers in particular parts of the UK. While some eighteen licences were awarded, the infant death rate was high, and, by the time serious consideration of post-switchover possibilities began in 2006, only around a dozen were still on air.

The principal broadcasts with local content otherwise were provided within the network structures of the BBC and ITV, with comparatively full provision for the nations of Scotland, Wales and Northern Ireland and relatively little output spread across large (and not always coherent) regional areas within England. While these services were simulcast on digital TV, Ofcom's regulatory regime for the approaching all-digital world involved reducing ITV's regional broadcasting commitments. Among countries with digital television, while the UK had the highest digital TV take-up in the world, it probably had the lowest provision of local and regional digital services.

In early 2006 Ofcom published a study of local television options for the future, supported by consultancy work carried out by Spectrum.[8]

Survey results showed 70 per cent of respondents declaring an interest in programmes reflecting their city, town or village, confirming potential demand for local content:

> Viewers say they like to see TV about a range of geographic areas, including their region and neighbouring areas as well as the UK as a whole. But they are most interested in programming that reflects their city, town or village, or even their neighbourhood… This is an interest which is not currently well-served…[9]

The study's economic modelling, however, suggested that multi-platform local services were only likely to be commercially viable in larger metropolitan areas and, even then, with limited scope for commissioning high-quality local original content:

> Other services are likely to rely to a greater or lesser extent on support from public agencies or community organisations.[10]

In this field, too, pilots and experiments sprouted, with an initial focus on satellite and broadband. The local TV station in Manchester, Channel M, having added cable coverage to its analogue terrestrial service in 2004, announced a satellite initiative as well in 2006. ITV launched ITV Local on broadband in Brighton and Hastings, while the BBC offered six locations in the Midlands a ten-minute local news bulletin by satellite and the option of access to the individual news stories at any time on the Internet via broadband.

The debate about the future of local television was timely in the run-up to switchover since, in addition to the frequency channels which would be cleared completely across the UK, switchover would yield some unoccupied 'interleaved frequencies' within the spectrum retained for digital terrestrial television which could potentially be used for local or regional services. For operators of the temporary Restrictive Service Licences, and any others wishing to enter the field, switchover offered a possible digital opportunity.

The transformation of traditional broadcasting

Trying to look beyond switchover to the time when some or even all of these technology and service experiments may be mature, we can see the beginnings of a far-reaching transformation of traditional broadcasting. Through the cloud of confusion generated by a multiplicity of set-top boxes and remote controls, we can perceive the emergence of a richer and more fluid broadcasting and communications pattern characterized by

- improved quality (HDTV, high-quality sound);
- greater choice (multiplicity of channels, archived programmes, interactive features);
- greater convenience (simplified recording and time-shifting, on-demand, mobile reception);
- greater personalization (more local services, interactive options, potential for self-scheduling).

Back in 1995 Nicholas Negroponte had observed:

> Television networks and computer networks are almost the opposite of each other. A television network is a distribution hierarchy with a source (where the signal comes from) and many homogeneous sinks (where the signals go to).
>
> Computer networks, on the other hand, are a lattice of heterogeneous processors, any one of which can act both as source and sink. The two are so different from one another that their designers don't even speak the same language.[11]

He predicted that this would change – and he was right. In the home most users still maintain a distinction between 'lean forward' active engagement at the computer screen at a desk and 'lean back' passive TV viewing from the couch, but editorially, technically and commercially the boundary line between TV and the Internet has become blurred. Already the broadcasters are breaking out of the analogue constraint of broadcasting the same material to everyone at times of the broadcaster's choosing, using interactive features and online services to provide a fuller service on a self-selective basis.

Different media gurus have portrayed the transformation of traditional television in various ways but it has become common to speak of a revolution in which the universal move to multi-channel achieved by digital switchover is only the first phase, leading to an on-demand, interactive and personalized pattern of services and devices. In 2005, Lord Birt, as John Birt had by then become, giving the MacTaggart lecture at the Edinburgh Television Festival, predicted:

We are not many steps away now from the ultimate digital vision – what you want, when you want it, where you want it. If you want it to be, your mobile device will be your all-in-one broadcast TV and radio receiver, your video telephone, your video camera, your PC, your games console, your music and video store, and your on-demand video player. A single, wireless system in the home – one box at its hub – may manage your media, your communication, your computing, and your household security and utilities.[12]

Barry Cox, in a 2003 series of lectures subsequently augmented in a booklet, predicted that changes to the services and distribution would also transform broadcasting economics and funding. The main thrust of his argument was that new delivery methods, coupled with the growth of pay TV, pay-per-view and pay-per-transaction, would provide the basis for an open, competitive market hitherto impossible in broadcasting:

> In the digital world all broadcasters and producers should be free to choose how they get their programmes to us, and we should be free to choose how we want to receive them – in particular how we want to pay for them.[13]

While some of the technology was still at an early stage of development, how this might work in practice, he argued, could readily be imagined, especially given the ability of the PVR (personal video recorder), once armed with enough historic data, to record material it anticipates its user might like.

> Let's say you subscribe to 20 channels, half of them premium standalone services, the rest a bundle of cheaper channels that you buy en bloc. Your PVR has automatic access to these, plus all the free advertising-funded channels. Before you go to work you tell it the two films or programmes you want it to record. It might, of its own accord, also record a couple of hours of other programmes it thinks you will like.
>
> When you get back in the evening you choose one of the recorded shows to watch. In addition, you have heard about – and read newspaper reviews of – a programme on a channel you don't subscribe to that went out the day before and that sounds very interesting. You go to the relevant website – it could be the broadcaster's, it could belong to the programme producer, or it could be a video-on-demand service – and order it to be downloaded so you can watch it when convenient. You will pay for it in your next bill from the telephone or cable company.
>
> The next day you realise there was something on one of the free channels that you missed, but fortunately your PVR did spot it and recorded it for you. You choose to watch it with the adverts cut out – so you will be charged for this at the end of the month.

There are all kinds of variations on that model, but I trust you get the idea. It is what the combination of personal video recorders, broadband distribution and micro-payment systems can do.[14]

Barry Cox's lectures were a mixture of prediction and advocacy. He foresaw the erosion of advertising revenue for television, now that PVRs made it simple to skip the ads, giving advertising-funded commercial broadcasters an interest in obtaining a slice of BBC's traditional licence fee revenue and in unbundling BSkyB's satellite 'bulk buys', both of which he advocated. He acknowledged that the problem with his vision of a digital broadcasting market would be the loss of the idea of providing high-quality broadcasting to everybody free at the point of use. To counter this he proposed the use of tax funding to ensure universal coverage, the retention of the regulation requiring impartial news and a broadcasting equivalent of the Arts Council.[15] Much of this could be seen as a contribution to future debates about the broadcasting structures and regulatory ground rules appropriate for an all-digital world – a subject on which there would be many rival views. However, Barry Cox clearly showed that, after switchover, the context for long-term political decisions on the future of UK television would be very different. Broadcasting's convergence with broadband, coupled with new recording technology, will transform the television landscape.

Major communications organizations have started positioning themselves for convergence. The dramatic merger between AOL and Time Warner in the United States in 2001, proclaimed as the biggest business merger in history, did not prove a success and led to some of the biggest losses in corporate history.[16] However, a few years later, others began more cautiously stepping outside their traditional business boundaries.

In 2005, BT announced plans for a broadband TV service, supported by Philips set-top boxes, which would combine live *Freeview* channels with on-demand access to films and other archived programmes.[17] In 2006, NTL merged with Telewest and then sought a deal with Virgin Mobile – enabling it to move beyond offering the 'triple play' of cable television, broadband Internet access and wired telephony to a 'quadruple play' which would encompass mobile telephony as well. Meanwhile BSkyB had acquired the telecommunications company Easynet in order to offer a broadband video-on-demand service to complement its digital satellite business.[18] In his MacTaggart lecture, John Birt warned of

a new battle of the boxes, with BT and Sky likely to be the two Goliaths fighting it out to the death.[19]

The public policy framework for this hybrid broadcasting/communications market of the future remains to be decided. It is possible to picture an open commercial market, not unlike print publishing, where pluralism and competition determine the outcome and the role of public policy, other than regulating fair competition, is minimal. Alternatively, as citizens, we could decide that, alongside a flourishing commercial market, we are willing to support some form of obligatory citizen payment – a 'licence fee' which is not necessarily tied to a particular piece of equipment – to sustain public service broadcasting for the foreseeable future.

There is no technological determinism driving us away from acting collectively as citizens, but there is a shift in relationships which Ed Richards of Ofcom has characterized as

> a gentle, gradual, evolving, historic act of liberation – the liberation of consumers, viewers, listeners, to determine their own viewing, their own listening, their own schedule, their own compilations, their own content and even their own services. What's going on here… is a gradual transfer of power from broadcaster, distributor and supplier, to viewer, listener and consumer.[20]

Digital television and the digital divide

The spread of Internet use continues to alter social, economic and political patterns: alongside e-commerce and e-education, we talk about e-government and even e-democracy.

Writing in 1995, Lawrence K. Grossman, former president of America's Public Broadcasting Service, PBS, foresaw the emergence of what he called 'the electronic republic' in the United States:

> This is the first generation of citizens who can see, hear and judge their own political leaders simultaneously and instantaneously. It is also the first generation of political leaders who can address the entire population and receive instant feedback about what the people think and want…
>
> The emerging electronic republic will be a political hybrid. Citizens not only will be able to select those who govern them, as they always have, but increasingly they also will be able to participate directly in making the laws and policies by which they are governed. Through the use of increasingly sophisticated two-way digital broadband telecommunications networks, members of the public are gaining a seat of their own at the table of political power.[21]

Certainly some grand claims have been made on behalf of new technology's potential role in government and politics. In 2000 the G-8 group of countries published their Okinawa Charter:

> Our vision of an information society is one that better enables people to fulfill their potential and realise their aspirations. To this end we must ensure that IT serves the mutually supportive goals of creating sustainable economic growth, enhancing the public welfare, and fostering social cohesion, and

work to fully realise its potential to strengthen democracy, increase transparency and accountability in governance, promote human rights, enhance cultural diversity, and to foster international peace and stability.[22]

Harvard political scientist Pippa Norris does not subscribe to a starry-eyed expectation of mass political e-participation, but nor does she see the Internet as simply reinforcing existing power structures.[23] She sees digital politics as a potentially positive force in civic society, altering the balance between outsider challengers and established organizations:

> Hierarchical communication channels, typical in bureaucratic organisations like government departments and international agencies, are less effective and slower mechanisms of information transmission than horizontal networks shared by informal coalitions of alternative social movements. National boundaries to information flows dissolve, allowing global networks to flourish. Independent upstarts and multiple sources of 'news', where immediacy outweighs authority, threaten the legitimacy of traditional journalism in the newspapers and television. Communication costs fall, and information costs plummet even faster. With wider and easier access to official sources, opposition groups and social movements can challenge the authority and expertise of government ministers, civil servants and elected officials on their own turf.[24]

However, if digital technology holds out the prospect of a more participative digital democracy, there is one snag. It was the title of Pippa Norris' 2001 book and it has passed into the language – 'the Digital Divide'.

The term 'digital divide' has become shorthand for the concern that, while some people have access to the world of the Internet, others are in practice excluded from it, whether through poverty, education, technophobia or some form of handicap. Pippa Norris identified a global divide between industrialized economies and developing countries, a social divide between the information-rich and the information-poor within a country, and a democratic divide, within the community of those connected to the Internet, between those who use the new technology to engage actively in public life and those who do not:[25]

> The chief concern about the digital divide is that the underclass of info-poor may become further marginalised in societies where basic computer skills are becoming essential for economic success and personal advancement, entry to good career and educational opportunities, full access to social networks, and opportunities for civic engagement.[26]

Enthusiasts for digital television – especially enthusiasts for public expenditure on digital television – have claimed that it can help bridge the digital divide. Indeed the assumption that digital television has a role in delivering e-government, especially in reaching those without access to computers, was initially promoted by the UK Government.

In pursuit of its e-agenda, Tony Blair's New Labour Government created within the Cabinet Office an outfit called the Office of the e-Envoy and in early 2001 Andrew Pinder was appointed to the e-Envoy post. This new organization's responsibilities ran across the whole agenda of e-commerce and e-government and across all e-delivery channels. Digital television's role therefore formed part of its remit.

In 2002 the Office of the e-Envoy published a consultation document outlining a policy framework for delivering e-government services to the home. Its Preface, with enthusiasm undiminished by the recent collapse of ITV Digital, confidently proclaimed:

> The television screen in the home can become a window to a digital world of new experience, linking citizens to each other and to information and services. Digital television is set to become a medium for all kinds of communication. Reaching out to people in their homes, it presents many opportunities for Government to improve its services and the way in which they are delivered. It can provide greater choice in the ways to deliver information, interact and transact, allowing Government to tailor services more closely to citizens' needs and lifestyle.[27]

The main body of the paper went further, claiming that digital television

> potentially provides a means for Government to reach the whole population, giving people a new way of accessing government services, taking advantage of all the features of DTV to blend rich information content with interactivity. It can also help overcome social exclusion, bringing e-government services to people who may currently be reluctant or unable to use them over the internet.[28]

An early step was to persuade satellite and cable broadcasters to offer an interactive service called *UK online interactive*, mirroring – in nomenclature, though not in functionality – the e-government website www.ukonline.gov.uk. The latter subsequently became www.directgov.uk, bringing together Internet access to a wide range of national and local government services.

In 2002 Tony Blair gave an address to an e-summit, setting out his vision of a knowledge-driven economy built on e-commerce, e-learning and e-government. Drawing on the work of a Broadband Project and the advice of a Broadband Stakeholders Group, he praised broadband for making 'using the Internet just like turning on a light.' He pledged Government funding to deliver broadband connections to every school by 2006 and broadband connectivity for every GP surgery, every hospital and every Primary Care Trust. This vision, dubbed 'Broadband Britain', picturing a twenty-first-century information revolution matching the nineteenth century's Industrial Revolution, concluded with a commitment to

> tackle the digital divide to ensure that all can contribute to, and benefit from, rising prosperity.[29]

While national government services enthusiastically developed Internet access, they showed very limited interest in practice in digital television. Digital terrestrial TV was predominantly a one-way communication, which greatly restricted its appeal to the architects of e-government. Cable and satellite (via a telephone return path) had two-way capability but, as we saw in Chapter Three, consumer reaction to the early interactive services on offer had been lukewarm.[30] The operation often seemed rather clunky, lacking the speedy response times to which computer users were increasingly accustomed. The popular verdict was that interactive television services were fine for gambling, but this would never be the route through which you applied to renew your passport.

The Department of Works and Pensions ran a pilot interactive television service but discontinued it. The NHS extended aspects of its *NHS Direct* Internet and telephone service to interactive TV. The Department for Education and Skills launched *Teachers' TV*, a service specifically for teachers, on satellite and cable, with overnight transmissions for recording carried on *Freeview*. Generally, though, national government services viewed the potential of digital television for the provision of e-government services as marginal. In 2004 the Office of the e-Envoy was abolished. Under a new head of e-government the emphasis shifted to improving the effectiveness of government online services so that efficiency savings could be made in paper-based and staff-intensive government administration.

Local government took more interest in using digital television for e-services and citizen feedback, albeit on a selective and experimental basis. A variety of local initiatives were given impetus by the evangelism of the Office of the Deputy Prime Minister (ODPM), the super-department headed by John Prescott until a 'demerger' in 2006.

In 2000 Knowsley Council began to offer a range of its Council services via the Telewest cable network – with a payments facility for housing rent and council tax, information on job vacancies and training, maps of local walks and local history information and an e-mail facility for citizen feedback. A few months later Newcastle City Council also introduced local e-services in conjunction with Telewest.[31]

In 2001 the Department of Transport, Local Government and the Regions, which was incorporated into the Office of the Deputy Prime Minister, published a paper called *Modern councils, modern services – access for all*. This encouraged every council in the land to produce its own Implementing Electronic Government statement which would be 'its local route-map to the e-revolution'.[32] Digital television was presented as one of the possible routes to take:

> Digital TV offers real opportunities to bridge the digital divide. It has the potential to be an almost universal technology. Online services will be available through this medium, as well as an enormous range of public information and learning opportunities.[33]

Central government finance was made available to local authorities through pilot schemes called Pathfinder projects. There were 25 Pathfinders, providing a wide-ranging miscellany of initiatives. For Ipswich and south Suffolk, for example, funding was granted to develop digital TV channels and on-street interactive kiosks. In Somerset a partnership was formed between all the local authorities and the police to launch a hybrid service called SomersetOnLine Digital TV.[34] A national DigiTV project, led by Kirklees and run in partnership with Knowsley, Suffolk, Somerset and the London Borough of Hillingdon, offered to provide local authorities with a 'starter kit' of technology and support for local e-services, to avoid reinventing the electronic wheel. The focus was on satellite and/or cable: digital terrestrial TV was regarded as unsuitable since, normally, it was one-way, with no return path.

As broadband became a potential television platform, new possibilities for local authorities opened up under the Government's Wired Up Communities Programme. A small experimental project covering around 500 households on the Carpenters Estate in Newham in East London was mounted by Newham Council. Via broadband , the service offered a range of digital television services, civic information, community-produced films and local current affairs, access to the Internet, an e-mail facility and an estate website for interactive feedback.[35]

Research was undertaken to assess the scheme's impact in terms of access, learning, employment and social cohesion. About 300 households had taken up the offer to participate in the project (which, since it was an experiment, they were able to do without any charge). Following training, a majority had used their boxes to surf the Internet and a minority with school-age children had done so for homework or other learning purposes. Use of the Internet to search for jobs was low but using it to find information about community groups was more significant. The local production of videos was found to have 'fostered greater awareness and cohesiveness'. However, a key challenge, both for this and for similar projects, would be

> the development of a financial model which meets the ongoing cost and support which ensures that the community continues to develop local content and benefit from the system.[36]

The technology used for the Carpenters Estate, called RegenTV, was also taken up by the East Thames Housing Group in Tower Hamlets,[37] while in Shoreditch, a Trust, helped by government funding, provided housing estate residents with the *HomeChoice* range of 55 digital TV channels and video-on-demand; computer services by television, including e-mail and word processing; a community safety channel, based on CCTV cameras on the estate; a health channel, including a GP appointments booking service; and an employment channel, providing NVQ courses, a local jobs website and virtual interview mentoring.[38]

Experimental local initiatives such as these have started to show that broadband, with its ability to combine TV and the Internet, could make a contribution to e-government. Even so, the funding arrangements underpinning imaginative local schemes for relatively small numbers of households are not easily scalable.

In producing their guide to assist housing professionals in charge of switchover for blocks of communal housing, the DCMS and the Chartered Institute of Housing did cite the RegenTV scheme and a *HomeChoice* pilot as case studies:

> Preparing for digital switchover provides an excellent opportunity, particularly for housing organisations, to look beyond the provision of broadcast television services. For example, it is possible to deliver via digital television internet access (if there is a telephone line or cable connection), local community TV, e-government and public sector services in education, health, employment etc. This helps fulfil the Government's vision of 'Broadband Britain' and bridges the 'digital divide'.[39]

In practice, however, the UK's switchover strategy tended to uncouple analogue switch-off from the transition to the full-blooded Information Society. For most households, the compulsory element of the switchover policy was likely to relate to converting second and third TVs. Here the emphasis would inevitably be on cheap set-top boxes, without return path features for interactive services. Moreover, cheap and simple set-top boxes were important in enabling the Government to affirm that it had met its commitment to ensure that digital switchover would be affordable for the vast majority of people.

In evidence to the Commons Select Committee, Video Networks, the provider of *HomeChoice*, noted that *Freeview* was unsuitable for HDTV and

> fails to meet the home entertainment and communication needs of the modern household, particularly at a time when the Government is committed to developing Broadband Britain and lessening the digital divide.[40]

Jocelyn Hay, representing the Voice of the Listener and Viewer (VLV), also told the Committee:

> Our fear in VLV about future boxes is that there is going to be a big divide between the cheapest boxes and the most sophisticated boxes. I think there is a huge danger there that a large swathe of people, particularly the most vulnerable, will either be given or acquire the cheapest boxes which will have very, very limited functionality.[41]

The Commons Select Committee report reflected their concerns.[42]

The fact remained, however, that access to the more sophisticated technology normally entailed paying a subscription. While the public policy of switchover involved compelling households, if they had not already done so voluntarily, to purchase new reception equipment for a one-off cost, subscription had to remain a voluntary option. Compulsory digital television did not, and could not, mean a compulsory interactive connection to the Information Society.

UK digital switchover in perspective

With the highest digital take-up in the world, surpassing 70 per cent in 2006, the UK tended to see itself very much in the vanguard of digital television, but, as other countries named earlier analogue switch-off dates, a different perspective emerged. The UK had been first to launch a national pattern of digital terrestrial television, but it would not be the first to switch off analogue terrestrial – nor, when switchover was complete, was it certain to be in the front rank of the information revolution.

In the UK, with its high dependence on terrestrial television (as indeed in other countries similarly dependent), the political challenge slowed the pace. In Germany and the United States, the dominance of cable and satellite meant that, from the outset, switching off analogue terrestrial television would only seriously affect a minority of consumers (and voters). In the UK, only by dint of a high voluntary take-up of digital TV (across a combination of platforms) could the number of households whose main sets would be affected by compulsory switchover be reduced to a minority. Achieving high voluntary take-up required time, so the UK's switchover timetable, chosen by prudent politicians on the recommendation of analogue terrestrial broadcasters who were in no rush, became more protracted than the schedules of several other pioneering countries.

During this extended switchover period the introduction of new software and new technical standards had to be treated with care. With the Government proudly announcing the ever-growing percentage of homes which had switched voluntarily, the broadcasters could not easily adopt new technology which rendered existing digital receivers obsolete and diminished the number of households equipped for switchover. As late as 2012–13 the broadcasters may still feel obliged to broadcast to set-top boxes purchased a decade previously, whereas in other countries with a later start and a shorter timetable this legacy issue poses less of a constraint.

Other countries are becoming digital pacesetters in their own ways too. The United States and Japan have adopted high-definition television. France has introduced the more advanced MPEG-4 compression technology for its digital terrestrial pay TV services. Japan has incorporated mobile TV into its digital terrestrial proposition. Italy, with the help of its subsidy policy, has embraced MHP as an Applications Programming Interface capable of supporting sophisticated interactive services, and some MHP receivers have been introduced in Scandinavia and Germany (though the technology still remains expensive and the European Union has decided against any attempt to mandate it).[43] Broadband TV has taken off rapidly in France and Italy.

Meanwhile, in contrast to some other countries, where free-to-view digital satellite is seen as an acceptable substitute for terrestrial transmission, the UK has committed to near-universal digital terrestrial coverage, designed to match the analogue terrestrial pattern as closely as possible. Terrestrial reception will continue to be subject to erosion by other platforms, the role of broadband will grow, and new BBC and ITV satellite initiatives may well take place. Even so, when switchover is finally complete, when new uses have been found for the released spectrum, and as the Information Society develops in new ways, the hilltop mast and the rooftop aerial seem set to maintain an important role in the UK's all-digital world.

Chapter Ten

Mapping Digital Switchover

In 2005 I was invited to talk to a seminar of New Zealand civil servants and broadcasters who wanted to know how transferable the UK experience was to New Zealand. My answer was that, looking at the varied pattern of digital television around the globe, it was becoming possible to distinguish between factors specific to particular national markets and some emerging common principles. Market specific factors were very important (so New Zealand needed to analyse its own market, not simply copy the UK). I subsequently developed this thinking further with Oxford colleagues for our submission to the Commons Select Committee and for separate publication.[1]

(a) Market-specific factors

On the cumulative evidence available, features of digital television which are specific to individual countries and help explain their significantly different experiences and switchover strategies include:

- Market size
- The extent of analogue multi-channel TV before start of digital
- The appetite for HDTV versus more standard definition channels
- The relative importance of terrestrial in relation to satellite and cable
- The strength of satellite and/or cable pay TV
- The availability of frequencies for digital terrestrial before analogue switch-off
- The role of public service or state television and of public funding
- The nature of competition among commercial TV companies
- The strength of concern about the prevention of copying (greater for HD services)
- The degree of government interest in promoting interactive services via digital television
- Detailed plans for auctioning and/or re-using released spectrum.

(b) Common principles

Confidently identifying common principles which some new development may yet contradict is risky, but here is a working hypothesis:

1. No country has yet decided to 'skip' digital terrestrial completely, even countries where terrestrial reception plays a very small role.
2. No country has launched digital terrestrial without also adopting an analogue switch-off goal (implying a compulsory final phase).
3. To facilitate analogue switch-off, digital terrestrial spectrum needs to be allocated to existing terrestrial broadcasters (not necessarily exclusively).

4. To facilitate analogue switch-off, consumers need to be offered a free-to-view option, usually digital terrestrial and/or free-to-view satellite: it is not, at any rate in the short term, politically realistic to make subscription compulsory.
5. Digital terrestrial pay TV is commercially risky where satellite and cable pay TV is well established and/or strong – but hybrid free-pay digital terrestrial can work.
6. Analogue switch-off dates which are set politically without regard to consumer take-up of digital TV tend to be postponed.
7. Full switchover is generally easier in countries where terrestrial reception is of limited importance and, at least in respect of their main TV set, a relatively small minority of households is affected.
8. In countries where terrestrial reception is dominant, high digital penetration achieved during the period of voluntary take-up is important as a pre-condition of switchover, since this reduces the number of households whose main TV set is likely to be analogue at the point of compulsion. Such take-up does not have to be exclusively digital terrestrial but other platforms only contribute if they carry digital versions of the analogue terrestrial services to be withdrawn.
9. Coordination between government, regulatory bodies, broadcasters, TV manufacturers and retailers is important for a number of purposes – from standard-setting at the outset through to the practicalities of implementing switchover.
10. Possible re-uses for released spectrum generally include HDTV, mobile television, and more local and/or regional channels, but also go wider than broadcasting, reflecting the convergence of broadcasting, computer and telecommunications technologies.

Fewer surprises?

Looking back at the early history of the UK and other pioneering countries, we can see that switchover was an uncertain goal at the outset and that some of the impetus for digital terrestrial television came from other forces, such as American concern about the risk of Japanese domination of high-definition television development and British terrestrial broadcasters' search for a new way of competing with BSkyB. The idea of switching off analogue terrestrial, while recognized as an attractive goal, was seen as a long-term prospect and, at times, a rather elusive one. Berlin's achievement in 2003 showed that switchover could be achieved in a limited area in a favourable environment, but only in 2005 did national governments begin to feel ready to elevate analogue switch-off from a broad aspiration to a timetabled practical commitment.

However, for the next wave of countries embarking on digital switchover, the pattern could be very different. Essentially there should be more certainty about the goal at the start and fewer surprises along the way.

The most common purpose is likely to be 'to improve spectrum efficiency and release frequencies for alternative use'. Another motive may be to increase broadcasting plurality and diversity and/or to safeguard for the digital age broadcasting cultural values originally enshrined in analogue institutions. In the end simply keeping up with the technology transition happening internationally will become a further motive, as analogue equipment, both for transmission and reception, is replaced by digital in the global market and digital TV skills become an industry requirement, from R&D through to programme – making. However, the notion that switching off analogue terrestrial television will usher in the Information Society, bridge the digital divide and open the way to electronic democracy should be treated with judicious scepticism – except insofar as the release of analogue spectrum assists the growth of new Internet-based interactive services.

The technology of digital television transmission and reception is much more mature. The second generation of countries launching digital television will not have to invent it, test it and standardize it in the same way: they can simply pick up the European DVB, the American ATSC, the Japanese ISDB or (in due course) the Chinese handbooks and follow established system designs. Obviously, the technology continually moves on, so newcomers' perspectives on HDTV, MPEG-4, mobile TV, broadband and on-demand services will be different from those of the pioneers (Norway and Estonia, for example, have decided to adopt MPEG-4) – but the framework of digital television technology has been firmly established.

Moreover, not only is the technology now largely standardized and documented, but the whole digital switchover policy process can also be charted. Newcomers can begin to picture the transition from start to finish, from a predominantly analogue television system through to the creation of a fully digital one.

Differences in market conditions and in political and social factors will no doubt remain critically important and each nation therefore needs to plan its own itinerary accordingly. Blindly following the driver in front will not work. However, it is no longer necessary to start with an almost blank sheet of paper. It is possible now to map the digital switchover process, stage by stage, and begin identifying conditions favourable to success.

Establishing feasibility

The baseline for a feasibility study is the 'do nothing' alternative, letting the market take its course. It is an option not to have a switchover policy, but simply to allow broadcasters and the receiver industry to make their own transitions to digital at their own pace.

The first drawback of this course, however, could be the postponement of spectrum release. There could be an excessively long period of inefficient spectrum use, with an open-ended long-term obligation to protect analogue terrestrial transmissions for broadcasters with no market incentive to switch, and with corresponding constraints on digital development.

Secondly, under this option, digital television could in practice come to equate with internationally based satellite TV, broadcast direct to the home or delivered by cable, leaving domestic (including public service) television declining with an obsolescent analogue infrastructure. For some policy-makers this may be entirely acceptable. For others, wishing perhaps to safeguard their national language, their domestic TV production base and/or the educational and cultural contributions made by their national public service television, concern at such a prospect may provide the incentive to adopt a planned digital switchover policy.

Merely having a public policy motive for digital switchover does not, however, make such a policy feasible. Unless the intention is to provide all the necessary consumer equipment on the basis of public finance (and no Cost-Benefit Analysis has yet recommended this option), then an essential ingredient is a flourishing consumer market. Consumers need to be willing buyers of new digital receivers, or at least persuadable potential buyers. That way, voluntary consumer take-up in the market can drive the switchover policy.

One fundamental test of switchover feasibility is an answer to the simple question: why should consumers wish to buy digital receivers? This question may not trouble pay TV broadcasters who supply the reception equipment free in return for a commitment to subscribe. However, in a democratic society accustomed to free-to-view analogue television, a free-to-view digital option – most obviously, digital terrestrial, digital satellite, or both – is essential. The economics of free-to-view digital television, whether financed by advertising or a mixture of advertising and public funding, do not permit the providers to give away free digital receivers. Therefore, consumers need to be willing to buy (or rent) the digital receivers required for the free-to-view option. Why should they?

It is surprisingly easy to overlook this fundamental issue. Governments and regulators may feel that it is not directly their problem and may lack the market expertise to answer it. Free-to-view analogue broadcasters may be preoccupied with persuading governments and regulators to give them spectrum or extra funding and may also be unaccustomed to dealing with the TV receiver market which, for analogue, they have long been able to take for granted. However, to launch a digital switchover policy without adequate prior analysis of the receiver retail market is a recipe for expensively broadcasting digital programmes into the ether with no one on the receiving end. This is how digital audio broadcasting started in the UK (though it then skilfully recovered) and it explains some of the postponed digital television switchover timetables in other countries.

The consumer motive for buying a new digital receiver could be:

- directly related to the equipment, e.g. improved picture and sound quality, greater portability/mobility, widescreen, or easier navigation and recording;
- more incidental to the receiver and primarily a function of the new services it provides, whether new channels or interactive features.

In reality, the consumer proposition could be based on some combination of these factors but there is a distinction between

- a consumer strategy based solely on features, such as HDTV, which essentially require the purchase of a new TV set (or equivalent in terms of a new display monitor as well as a set-top box)
- a consumer strategy based on services, such as extra channels, which can be based on the purchase of set-top boxes working with existing analogue TV sets.

The latter involves a smaller consumer outlay and a switchover policy based on it should generally be achievable over a shorter timescale.

The next question for policy-makers is whether digital terrestrial TV should necessarily be an integral part of the mix. In principle, consumers should have platform choice within a regulatory regime of platform neutrality, but there is no avoiding a political decision on whether to create a regulatory framework to enable digital terrestrial to become one of the consumers' platform options.

We noted that, among the early pioneers, no country had embarked on full digital switchover without first launching digital terrestrial TV and that no country has launched digital terrestrial TV without also intending ultimately to switch off analogue terrestrial. The connections are clear. If the policy aim is to wean the consumer from analogue terrestrial, in the end on a compulsory basis, then digital terrestrial is both cheap and familiar as a free-to-view substitute. Persuading reluctant viewers to acquire a set-top box and install it between their existing aerial and their existing analogue TV set is simpler than persuading *everyone* to buy a satellite dish and set-top box installation or become a subscriber.

Introducing digital terrestrial TV as a prelude to switchover is, therefore, probably the route of least political resistance, though not, of course, the only possible route. Countries where 'skipping' digital terrestrial is most likely to be considered will be those where some combination of satellite, cable and broadband reception is near-universal and/or where the topography makes a continuing investment in terrestrial transmitters uneconomic. Otherwise some allocation of digital terrestrial spectrum to existing analogue terrestrial broadcasters for a period of simulcasting is the orthodox choice.

The nature of the digital terrestrial consumer proposition which will work in any given country, in conjunction with the service propositions on other platforms, depends greatly on national market conditions – the balance of the pay and free-to-view markets, the extent to which multi-channel TV has already become established, the role of public service broadcasting, reception quality, service quality, and levels of consumer electronics expenditure. The structure and the extent of competition is also a critical factor. The Finnish researcher, Antti Sillanpää, contrasting high digital take-up soon after launch in the UK with Finland's 'more stagnant' early experience, attributed the difference to the strength of commercial competition in the UK.[2] However, he also noted that the imitative nature of the pay TV competition between BSkyB, ITV Digital, NTL and Telewest had culminated, financially, in one winner and three losers, whereas commercial strategies based on greater differentiation might have produced a different outcome.

While the pattern of competition must be largely a matter for the market participants to shape, the presence or absence of attractive free-to-view services is an important consideration for switchover policy-makers. If ultimately some segment of the population will be compelled to buy a free-to-view receiver, some demonstrable improvement to the free-to-view service offering is a vital component. Digital duplication of the analogue services does not, of itself, constitute an attractive consumer proposition. There has to be enough added value to encourage consumer expenditure on a digital receiver.

Identifying a potential consumer strategy including free-to-view digital terrestrial TV which will advance the public policy goal of switchover will almost certainly raise a number of consequential issues:

- the pricing of spectrum for digital terrestrial transmission
- sources of funding for broadcasters' digital transmission costs
- sources of funding for broadcasters' new service production costs
- sources of funding (if relevant) for broadcasters' new HDTV production equipment.

It would be simple if market mechanisms could supply all the answers here – if the broadcasters' new commercial revenue from digital television could finance all their costs, including the price of spectrum, and if their business interests spontaneously delivered the necessary technical collaboration between rivals. However, blind faith in the market could be a high-risk strategy, leaving the public policy of digital switchover vulnerable to major commercial failure. The logic of intervention leads on to consideration of the regulatory regime for the commercial terrestrial broadcasters and the funding of publicly financed broadcasters. Policy interventions here need to be carefully judged so as to be non-discriminatory, maintaining appropriate platform neutrality, and proof against legal challenges. Designing switchover policy is not for the legally faint-hearted.

The other key step in assessing feasibility at the outset is to estimate the potential impact of analogue switch-off. How many households are in danger of being directly deprived (a) in respect of their main TV set (b) in respect of secondary sets and recording equipment?

If satellite and cable TV (whether analogue or digital or both) are widespread and carry the services of the analogue terrestrial broadcasters, then the impact of analogue terrestrial switch-off could be relatively small. The greatest challenges will be in countries where terrestrial television accounts for reception on the main TV set of a great majority of households. Generally speaking, provided that sufficient spectrum is available for simulcasting, the transition period may need to be a long one here to ensure that the voluntary phase does much of the work. By modelling growth in the satellite and cable markets and realistic expectations of digital terrestrial take-up, it is possible to judge how long it might take for the number of households in danger of deprivation to be reduced to an acceptably small minority.

Having undertaken a feasibility study, perhaps supported by trials or pilot initiatives, the next stage – if feasibility is confirmed – is to prepare systematically for 'switch-on'.

Preparing for digital terrestrial switch-on

Creating the regulatory and financial framework for the introduction of digital terrestrial television alongside other digital platforms is best done with extensive consultation, taking full account of the distinctive characteristics of the nation's broadcasting and receiver markets.

Perhaps the first step is to ensure that the regulatory organization is geared up to cope. Does it need any reform, e.g.

- to give it the powers necessary for creating the digital terrestrial framework
- to give it the powers required to withdraw analogue terrestrial frequencies at the end of the switchover transition
- to alter the balance of its regulatory duties in readiness for the more pluralist broadcasting industry which digital will bring – less emphasis on content regulation, more focus on fair competition
- to equip it to face wider regulatory challenges which may come with communications convergence?

Spectrum planning is another central activity at this stage, to determine how the launch of digital terrestrial television can be made compatible with the protection of analogue transmissions during the transition period and how many digital terrestrial multiplexes might be possible pre-switchover. It is also essential to decide whether provision will be made for high-definition terrestrial television pre-switchover, since this will be a major factor in assessing how much digital spectrum might be available for what purposes.

Another spectrum planning issue to be addressed is whether, as in the UK, the plan should be based on the principle of using temporary frequencies for digital terrestrial television initially and then switching the digital services to the old analogue frequencies at the point of analogue switch-off. The alternative, adopted in Japan, is to bring up the new digital terrestrial services on the frequencies where they will remain for the long term, to publicize them, and to encourage viewers to migrate from the analogue frequencies due to be closed down. While this approach reduces viewer disruption at the point of switchover, it could well entail disruptive and expensive frequency changes for some analogue services before digital terrestrial can be launched. The options should be assessed in the light of each country's current spectrum plan and future spectrum aims.

Then the allocation of digital terrestrial spectrum to incumbent analogue terrestrial broadcasters needs to be considered. The central questions include whether merely to allocate them enough for simulcasting or whether to allow them scope to develop new services as well; whether simulcasting should be mandatory; and what charges, if any, should be levied. For switchover to be smoothly accomplished, it makes sense to offer them sufficient incentive to persuade their viewers to switch from their analogue to their digital services, without unfairly discriminating against satellite and cable broadcasters or unduly restricting the scope for new digital terrestrial entrants.

Other key governmental and regulatory decisions at this stage include:

- whether mobile television should feature (as in Japan);
- the balance between national, regional and local services and between scheduled channels of programmes, on the one hand, and on-demand data and interactive features, on the other;
- how far to set public service content objectives for the new digital environment and how far to deregulate, leaving content to be determined by the more pluralist market due to emerge;
- the balance between public funding, advertising revenue and subscription and transaction revenue and thus between free-to-view and pay TV;
- the qualifications required of organizations seeking to be awarded digital terrestrial multiplex licences, including their financial strength, any ownership restrictions related to broadcasting dominance or cross-ownership with other media, their coverage obligations and any content requirements;
- the relationship envisaged between those licensed to run digital terrestrial multiplexes and (a) prospective transmission suppliers and (b) prospective programme channel suppliers;
- the role of competition – whether by 'beauty contest', auction or some combination – in selecting the organizations to be granted digital terrestrial multiplex licences;
- the financial framework for analogue terrestrial commercial broadcasters and public broadcasters;
- the rules governing existing analogue terrestrial broadcasters' cross-promotion of their digital services, to provide legitimate consumer information without unfair competition;
- any copyright protection issues.

Technical regulatory decisions include whether to specify transmission technical standards in any close detail in order to ensure consistency, or compatibility, between different multiplexes. Then there is the hornet's nest of whether to specify common conditional access arrangements, a common API (Application Programming Interface), and/or any obligations to facilitate open standard EPGs (Electronic Programme Guides) to ensure consistency, or compatibility, between different multiplexes or even between different platforms. The European Union framework of regulation allows for diversity here, including proprietary technology, but requires fair and reasonable terms of access to allow reception of other broadcasters' services on proprietary set-top boxes – and a common interface for conditional access is required on integrated digital TV sets.

It is also possible to require a degree of collaboration between different multiplexes over technical and commercial matters where the regulator favours a common approach but does not wish to be prescriptive in detail, e.g. in providing advance programme information to facilitate easy recording via an EPG.

The design of the digital terrestrial licences granted to existing analogue terrestrial broadcasters should have the switchover goal clearly in mind. Spectrum for simulcasting could be treated as a loan. An obligation to cease analogue broadcasting within a certain time frame could be incorporated in the digital licences, subject to certain caveats. An obligation to publicize, and participate in the organization of, switchover at some later date could be made explicit, if desired, at the point when the licence is first granted, as in Norway, avoiding the need for the prolonged dialogue about switchover responsibilities that took place in the UK.

Relations with other platforms are of critical importance, and not only from the standpoint of fair competition. There are policy decisions on 'must carry' obligations for cable and satellite which bear directly on the ease and cost of switchover. If cable and satellite relay the analogue terrestrial services, then cable and satellite households – at any rate in respect of their main TV sets – will not be deprived at analogue switch-off.

Finally, there are two areas of optional regulatory intervention from which the UK public policy-makers shied away but which featured in approaches taken elsewhere – subsidizing start-up and/or regulating the receiver industry.

(a) Subsidizing start-up

A cold start for digital terrestrial television does carry the risk of a vicious circle. Receivers are initially produced in modest volumes, since there is not yet the confidence to justify mass production; receiver prices are therefore high; consumer take-up is small; revenues are small; investment in new programming is low; programme content is not very compelling; consumer take-up remains small; therefore, receiver production volumes stay down and receiver prices stay up. Hence, some kind of subsidy to kick-start a virtuous cycle of growth is a policy option.

In the UK, of course, the initial subsidizing of the launch of digital terrestrial television was undertaken by ONdigital who, under its later name of ITV Digital, subsequently went bankrupt. In terms of public policy, the Government managed the BBC's funding and the regulator reduced the commercial analogue terrestrial broadcasters' licence charges as digital take-up grew but there were no direct public subsidies for start-up.

In Berlin, however, some government assistance supported digital transmission, while in Italy the government financed a receiver subsidy. These early subsidy schemes were controversial and gave rise to legal challenges and European Commission investigations. The central question was whether the subsidies had breached platform neutrality by discriminating in favour of digital terrestrial, unfairly disadvantaging satellite and/or cable.

Significantly, even when it found fault in particular cases, the European Commission recognized that subsidies may need to have a role in digital switchover policies. It approved a support package proposed by Austria and, on the basis of this and of its Berlin investigation, set out guidance on how to design public subsidy schemes without falling foul of competition law. The principles to be followed, it advised, are transparency, necessity, proportionality and technological neutrality and

> The Commission recognises that digital switchover may be delayed if left entirely to market forces and that public intervention can be beneficial, through for example regulation, financial support to consumers, information campaigns or subsidies to overcome a specific market failure or to ensure social or regional cohesion...

The Commission would in particular view favourably:

- funding for the roll-out of a transmission network in areas where otherwise there would be insufficient TV coverage
- financial compensation to public service broadcasters for the cost of broadcasting via all transmission platforms in order to reach the entire population, provided this forms part of the public service mandate
- subsidies to consumers for the purchase of digital decoders as long as they are technologically neutral, especially if they encourage the use of open standards for interactivity
- financial compensation to broadcasters which are required to discontinue analogue transmission before the expiry of their licences, provided this takes account of granted digital transmission capacity.[3]

The European Commission's guidance underlines the complex and highly sophisticated relationship between public policy and the market involved in accomplishing digital switchover.

(b) Regulating the receiver industry

As exemplified in the United States, one tool open to governments is to require manufacturers, from a particular date, to include digital receivers in any integrated TV sets they bring to market. The purpose is to curtail the continuing sale of analogue TV sets and to ensure that the TV set replacement market becomes a driving force in delivering digital switchover.

Policy-makers considering this option need first to be sure of their legal ground. In the United States, the Federal Communications Commission used powers it had been granted in different circumstances forty years earlier and this was upheld in court when challenged by the receiver manufacturers. In the European Union the Commission can make proposals for the common use of standards and, if appropriate, mandate them, providing the regulation is non-discriminatory between platforms and proportionate to its purpose. However, without European-level action, national governments within the EU are not free to mandate digital TV sets and any informal 'concordat' between manufacturers would need to comply with EU competition rules.[4]

The principal arguments in favour of mandating integrated digital TV sets are that it:

- provides evidence of the seriousness of the switchover commitment;
- takes full advantage of the TV set replacement market;
- kick-starts the volume production of integrated digital TV sets, which brings down consumer prices, which provides further impetus to sales and to switchover.

The principal arguments against mandating are:

- imposing an unnecessary cost on TV set purchasers who rely on set-top boxes for their digital technology (including, of course, most pay TV households);
- the difficulties of a 'one answer suits all' policy in a set of national markets with such diverse switchover approaches and timetables as those in Europe and the consequent risks of market distortion.

As a general principle, the case for imposing a mandatory digital regime on the TV receiver market is stronger where the switchover strategy is based on new HDTV-capable TV sets than where it primarily relies on adding set-top boxes to existing analogue TVs.

Either to complement mandating, or as an advisory alternative, labelling digital TV sets so that consumers can readily identify them is a further policy option. A corollary is to place warning labels on analogue TV sets, as the Japanese have done.

The practicalities of implementing and enforcing a labelling policy need to be thought through: does the responsibility arise in the factory (which could well be abroad), at the point of import, or in the shop? To succeed, a labelling policy requires active support from within the retail and manufacturing sectors of the industry. This should include commitments by retailers to brief and, where necessary, train their staff on the implications of switchover, to ensure clear and consistent communication to consumers.

Preparing for analogue terrestrial switch-off

Assuming that digital television switch-on, with or without subsidy, with or without receiver regulation, has been satisfactorily planned, the next stage is to prepare for analogue switch-off. This can be done, depending on circumstances, either several years after the preparation for digital terrestrial switch-on, as in the case of the UK, or at the same time, viewing the two as essentially one integrated process, on the German model.

It makes sense to separate the two stages in a large country with a high dependence on terrestrial television, with sufficient spectrum for a prolonged period of simulcasting, and where some commercial and political uncertainty surrounds the switchover commitment. That way, the effectiveness of the launch of digital services and the speed of take-up can be assessed before analogue switch-off is firmly timetabled. The German model – planning digital terrestrial switch-on and analogue terrestrial switch-off as a single strategy – is more appropriate where the number of terrestrial households to be switched is small, terrestrial spectrum is scarce, and the political commitment to completing switchover is much less dependent on the level of commercially driven digital take-up.

Spectrum planning

The essential requirement at this stage is a spectrum plan for terrestrial broadcasting's post-switchover requirements and an operational plan for implementing it. As we saw in the case of the UK, there could well be a trade-off between the amount of upheaval for the transmitters of existing terrestrial broadcasters and the aerials of their viewers, on the one hand, and the amount of spectrum which can be released, on the other. The complex technical planning work here includes developing a strategy for handling international frequency coordination issues, which affect frequency selection, transmitter power and the degree of flexibility surrounding the reuse of spectrum due to be released.

Deciding the desired level of post-switchover digital terrestrial transmission coverage is fundamental to spectrum planning. If the country's reliance on terrestrial reception is high and likely to remain so, matching analogue terrestrial coverage becomes a serious option. Even so, it is an expensive one, especially as the long-term trend is likely to be towards a diminution in the role of terrestrial as satellite, cable and broadband TV spread. Near-universal digital terrestrial coverage is likely to be most appropriate for public service television, and fully commercial services will want to be able to make their own coverage decisions on a commercial basis.

If, for public service television, the intention is to limit digital terrestrial coverage to a level below that of analogue, e.g. to 90 per cent or 95 per cent instead of 98 or 99 per cent, then a viable alternative needs to be available for the communities to be deprived of a terrestrial option. Free-to-view digital satellite television, under secure and reliable management and regulatory arrangements, is the most obvious candidate. Restrictions on satellite reception, whether topographical or resulting from planning restrictions on dish aerials, need to be investigated. If the cost of switching from analogue terrestrial to digital satellite exceeds the cost of switching from analogue terrestrial to digital terrestrial, should there be any subsidy for households which will have no digital terrestrial option? If so, who should provide and administer it?

The post-switchover frequency plan will almost certainly involve existing terrestrial broadcasters in making some frequency changes and, in some cases including the UK's, very extensive ones. The implications for viewers in terms of aerials and receiver rescanning need to be assessed.

Cost-Benefit and Risk Analyses

A formal Cost-Benefit Analysis (CBA) can be undertaken for analogue switch-off. As a policy tool, it has its limitations: the outputs are dependent on the quality of the inputs and the value of released spectrum may be difficult to estimate reliably. Nonetheless, as we saw in the UK study described in Chapter Five above, the findings can give a broad picture which helps consolidate political decisions. Moreover, the systematic approach required to undertake the exercise can itself have benefits in prompting a comprehensive review of all the implications of switchover.

The CBA can be undertaken, as in the UK, after the digital terrestrial launch and prior to analogue switch-off. Alternatively, if both digital terrestrial switch-on and analogue terrestrial switch-off are to be undertaken in relatively quick succession, and planned as a whole, then a Cost-Benefit Analysis could be done for the whole process, encompassing both switch-on and switch-off.

The difference between these two approaches helps illustrate the limitations of the policy tool. A key factor is the selection of the *status quo* base case. If the CBA is undertaken after digital terrestrial launch and ahead of analogue switch-off, then the base case is digital and analogue terrestrial co-existing in perpetuity. If at this point the terrestrial broadcasters are simulcasting, then analogue switch-off should reduce their transmission costs and, for the analysis, this will constitute a benefit. However, if the CBA is undertaken before digital terrestrial starts, then the base case becomes analogue terrestrial without digital terrestrial: in this case, the period of simulcast transmission will show as an extra cost.

While undertaking a CBA right at the outset has the merit of being more comprehensive, the disadvantage may be that so little is known in practice about digital transmission costs, digital service content, digital receiver prices, and the viewer appeal of the services that the quality of the inputs becomes an issue. It may be sensible, nonetheless, to do the analysis at this point if there is political uncertainty about whether to embark on digital terrestrial and digital switchover at all, but the calculations should probably then be re-worked as better quality data becomes available. Conversely, the advantage of undertaking the CBA well after digital terrestrial has been established is that modelling and forecasting take-up and making assumptions about consumer costs can be based much more firmly on directly relevant market experience.

By modelling predicted take-up and showing a sliding scale for net cost or net benefit year by year, some insight can be gained into the optimum timing for analogue switch-off. However, it is important that this is accompanied by a Risk Analysis. The year in which the benefits most fully exceed the costs may also be a year in which the risks are very high and may therefore not be the optimum time at all.

Risk Analysis is thus another critical step in preparing for analogue switch-off. This should be done systematically for all the major risk factors, identifying the potential consequences of each risk, assessing its severity and probability, brainstorming countermeasures to eliminate or at least reduce it and assigning responsibility for action. This analysis, which should cover the full span of risks, from technical hitches or equipment shortages through to the possibility of politicians changing their mind, should be set out as a Risk Register. Each risk reduction action should then be monitored: once an action has been taken, the severity and/or probability rating in the Risk Register can be reduced. Steadily, and proactively, the overall risk of analogue switch-off can be brought down to the point of acceptability.

Guides on Cost-Benefit and Risk Analysis methodology are available from government and other centres of project management expertise.

Implementation planning

Given the different risks likely to arise in different countries, attempting to set out any comprehensive framework for the final phase would be unwise. Nonetheless, some guidance can be drawn from the experience of the pioneering countries. A regulatory checklist for preparing for analogue switch-off should probably include:

- undertaking any switch-off pilots to test feasibility and readiness;
- identifying any groups for whom analogue switch-off could be seriously difficult and assessing what measures to take to assist them;
- setting or amending the broadcasters' licence conditions and clarifying responsibility for switchover operations at the transmitters;
- establishing whether any qualifying criteria (e.g. coverage, take-up and/or affordability) for analogue switch-off have been met;
- deciding whether some cable transmission can continue in analogue;
- in the light of the Cost-Benefit Analysis, the Risk Analysis, other stakeholder inputs and appropriate consultation, selecting the timetable for the compulsory analogue switch-off;
- deciding whether analogue terrestrial switch-off will be implemented region by region or with a single national deadline;
- deciding whether analogue switch-off will be implemented channel by channel or with all broadcasting channels switched on the same day;
- ensuring sufficient advance training within the industry, especially of retail and installation staff;
- ensuring sufficient advance financial and practical planning by social and private landlords and by a wide range of institutions from hospitals to hotels and from pubs to prisons;
- developing a communications strategy to
  - (a) encourage as much voluntary switching to digital TV as possible
  - (b) explain the compulsory phase and win broad support for it
  - (c) explain the implications of compulsory switchover to those directly affected with as much local and individual focus as possible and with back-up advice and support.

Responsibility for leading implementation can be entrusted to a regulatory body. Alternatively, some specially constituted body, with strong links to broadcasters, retailers and installers, could be appointed to coordinate the various bodies involved and spearhead consumer communications. In the latter case, the body could be appointed by the relevant government department, as in Sweden, or else, on the UK model, the Government and regulator could ask the broadcasters to appoint it in conjunction with the receiver industry. As discussed in more detail below, organizational innovation, if carefully scoped, can make a very positive contribution to digital switchover generally.

While organizational responsibility is being settled, public relations experts can be relied upon to advise their clients how best to safeguard their respective reputations, and lawyers to advise them how best to limit their respective liabilities, should the switch-off operation go badly wrong. The challenge, amid all this advice, is to ensure that fear of the worst does not produce the conflict or paralysis most likely to deliver the worst. It is in every party's interest to devise effective organizational arrangements with the capability to do the job well.

Public persuasion

Throughout the whole switchover policy process, public explanation and persuasion play a central role. If the strategy is to allow an extended period of time for voluntary migration before the compulsory timetable starts to bite, it may make sense for the initial communications drive to come primarily from broadcasters, retailers and the receiver industry, engaging with the public as consumers, without complicating commercial marketing with political arguments. The benefit of a 'softly, softly' approach from a political standpoint is that it can help avoid a major storm of adverse publicity of the kind that might trigger a mass consumer revolt. The drawback, however, could be a continuing low level of public awareness.

Switchover cannot in the end be implemented without high public awareness. Everyone has to buy, or have already bought, a digital receiver in order to continue receiving television at the point at which the analogue signal from their local transmitter is switched off. So a gear-change in communications is required when the timetable is named. No one really wants to shoulder all the potential unpopularity for the compulsory element. The orthodox solution is for politicians to explain the rationale for the policy and take responsibility for the consumer implications of the timetable, while leaving communication of the practicalities to some combination of the regulator, the industry and any specially created body with switchover responsibility.

In the later stages the focus will be less on those who have already converted their main sets voluntarily and more on those – especially the elderly, the severely disabled and the poorest households – for whom switching presents serious difficulties. Targeting such groups with advice and information, practical help and charitable or publicly financed assistance is the key both to helping the groups themselves and to winning the consent of the wider population who would otherwise be concerned on their behalf.

One final observation about subsidy schemes: they impact on consumer behaviour. If a policy-maker announced an intention to subsidize receivers for anyone who had not bought voluntarily by a particular date, many consumers would wait for the taxpayer handout, distorting and frustrating the market. It makes more sense to define those who would qualify for any subsidy on the basis of need, not timing, and by implication to make it clear to everyone else that they will be paying the receiver cost themselves, whether they buy sooner or later.

Organizational innovation

Is it possible to go beyond mapping out the process of digital switchover in terms of checklists and options and to be more prescriptive? Academic analysis of the differences between countries acts as a caution against this. Hernan Galperin, noting that state intervention has been of striking importance in shaping the switch to digital television, contrasts the different political strategies adopted by the USA and the UK:

The transition has unfolded differently in ways that reflect each nation's political institutions and their legacies in the organisation of the broadcasting sector.[5]

The evidence from France, Japan and Germany confirms his finding that

Each nation has taken a distinct course of action, driven by different domestic concerns and regime legacies.[6]

Without dissenting from this, I would suggest that it is nonetheless possible to suggest one approach which may be applicable across different nations, though here we enter the field of political art, not political science. It is to consider developing new organizational structures which, flexibly and informally, yoke together public policy and market decision-making.

With settled technology, industry players know how to compete – individually, in traditional supply-chain relationships and in purpose-designed alliances and joint ventures. However, the arrival of a new technology brings a need for pan-industry collaboration to help set technical standards, ensure the desired levels of compatibility and inter-operability, and promote consumer awareness and understanding. In the field of broadcasting and spectrum management this work is closely related to the responsibilities of government and regulatory policy-makers. The birth of digital television and the pursuit of digital switchover have therefore given rise to new forms of pan-industry and government-regulator collaboration.

As illustration, it is worth re-looking briefly at five organizations: the FCC's Advisory Committee on Advanced Television Services (ACATS) in the United States; the Digital Video Broadcasting (DVB) organization in Europe; the Digital TV Group in the UK; the UK Digital TV Project; and Digital UK. The first three were instrumental in facilitating the launch of digital terrestrial television, while the last two focussed on analogue terrestrial switch-off.

ACATS

As Joel Brinkley tells the history, the FCC originally set up its Advisory Committee on Advanced Television Services as a time-honoured solution to a dilemma over competing claims on spectrum:

Appointment of an advisory committee was hardly a momentous event in Washington. Dozens were formed every year. The leaders of almost every agency in government established them anytime they had a thorny problem they could not solve – and they could not ignore.[7]

Yet this Committee, chaired by Richard E. Wiley, himself a former FCC chairman, and including a wide range of broadcasting members, proceeded to mount a competition which stimulated the technological breakthrough of high-definition digital terrestrial television.

Having initially reviewed a wide range of analogue and digital options, the Advisory Committee decided to proceed down the digital road. It commissioned tests of four rival digital systems and prompted the formation of a Grand Alliance which designed a solution incorporating the best features of each. As we saw in Chapter Eight, this became the basis for the standard developed and documented by the Advanced Television Systems Committee (ATSC) and adopted by the FCC.

ACATS was set up in 1987. It published its final report and disbanded at the end of 1995. In those few years, during which over a thousand industry experts were drawn into its work, this temporary creation changed the course of television history, directly in the United States and indirectly across much of the wider world. Its role, though, was advisory.

The DVB

Europe's equivalent body for hammering out digital television technical standards was the Digital Video Broadcasting Project (DVB), set up in the aftermath of the failure of the analogue MAC technology. As we saw in Chapter Two, a reaction against the MAC experience and a desire to learn its lessons led European Union policy-makers to stand back and allow the industry to take more of a lead, while industry was insistent that technical standards should reflect commercial viability and not technical perfectionism.

Credit for the initiative which led to the creation of the DVB has been given to two national government officials, Peter Kahl of Germany and Stephen Temple of the UK, who, following the American technological breakthrough, realized the importance of developing digital television and agreed to push for it bilaterally.[8] As other countries began to arrive at the same conclusion, and as various European satellite broadcasters started to take a direct commercial interest in launching digital pay TV operations, an informal European Launching Group emerged in 1991. Two years later it was re-formed and inaugurated as the DVB, based on a Memorandum of Understanding among a membership comprising broadcasters, transmission network providers, TV manufacturers, R&D organizations, electronics equipment manufacturers, regulators and government officials at both European and national level. Peter Kahl became the chairman.

The DVB's objective was to determine transmission specifications for the different digital TV platforms which would then be passed to the official standard-setting bodies for formal agreement. It was remarkably and swiftly successful in formulating draft standards for digital satellite, digital cable and, shortly afterwards, digital terrestrial television.

On conditional access the DVB was unable to agree Europe-wide open technology, given the *realpolitik* of pay TV companies in a number of national markets subsidizing their own proprietary receivers protected by their own proprietary conditional access systems. It could go no further than agreeing a voluntary Code of Conduct for conditional access which the European Commission and Parliament strengthened through a Directive requiring fair, reasonable and non-discriminatory access to proprietary systems.[9] However, the DVB's achievement in respect of transmission standards was impressive – and influential internationally.

The DVB's success was attributable to its ability to secure agreement within industry and between industry, governments and regulators without any sanctions-backed authority. David Levy, a senior BBC manager who in 1999 published a study on the European broadcasting regulation of digital television, observed that

> DVB occupies a strange halfway house between the formal standard setting world and the plethora of private industry groups. Technically a private industry grouping it took a role which was much more than that might suggest. The fact that it had been established and was chaired by a highly placed German civil servant and that it included European Union and national officials and consciously attempted to reach out to the entire European TV industry did much to enhance its status... DVB specifications usually made rapid progress through the formal standard setting procedures...[10]

UK Digital TV Group

The DVB model set the context for the Digital TV Group, the new organization which we created in the UK to support the launch of digital television in general, and digital terrestrial television in particular. While the satellite and cable operators were able to plan their own vertically integrated systems in-house, using their own proprietary technology, digital terrestrial TV promised to be a horizontal market with a range of broadcasters, four licensed multiplex operators, at least two transmission providers, and a wide range of TV set and set-top box manufacturers who would need to design their respective technical systems in a consistent manner. Diverse components – from programmes through to silicon chips – needed to be brought together from a wide variety of sources to create a chain linking transmission and reception. In order for the receivers to display, and navigate between, the channels and programmes on offer, detailed 'Service Information' needed to be integrated into the transmissions. The DVB standards provided a framework but many more detailed technical choices and specifications needed to be agreed.

So in 1995 we formed the Digital TV Group, again based around a Memorandum of Understanding and again including members from all parts of the industry, to undertake this work. Government civil servants opted for observer status. Early meetings enabled the different members – broadcasters, receiver manufacturers, chip manufacturers – to begin to understand one another's businesses and timescales, so that we could see the Critical Path towards launch. Subsequent detailed technical work produced a reference handbook, called the 'D-book', mapping out the practicalities of achieving interoperability.

Once the multiplex licensees had been appointed and we had set up The Digital Network (TDN), a more commercial organization came into place for the broadcaster-transmission end of the chain and the ITC had formal responsibility for technical standards. However, the Digital TV Group, under the chairmanship of Professor David Youlton, continued to provide a bridge between broadcasters and the receiver industry. It lubricated and underpinned cooperation across the industry in a variety of ways, including offering a postcode guide to reception, developing a receiver test centre, managing a software download channel and providing practical support for stakeholder activity. It carried out technical studies and facilitated joint R&D work, e.g. on the digital terrestrial transmission of advance programme information. It also constructed the supply chain grouping which brought together receiver manufacturers, retailers and aerial and installation businesses.

The Digital TV Group thus provided the glue needed in the horizontal market of digital terrestrial television, yet made sure that it also considered the interests of the satellite and cable industries. Its membership grew and its ethos helped foster collaborative behaviour within the UK Digital TV Project and Digital UK.

The UK Digital TV Project

Whereas the Digital TV Group was first and foremost an industry-led body which welcomed government and regulatory involvement, the UK Digital TV Project was a Government-led initiative, accountable ultimately to a Steering Board chaired by Ministers. It drew up and implemented the Action Plan with the aim of full digital switchover.

The Project's style of working, again, was collaborative. It was essentially a joint project between Government, Ofcom, industry and consumers. Following a set-up period in 2001, it ran from early 2002 to the end of 2004.

The structure was flexible. The Project had Task Groups with mixed (and mostly open) membership. It worked closely with a Stakeholder Group, spanning all sections of the industry and consumer interests, which in turn had its own specialized sub-groups. The Steering Board had both industry and consumer members.

The output was in part practical – in terms of frequency planning, marketing proposals and trials, for example – and in part a body of advice to Ministers, carrying broad industry and consumer representative support, on how switchover could best be accomplished. It provided the foundations for the creation of the 'Switchco' organization which was subsequently christened Digital UK.

Like ACATS, the DVB and the DTG, it experienced some clashes of interest between different stakeholders but, also like them, because it was essentially advisory and consensual, it had the ability to resolve most such differences and, in consequence, developed a standing which ensured that its findings and proposals influenced decision-making.

Digital UK

While on the face of it Digital UK is an organization with a small number of shareholders and a defined remit within which it has executive authority, it also displays features of collaborative working across a broader field. Its approach to communications includes consultation and coordination with satellite and cable broadcasters. It enlists the skills and commitment of voluntary organizations in dealing with vulnerable groups. Its links to the supply chain of receiver manufacturers, retailers, aerial manufacturers and installers are fundamental.

The management of the programme of projects which links its responsibilities to those of the Government and Ofcom is also a piece of consensual design. A Switchover Programme Group, chaired by Barry Cox as the chairman of Digital UK, brings together representatives of the Department for Culture Media and Sport, the Department of Trade and Industry, the regulator Ofcom, and Digital UK, working to a set of ground rules which include:

The Group will not take decisions on policy, only on implementation...

Group members are only able to action decisions that affect their organisation, so decisions that affect other organisations need the agreement of the relevant Group member.

Significant decisions on the direction of the programme require consensus agreement of all Group members (with approval from Group members' higher authorities or stakeholders where necessary).

The Group may, from time to time, invite other parties or stakeholders to attend its meetings to update on progress or discuss a particular issue...

If a decision is needed which would require any Group member to act outside their delegated authority then the decision will be deferred until that Group member is able to consult their higher authority or relevant stakeholders.[11]

Thus the body which coordinates the practicalities of switchover implementation, while more than advisory, has its formal powers severely constrained in order to avoid compromising Government, Ofcom and industry responsibilities – and is then, in practice, able to get on with the job.

The House of Commons Culture, Media and Sport Committee expressed concern that Digital UK might lack the authority and resources to implement switchover because of possible restrictions imposed by its broadcaster shareholders, whose interests were not all identical and could come under strain. Questioned about this hypothetical risk, Barry Cox replied:

> In the end the people who resolve it would be either Ofcom or Government because they are the people to whom the broadcasters are accountable. We have very active working relationships with both Government and Ofcom, we meet them regularly. If these things begin to surface they will be sorted out long before they cause a crisis.[12]

Like Walter Bagehot's Victorian English Constitution, the switchover organization has both its 'dignified' and its 'efficient' elements.

Common organizational features

The five examples of organizational innovation reviewed above are very different from one another, doing different jobs at different times within different national or international settings. Nor are they the only examples of new collaborative organizations: Japan's D-pa and Finland's TV2007 can also be considered.

However, while the organizational forms may vary significantly by country and by context, four characteristics seem to be common

- they are, or were, all newly created bodies;
- each was constituted with a strong task-focus, with no organizational aspiration to exist in perpetuity;
- their working methods are based on a commitment to involving participants from across the whole industry, either through open terms of membership or through arrangements for stakeholder dialogue and consultation;
- they have a low level of formal responsibility: thus the organization might have advisory or restricted executive status, so that formal government, regulatory and standard-setting roles are not compromised and companies preserve their freedom of decision-making. The removal of any threat here helps business to be done with the expectation that the collaborative organization's 'advice' will very probably be accepted by all the relevant parties.

Other countries embarking on digital switchover might wish to consider applying this generic approach to organizational development within their own political and commercial structures. The aim would be to facilitate cooperation between political, regulatory and industry decision-makers, all playing in position (doing their own jobs and not attempting to do one another's), yet collaborating in more creative ways than would perhaps otherwise have been possible.

In conclusion: public policy and the market

What the story of the UK's switch to digital television and parallel experiences in other pioneering nations illustrate – and bequeath as guidance for the benefit of countries pursuing switchover in the future – is the fundamental importance of collaboration between public policy and the market. Essentially, this collaboration is a kind of mutual risk reduction scheme.

Governments and regulators cannot easily switch off analogue terrestrial broadcasting without migrating existing terrestrial broadcasters to digital television – and that migration is too risky for the broadcasters unless there is public policy support, at the very least in terms of spectrum allocation, allowing a viable free-to-view market to develop alongside pay TV. Broadcasters cannot embark upon the transmission investment and new content creation without some assurance from the receiver industry on the supply and marketing of digital receivers.

Neither broadcasters nor the receiver industry will switch out of the analogue market fully without some announcement from government of a firm and reliable switchover timetable which will be enforced. Governments will only commit to a firm timetable if the consumer proposition of the broadcasters' services and the industry's receivers is strong enough to carry most analogue terrestrial households across to digital TV of their own volition and to minimize the risk of a consumer revolt.

Consumers will only accept the policy without rebelling if they understand the reasons for it, if the consumer proposition offers real benefits (one measure of which is voluntary take-up), if the element of compulsion is relatively low, and if help is provided to those who will find switching most difficult. Governments and industry need to deliver those assurances.

This mutual risk-reduction is not capitalism, it is not socialism, it is not a formal public-private sector partnership or joint venture: it is more like a dance, in which, while the dancers may make up the steps as they go along, they know, and respect, their positions in relation to one another. On the evidence of this case study, it is how, in an area of high risk, the mixed economy actually functions.

Notes

Chapter One

1. The Labour Party, *Britain **forward** not back*, election manifesto, April 2005, p. 98.
2. Famously studied in Wilson, H. Hubert, *Pressure Group – The Campaign for Commercial Television*, London, Secker & Warburg, 1961.
3. 1989 European Council Directive 89/552/EEC, amended in 1997 by the Council and European Parliament as Directive 97/36/EC and under further revision in 2005–6.
4. Galperin, Hernan, *New Television, Old Politics*, Cambridge and New York, Cambridge University Press, 2004, pp. 15–23.
5. Elstein, David, *The Politics of Digital TV in the UK*, at www.opendemocracy. net 2002.

Chapter Two

1. MIT Commission on Industrial Productivity, 1989, cited in Galperin, Hernan, op. cit., p. 31.
2. Galperin, Hernan op. cit., p. 35.
3. Ibid., p. 45.
4. Home Office, *Report of the Committee on Financing the BBC*, London, HMSO, Cmnd. 9824, 1986.
5. Milne, Alasdair, *DG – The Memoirs of a British Broadcaster*, London, Hodder & Stoughton, 1988, pp. 109–110.
6. Ibid., p. 118.
7. Murdoch, Rupert, James MacTaggart lecture at the Edinburgh Television Festival, 1989.
8. Quoted in Chippindale, Peter, and Franks, Suzanne, *Dished! The Rise and Fall of British Satellite Broadcasting*, London, Simon and Shuster, 1991, p. 260. Sky losses p. 262.
9. Ibid., p. 306.
10. Ibid., p. xi.
11. Quoted in *The Times*, 3rd February 2005.
12. ITC, *Discussion Paper on Digital Television*, 1993, p. 10.
13. Statement by Peter Brooke, Secretary of State, Department of National Heritage, July 1994.
14. Department of National Heritage *Digital Terrestrial Broadcasting – The Government's Proposals*, London, HMSO, Cmnd. 2946, 1995.
15. Ibid., p. 4.
16. Ibid., p. 1.

17. Ibid., p. 12.
18. Birt, John, *The Harder Path*, London, Time Warner Books, 2002, p. 456.
19. Ibid., p. 455.
20. Speaking at the Royal Television Society, November 1994.
21. Birt, John, op. cit., p. 456.
22. ITV Association press release 15th October 1996.
23. Starks, Michael, *Public Service Digital Television*, presentation to IBC & CDG conference on Digital Terrestrial Television, 7th March 1996.
24. Starks, Michael, *The Dark Horse which Changed its Spots*, speech to the Royal Television Society published in the *Journal of the Royal Television Society*, May 1997.
25. Birt, John, op. cit., p. 455.
26. Quoted in *Sunday Business*, 1st December 1996.

Chapter Three

1. Department of National Heritage, press release, 15th December 1995.
2. Walters, Geoff, Shoenberg lecture to the Royal Television Society, 28th November 2000.
3. Bell, Emily, *The Observer, Business*, 11th May 1997.
4. Birt, John, op. cit., p. 461.
5. Quoted in Horsman, Mathew, *Sky High*, London, Orion, 1997, p. 195.
6. Walters, Geoff, op. cit.
7. Goodwin, Peter, *United Kingdom: Never Mind the Policy, Feel the Growth*, in Brown, Allan, and Picard, Robert G. (eds.), *Digital Terrestrial Television in Europe*, New Jersey, Lawrence Erlbaum Associates, 2005, p. 162.
8. Quoted in *Broadcast*, 20th June 2003.
9. Reported in *New Media Markets*, 20th November 2000, and *The Guardian*, 5th January 2001.
10. Milne, Alasdair, op. cit., p. 111.
11. Home Office, *Report of the Committee on Financing the BBC*, London, HMSO, Cmnd. 9824, 1986, p. 113.
12. Mergers summarized in *The Independent*, 8th August 2000.
13. *The Financial Times*, 8th February 2001.
14. *Inside Digital TV*, 29th January 2001.
15. *The Times*, 14th December 2000.
16. *The Times*, 27th September 2001.
17. *Sunday Business*, 16th December 2001.
18. Author interview with Martin Bell, June 2006.
19. *The Sunday Times*, 31st March 2002.
20. *Financial Mail on Sunday*, 7th October 2001.
21. *The Times*, 26th June 2001.

22. Radiocommunications Agency and Department for Culture, Media and Sport (DCMS), *A Study to Estimate the Economic Impact of Government Policies towards Digital Television*, report by NERA and Smith System Engineering, 1998.
23. Radiocommunications Agency and DCMS, *Television: the Digital Future*, Consultation, 1998.
24. ITC, *The Genesis Project*, prepared by NTL and the Smith Group, 2000.
25. Chris Smith, speech to the Royal Television Society Cambridge Convention, September 1999, published in the *Journal of the Royal Television Society*, October 1999.
26. *The Sunday Times*, 27th August 2000.
27. *Joint ITC, Oftel and OFT advice to Government on Digital Television*, 2000.
28. DCMS, *Digital Decisions: Viewer Choice and Digital Television*, report by the Viewers' Panel to the Secretary of State for Culture, Media and Sport, 2001, p. 4.
29. *The Financial Times*, 5th November 2001.
30. European Commission, *Europe and the Global Information Society: Recommendations to the European Council*, report from the High Level Group on the Information Society, May 1994.
31. Virginia Bottomley, letter to *The Times*, 11th August 1995, quoted in Galperin, Hernan, op. cit., p. 173.
32. Chris Smith, op. cit.
33. DTI & DCMS, *A New Future for Communications*, December 2000.
34. CITU, *Modernising Government – Framework for Information Age Government, Digital TV*, 2000, p. 2.
35. DTI, *Enterprise, Skills and Innovation*, February 2001, paras 4.52 and 4.53.
36. *The Financial Times*, 3rd November 2001.
37. *The Times*, 22nd December 2000.
38. DVB press release, 24th August 2001.
39. Oftel, *Digital Television – Consumers' Uses and Perceptions*, report prepared by Counterpoint Research, 2001, pp. 10–11.
40. Ibid., p. 11.
41. *Joint ITC, Oftel and OFT advice to Government on Digital Television*, 2000, p. 3.
42. Ibid., p. 7.
43. Ibid., p. 4.
44. Consumers' Association, *Turn On, Tune In, Switched Off – Consumer Attitudes to Digital TV*, 2001.
45. Department for Culture, Media and Sport, *Digital Television 2001, Research Study conducted by MORI*, 2001.
46. National Consumer Council, *Digital Mystery Shopping*, press release 18th June 2001.

Chapter Four

1. *The Guardian*, 15th December 2001.
2. *The Independent*, 13th February 2002.
3. *The Financial Mail on Sunday*, 13th January 2002.
4. *The Independent Review*, 29th January 2002.
5. ITV Response to the House of Commons Culture, Media and Sports Committee: Inquiry into Communications, January 2002, pp. 11–12.
6. Testimony to the House of Commons Culture, Media and Sport Committee: Inquiry into Communications, 29th January 2002.
7. BBC, *Annual Report & Accounts*, 1998/99, p. 40.
8. BBC, *The BBC Beyond 2000*, 1998, p. 83.
9. Department for Culture Media and Sport, *The Future Funding of the BBC, Report of the Independent Review Panel, Chairman: Gavyn Davies*, 1999.
10. Thompson, Mark, *Why public service TV has to change*, speech in Banff, Canada, 12th June 2000.
11. Dyke, Greg, *A Time for Change*, James MacTaggart Memorial Lecture, Edinburgh Television Festival, August 2000.
12. Department for Culture, Media and Sport, press release including schedule of conditions, 13th September 2001.
13. Kim Howells, speaking at a Royal Television Society dinner, 12th March 2002, published in the *Journal of the Royal Television Society*, April 2002.
14. Conference of *The Voice of the Listener and Viewer*, 28th November 2001.
15. *The Times, Business*, 12th January 2002.
16. *The Financial Times*, 7th November 2001; *The Daily Telegraph*, 8th November 2001; *The Guardian*, 8th November 2001.
17. *Sunday Business*, 11th November 2001.
18. *Broadcast*, 14th December 2001.
19. *The Financial Times*, 18th January 2002.
20. Reported in *Broadcast*, 22nd February 2002.
21. Dyke, Greg, *Inside Story*, London, Harper Collins, 2004, p. 185.
22. *The Evening Standard*, 20th March 2002; *The Times*, 21st March 2003.
23. *The Financial Times*, 21st March 2002.
24. *The Independent*, 22nd March 2002; *The Sun*, 22nd March 2002.
25. Tessa Jowell, Statement to the House of Commons, 26th April 2002.
26. *The Sunday Times*, 4th August 2002.
27. Quoted in *The Sunday Express*, 5th May 2002.
28. Quoted in *The Guardian*, 29th April 2002.
29. *The Sunday Telegraph*, 5th May 2002.
30. Stuart Prebble interviewed by Peter Goodwin. See Goodwin, Peter, op. cit., p. 164.
31. *The Independent*, 29th January 2002.
32. *The Daily Mail*, 17th April 2002.

33. *Mediaweek*, 10th May 2002.
34. *The Daily Express*, 9th August 2002.
35. Elstein, David, *The Politics of Digital TV*, UK Digital TV conference, 29th April 2002.
36. Dyke, Greg, in *The Sunday Telegraph*, 28th April 2002.
37. *Broadcast*, 24th May 2002.
38. *The Times*, 18th May 2002.
39. ITC News Release, 13th June 2002.
40. Dyke, Greg, *Inside Story*, London, Harper Collins, 2004, p. 187.
41. ITC News Release, 4th July 2002.
42. Ibid.
43. ITC News Release, 20th September 2002.
44. *The Guardian*, 10th December 2002.
45. *The Guardian*, 21st August 2002.
46. *The Guardian*, 18th October 2002.
47. *The Guardian*, 3rd December 2002; *The Daily Telegraph*, 4th December 2002.
48. *Broadcast*, 3rd October 2003.
49. *The Times*, 23rd October 2002.
50. *The Times*, 18th December 2002.
51. *The Times*, 30th August 2002.
52. *The Evening Standard*, 21st October 2003.
53. *The Guardian*, 27th February 2004.
54. *Broadcast*, 3rd March 2003.
55. Dyke Greg, *Inside Story*, London, Harper Collins, 2004, pp. 190–1.
56. Quoted in *The Guardian*, 25th November 2002.

Chapter Five

1. Quoted in *The Guardian*, 28th January 2002.
2. Radiocommunications Agency and Department for Culture, Media and Sport (DCMS), *A Study to Estimate the Economic Impact of Government Policies towards Digital Television*, report by NERA and Smith System Engineering, 1998.
3. ITC, *The Genesis Project*, prepared by NTL and the Smith Group, 2000.
4. Digital TV Group, *A Study on the Technical Impediments to Analogue Switchover*, July 2000.
5. DTI, *The role of Integrated Digital Television Sets in achieving Digital Switchover*, a consultation, June 2002.
6. Teather, David, in *Mediaweek*, 30th August 2002.
7. DCMS and DTI, *Digital Television Action Plan*, version 5.1, published February 2003.
8. ITC and BBC, *A Report on Progress Towards Digital Switchover*, April 2003.
9. DCMS and DTI, *Digital Television Action Plan*, version 7.0, published July 2003.
10. ITC, *Go Digital*, report on trial, 2003.

11. GfK data cited in DCMS and DTI, *Report of the Digital TV Project*, November 2004, published 2005.
12. DCMS and DTI, *Report of the Digital TV Project*, November 2004, published 2005.
13. DCMS and DTI, *Cost Benefit Analysis of Digital Switchover*, published 18th September 2003.
14. DCMS press release, 17th June 2003.
15. Speech by Tessa Jowell, Secretary of State for Culture, Media and Sport, at the Royal Television Society Cambridge Convention, 18th September 2003.
16. DTI, *Paving the Way for a Digital Future*, information note, and *Statement on the principles for planning the use of the UHF spectrum once analogue terrestrial transmissions end*, 30th January 2003.
17. Ibid.
18. Ofcom, *Digital replacement licences to be offered to channels 3, 4 and 5 and public teletext*, consultation, 2004.
19. Ibid.
20. Ofcom, *Planning Options for Digital Switchover*, 2005.
21. Ofcom, *Spectrum management update: technical planning for digital switchover around the UK*, 2005.
22. Ofcom, *Driving digital switchover: a report to the Secretary of State*, 2004.
23. DTI Press release, *New labelling to promote digital TV take up*, 27th February 2003.
24. DCMS and DTI, *Report of the Digital TV Project*, November 2004, published 2005.
25. Ibid.
26. Ibid.
27. Ibid.
28. Ibid.
29. DCMS, *Communal TV systems and digital switchover*, Report for the DCMS by NOP World, 2005.
30. DCMS and DTI, *Report of the Digital TV Project*, November 2004, published 2005.
31. DCMS, *Persuasion or Compulsion? Consumers and Analogue Switch-off*, Report to the Broadcasting Minister by the Consumer Expert Group, 2004.
32. Ofcom Consumer Panel, *Supporting the most vulnerable consumers through digital switchover*, published by Ofcom, 2004.
33. DCMS and DTI, *Report of the Digital TV Project*, November 2004, published 2005.
34. Ibid.
35. DCMS, *Persuasion or Compulsion? Consumers and Analogue Switch-off*, Report to the Broadcasting Minister by the Consumer Expert Group, 2004.
36. Ibid.

37. Ministerial Statement to Parliament by the Secretary of State for Culture, Media and Sport and DCMS Minister of State, 22nd July 2004.
38. Ibid.
39. DCMS and DTI, *Report of the Digital TV Project*, November 2004, published 2005.
40. *The Guardian*, 25th November 2004.
41. DCMS and DTI, *Report of the Digital TV Project*, November 2004, published 2005.
42. Ibid.
43. DCMS and DTI, *Digital Switchover Technical Trial, Fact Sheet*, 30th March 2005.
44. DCMS and DTI, *Report of a Digital Switchover Technical Trial at Ferryside and Llansteffan*, 2005.
45. Sheila Cassells, speaking at Westminster e-Forum session on *Managing Digital Switchover*, 24th November 2004.

Chapter Six

1. DCMS press release, 15th September 2005.
2. Speech by Tessa Jowell, Secretary of State for Culture, Media and Sport, at the Royal Television Society Cambridge Convention, 15th September 2005.
3. DCMS and DTI, *Regulatory and Environmental Impact Assessment: the timing of digital switchover*, 2005, drawing on report by the Generics Group, *Attitudes to Digital Switchover*, 2004.
4. DCMS and DTI, *Regulatory and Environmental Impact Assessment: the timing of digital switchover*, 2005.
5. Ibid.
6. Ibid.
7. Speech by Tessa Jowell, Secretary of State for Culture, Media and Sport, at the Royal Television Society Cambridge Convention, 15th September 2005.
8. Ibid.
9. 'Switchco' press release, 13th April 2005.
10. DCMS and DTI, *Regulatory and Environmental Impact Assessment: the timing of digital switchover*, 2005.
11. At the Royal Television Society Cambridge Convention, September 2005, reported in *Television*, October 2005.
12. Digital UK press release, 15th September 2005.
13. Quoted in *The Guardian*, 19th September 2005.
14. DTI and HM Treasury, *Review of Radio Spectrum Management by Professor Martin Cave*, 2002.
15. DTI, Radiocommunications Agency and HM Treasury, *Government Response to the Review of Radio Spectrum Management*, 2002.

16. Speech by Tessa Jowell, Secretary of State for Culture, Media and Sport, at the Royal Television Society Cambridge Convention, 15th September 2005.
17. DCMS and DTI, *Report of the Digital TV Project*, November 2004, published 2005.
18. Duncan, Gary and Paterson, Lea, in *The Times*, 18th March 2004.
19. HM Treasury, *2004 Spending Review*, July 2004.
20. *The Sunday Times*, 13th June 2004.
21. At an Institute of Economic Affairs conference, reported by *The Guardian*, 18th June 2003.
22. At the Oxford Media Convention, reported by *The Guardian*, 21st January 2005.
23. Cox, David, in the *New Statesman*, 27th September 2004.
24. Statement by Paul Kenny, acting General Secretary, August 2005.
25. Sieghart, Mary Ann, in *The Times*, 6th October 2005.
26. DCMS, *Review of the BBC's Royal Charter*, consultation, 2003.
27. BBC, *Building Public Value – Renewing the BBC for a digital world*, June 2004.
28. Cox, Barry, *TV in the Digital Age*, set of lectures as Visiting Professor of Broadcast Media at Oxford University, lecture 2, *The Reformation of the BBC*, 4th February 2003.
29. Tessa Jowell in interview with Raymond Snoddy, *The Independent*, 18th October 2004.
30. Quoted in *The Guardian*, 7th February 2003.
31. Ed Richards, speaking at the Oxford Media Convention, quoted in *The Times*, 21st January 2005.
32. Ofcom, *Ofcom review of public service television broadcasting, Phase 2 – Meeting the digital challenge*, 2004, p. 71.
33. Letter from Lord Burns to the Secretary of State for Culture, Media and Sport, 27th January 2005 accompanying report of the Independent Panel.
34. BBC, *Building Public Value – Renewing the BBC for a digital world*, 2004.
35. Ibid.
36. DCMS, *Review of the BBC's Royal Charter, A strong BBC, independent of government*, Green Paper, 2005.
37. Ibid.
38. Lecture to the European Media Forum, 12th July 2005, edited version published in *Television*, September 2005.
39. Speech at the FT Broadcasting and New Media Conference, 9th March 2005.
40. Dyke, Greg, *Inside Story*, London, Harper Collins, p. 111.
41. Ibid. p. 118.
42. Ofcom, *Ofcom review of public service television broadcasting, Phase 2 – Meeting the digital challenge*, 2004, pp. 92–3 ff.
43. Ofcom, *Digital Replacement Licence Consultation*, 14th September 2004.
44. Ofcom, press release 14th December 2004.

45. Ofcom, press release 6th July 2005.
46. Ofcom, *Methodology for reviews of financial terms for Channel 3, Channel 5 and Public Teletext licences*, statement, 2004.
47. Ibid.
48. Ofcom, press release 6th July 2005.
49. ITV plc presentation, 7th September 2005, published at www.ITV.com.
50. DCMS and DTI, *Regulatory and Environmental Impact Assessment: the timing of digital switchover*, 2005.
51. *The Times*, 27th May 2005 and 18th August 2005.
52. *The Times*, 16th December 2005.
53. *The Times*, 28th April 2005.
54. Reported in *DTG News*, 14th October 2005, published at www.dtg.org.uk.
55. Speech at the Royal Television Society Cambridge Convention, 15th September 2005.
56. DCMS and DTI, *Regulatory and Environmental Impact Assessment: the timing of digital switchover*, 2005.
57. DCMS and Chartered Institute of Housing, *Digital Switchover – A Good Practice Briefing*, 2005.
58. DCMS and DTI, *Regulatory and Environmental Impact Assessment: the timing of digital switchover*, 2005.
59. Ofcom, press release 8th November 2005.
60. DCMS and DTI, *Regulatory and Environmental Impact Assessment: the timing of digital switchover*, 2005.
61. House of Lords Select Committee on the BBC's Charter Review, *The Review of the BBC's Royal Charter*, vol. 1, report, 2005, p. 5.
62. House of Lords Select Committee on the BBC's Charter Review, *Further Issues for BBC Charter*, 2006, p. 15.
63. DCMS, *A public service for all: the BBC in the digital age*, White Paper, 2006, p. 3.
64. Ibid., p. 26.
65. Ibid., p. 64.
66. Memorandum submitted by BSkyB to the House of Commons Culture, Media and Sport Committee, October 2005, published by the Committee in *Analogue Switch-Off: a signal change in television*, Second Report of Session 2005–06, Volume II, *Oral and Written Evidence*, 2006, p. 200.
67. House of Commons Culture, Media and Sport Committee, *Analogue Switch-Off: a signal change in television*, Second Report of Session 2005–06, volume I, 2006, p. 10.
68. Ibid., p. 44 ff.
69. Greg Dyke, speaking at Mipcom TV festival in Cannes, reported by *The Guardian*, 19th October 2005.
70. House of Lords Select Committee on the BBC's Charter Review, *Further Issues for BBC Charter Review*, 2006, p. 15.

71. Oral evidence to the House of Commons Culture, Media and Sport Committee, 15th November 2005, published by the Committee in *Analogue Switch-Off: a signal change in television*, Second Report of Session 2005–06, Volume II, *Oral and Written Evidence*, 2006, p. 67.

72. BBC, *The BBC Licence Fee Bid: what does the public think?*, report for the BBC Board of Governors by Professor Patrick Barwise, 2006.

73. BBC, *Review of the BBC's Royal Charter: BBC response to 'A strong BBC, independent of government'*, 2005, p. 45.

74. BBC, press release, *BBC launches case for new licence fee settlement*, 11th October 2005.

75. *The Times*, 12th October 2005.

76. DCMS, *Review of the BBC Value for Money and Efficiency Programmes*, by independent consultants PKF, 2006.

77. Ofcom, *Future pricing of spectrum used for terrestrial broadcasting*, consultation, 2006.

78. DCMS, press release, *Tessa Jowell announces cost of Digital switchover help scheme*, 18th December 2006.

Chapter Seven

1. Chris Smith, speech to the Royal Television Society Cambridge Convention, September 1999, published in the *Journal of the Royal Television Society*, October 1999.

2. DCMS, *Digital Decisions: Viewer Choice and Digital Television*, report by the Viewers' Panel to the Secretary of State for Culture, Media and Sport, 2001.

3. DCMS, *Digital Television 2002, Research Study Conducted for Department for Culture Media and Sport by MORI*, 2002.

4. DTI, *Digital Television For All, a report on usability and accessible design*, in association with the Generics Group, 2003.

5. DTI, *Attitudes to Digital Television, Preliminary findings on consumer adoption of digital television*, in association with the Generics Group, 2004.

6. DTI, *Attitudes to Digital Switchover, The impact of digital switchover on consumer adoption of digital television*, in association with the Generics Group, 2004.

7. DCMS, *Persuasion or Compulsion? Consumers and Analogue Switch-off*, Report to the Broadcasting Minister by the Consumer Expert Group, 2004.

8. Ofcom Consumer Panel, *Supporting the most vulnerable consumers through digital switchover*, published by Ofcom, 2004.

9. ITC, *Go Digital*, report on trial, 2003.

10. DCMS and DTI, *Report of a Digital Switchover Technical Trial at Ferryside and Llansteffan*, 2005.

11. DCMS, *Report of the Bolton Digital Television Trial*, 2006.

12. Ofcom Consumer Panel, *Consumers and the communications market: where we are now*, published by Ofcom, 2005, p. 32.

13. DTI, *Attitudes to Digital Television, Preliminary findings on consumer adoption of digital television*, in association with the Generics Group, 2004, pp. 4–5.

14. Ibid., p. 5.

15. Ibid., p. 6.

16. Ibid., p. 32.

17. ITC, *Go Digital*, report on trial, 2003.

18. DTI, *Attitudes to Digital Switchover, The impact of digital switchover on consumer adoption of digital television*, in association with the Generics Group, 2004, p. 3.

19. Ibid.

20. Ibid., p. 86.

21. DTI, *Digital Television For All, a report on usability and accessible design*, in association with the Generics Group, 2003, pp. 45–6.

22. Ibid., pp. 23–39.

23. DCMS and DTI, *Report of a Digital Switchover Technical Trial at Ferryside and Llansteffan*, 2005.

24. DCMS, *Ferryside and Llansteffan Digital Switchover Technical Trial: Research on Vulnerable Households*, 2005.

25. DCMS, *Report of the Bolton Digital Trial*, 2006.

26. *The Daily Mirror*, 4–15 December 2004.

27. DCMS and DTI, *Government Response to the Culture, Media and Sport Select Committee, Session 2005–2006: Report on Analogue Switch-Off*, 2006.

28. E.g., in *The Times* and *The Guardian*, 16th September 2005.

29. Quoted in *The Times*, 5th May 2006.

30. Digital UK press release, 5th May 2006.

31. Digital UK website, www.digitaluk.co.uk.

32. Ofcom Consumer Panel, *Consumers and the communication market: 2006*, published by Ofcom, 2006.

33. DTI, *The Border TV Region and Readiness for the Digital Switchover*, 2006.

34. Digital UK press release, 21st July 2006.

35. Ofcom, *Summary of research on the ease of use of domestic digital television equipment*, 2006.

36. DTI, *Equipment needs of consumers facing most difficulty switching to digital television equipment*, prepared by i2 media research, 2006.

37. DTI, *The equipment needs of consumers facing most difficulty switching to digital TV*, prepared by Scientific Generics, 2006.

38. www.ricability-digitaltv.org.uk.

39. *The Daily Telegraph*, 3rd July 2006.

40. DCMS and DTI, *Regulatory and Environmental Impact Assessment: the timing of digital switchover*, 2005.

41. Ibid., p. 26.
42. Ofcom, *Cost and power consumption implications of digital switchover*, prepared by Scientific Generics, 2005.
43. Energy Savings Trust, *The rise of the machines*, 2006.
44. DTI, *Energy Review: The Energy Challenge*, 2006, p. 13.
45. DCMS, press release, 20th July 2006.
46. DCMS and DTI, *Government Response to the Culture, Media and Sport Select Committee, Session 2005–2006: Report on Analogue Switch-Off*, 2006.

Chapter Eight

1. Programme in Comparative Media Law and Policy, Centre for Socio-Legal Studies, University of Oxford, *Overview on Switchover Policy: Europe, the U.S. and Japan*, by María Trinidad García Leiva, Michael Starks and Damian Tambini, submission to House of Commons Culture, Media and Sport Committee, December 2005, published by the Committee in *Analogue Switch-Off: a signal change in television*, Second Report of Session 2005–06, Volume II, *Oral and Written Evidence*, 2006, p. 316. Much of the material in this chapter draws on the same research as our submission – see also Note (1) to Chapter 10 below on our *Info* article.
2. *The 9/11 Commission Report*, authorized edition, New York, W. W. Norton, 2004, p. 397.
3. Federal Communications Commission, press release from the Office of Engineering and Technology Action, 9th July 1997.
4. Brinkley, Joel, *Defining Vision: The Battle for the Future of Television*, New York, Harcourt Brace, 1997, pp. 4–10.
5. Advanced Television Systems Committee, *Development of the ATSC Digital Television Standard*, published at www.atsc.org/history.
6. Galperin, Hernan, op. cit., pp. 86–7.
7. Hundt, Reed E., *You Say You Want a Revolution: A Story of Information Age Politics*, New Haven, Yale University Press, 2000, p. 65.
8. Federal Communications Commission, *Fifth Report and Order*, April, 1997.
9. Ibid.
10. Congressman Eliot Engel quoted in *Wired Magazine*, 25th September 2002, cited in Galperin, Hernan, op. cit., p. 125.
11. Albiniak, Page, *Stations 'waiver' on DTV*, in *Broadcasting & Cable*, 20th August 2001, cited in Galperin, Hernan, op. cit., p. 124.
12. Grimme, Katharina, *Digital Television – Standardization and Strategies*, Boston and London, Artech House, 2002, p. 239.
13. Published Consumer Electronics Association letter of 12th July 2002 to Federal Communications Commission Chairman Michael Powell.
14. Federal Communications Commission, *Second Report and Order*, August 2002.
15. Ibid.

16. Federal Communications Commission, *Second Report and Order*, November 2005.

17. Federal Communications Commission, press release on easing digital TV transition for consumers, 10th September 2003.

18. Federal Communications Commission, press release on resolving dual and multicast carriage issues, 10th February 2005.

19. Testimony of Kyle McSlarrow, President & CEO, National Cable and Telecommunications Association, to the Senate Committee on Commerce, Science and Transportation, 12th July 2005.

20. Testimony of Michael D. Kennedy, Senior Vice President, Motorola, to the Senate Committee on Commerce, Science and Transportation, 12th July 2005.

21. Testimony of Charles C. Townsend, President Aloha Partners, to the Senate Committee on Commerce, Science and Transportation, 12th July 2005.

22. Statement of Gary J. Shapiro, President and CEO Consumer Electronics Association, to the Senate Committee on Commerce, Science and Transportation, 12th July 2005.

23. Consumer Electronics Retailers Consortium submission to the Senate Committee on Commerce, Science and Transportation, 25th July 2005.

24. General Accounting Office, *Telecommunications: Additional Federal Efforts Could Help Advance Digital Television Transition*, (GAO 03-7, Washington D.C.), 2002.

25. General Accounting Office, *Digital Broadcast Television Transition: Estimated Cost of Supporting Set-Top Boxes to Help Advance the DTV Transition*, (GAO 05-258T, Washington D.C.), 2005.

26. Statement of Gary J. Shapiro, op. cit.

27. Testimony of Gene Kimmelman, Senior Director of Public Policy and Advocacy, Consumers Union, on behalf of the Consumers Union and the Consumer Federation of America, to the Senate Committee on Commerce, Science and Transportation, 12th July 2005.

28. National Association of Broadcasters, press release, 1st August 2005.

29. Testimony of Gene Kimmelman, op. cit.

30. Letter from John McCain (Senator, Republican), Joseph Lieberman (Senator, Democrat), Jane Harman (House of Representatives, Democrat) and Curt Weldon (House of Representatives, Republican), in *The Washington Post*, 19th September 2005.

31. Tracey, Michael, *The Decline and Fall of Public Service Broadcasting*, Oxford and New York, Oxford University Press, 1998, pp. 222–3.

32. Brinkley, Joel, op. cit., pp. 128–133.

33. Ministry of Public Management, Home Affairs, Posts and Telecommunications, Japan, *Major Aspects of Japan's Broadcasting Policy*, December 2002.

34. Ministry of Public Management, Home Affairs, Posts and Telecommunications, Japan, *Third Action Plan for the Promotion of Digital Broadcasting*, April 2003.

35. Ministry of Public Management, Home Affairs, Posts and Telecommunications, Japan, *Major Aspects of Japan's Broadcasting Policy*, December 2002.

36. Author interviews with NHK and TBS Media Research Institute, November 2005.

37. Japan Electronics and Information Technology Industries Association, November 2005.

38. Ministry of Public Management, Home Affairs, Posts and Telecommunications, Japan, *Third Action Plan for the Promotion of Digital Broadcasting*, April 2003.

39. Author interview with Norio Kumabe, Visiting Professor, Global Information and Telecommunication Studies, Waseda University, Japan, November 2005.

40. Japan Electronics and Information Technology Industries Association, November 2005.

41. Ministry of Public Management, Home Affairs, Posts and Telecommunications, Japan, *Information and Communications in Japan – Building a Ubiquitous Network Society That Spreads Throughout the World*, White Paper, 2004.

42. Ibid.

43. European Commission, *Communication on the transition from analogue to digital broadcasting (from digital switch-over to analogue switch-off)*, COM (2003) 541 final, 2003.

44. Ibid.

45. Ibid.

46. European Commission, *Public policy treatment of digital terrestrial television in communications markets*, Report by Analysys Consultants, 2005, Annex A.

47. Author interviews with Finland's Ministry of Transport and Communications, the TV2007 project, and YLE (Finnish national broadcasting), September 2006.

48. Programme in Comparative Media Law and Policy, Centre for Socio-Legal Studies, University of Oxford, op. cit.

49. Ibid.

50. European Commission, *Public policy treatment of digital terrestrial television in communications markets*, Report by Analysys Consultants, 2005, Annex A.

51. Programme in Comparative Media Law and Policy, Centre for Socio-Legal Studies, University of Oxford, op. cit.

52. Ibid.

53. European Commission, *Communication on EU spectrum priorities for digital switchover in the context of the upcoming ITU Regional Radiocommunication Conference 2006 (RRC-06)*, COM (2005) 461 final, 2005.

54. European Commission, *Communication on accelerating the transition from analogue to digital broadcasting*, COM (2005) 204 final, 2005.

55. Ofcom, press release, 30th June 2006.

Chapter Nine

1. Ofcom, press release announcing the Digital Dividend Review, 17th November 2005.
2. DVB: see www.dvb-h-online.org/services.
3. Preliminary report given by Mike Short, Vice President, Research and Development of O2, to the Oxford Media Convention, 19th January 2006.
4. Foster, Robin, *IPTV: China maps out a route to success*, in *Television*, February 2006.
5. Ofcom, *The Communications Market 2005*, published July 2005.
6. BBC, press release, 16th May 2005.
7. *The Times*, 6th October 2005.
8. Ofcom, *Digital Local: Options for the future of local video content and interactive services*, 2006.
9. Ibid.
10. Ibid.
11. Negroponte, Nicholas, *Being Digital*, London, Hodder & Stoughton, 1995, p. 180.
12. Birt, John, *TV needs more truth and beauty*, James MacTaggart Lecture, Edinburgh Television Festival, August 2005.
13. Cox, Barry, *Free For All? Public service television in the digital age*, London, Demos, 2004, p. 16.
14. Ibid., p. 27.
15. Ibid., pp.17–19.
16. *The Times*, 30th January 2003.
17. *The Times*, 27th October 2005.
18. *The Times*, 22nd October 2005.
19. Birt, John, *TV needs more truth and beauty*, James MacTaggart Lecture, Edinburgh Television Festival, August 2005.
20. Richards, Ed, *Trends in Television, Radio and Telecoms*, Ofcom Annual Lecture, Westminster Media Forum, 20th July 2005.
21. Grossman, Lawrence K., *The Electronic Republic*, New York, Viking Penguin, 1995 and New York and London, Penguin, 1996, p. 4.
22. G-8, *Okinawa Charter on Global Information Society*, 23 July 2000, quoted in Norris, Pippa, *The Digital Divide*, Cambridge and New York, Cambridge University Press, 2001, p. 6.
23. Norris, Pippa, op. cit., p. 23.
24. Ibid., p. 20.
25. Ibid., p. 4.
26. Ibid., pp. 68–9.
27. Office of the e-Envoy, *Digital television – A policy framework for delivering e-government services to the home, draft for public consultation*, 2002.

28. Ibid.
29. Prime Minister's keynote speech to e-Summit, 19th November 2002.
30. Oftel, *Digital Television – Consumers' Uses and Perceptions*, report prepared by Counterpoint Research, 2001, pp. 10–11.
31. Office of the e-Envoy, op. cit.
32. Department of Transport, Local Government and the Regions, *Modern Councils, modern services – access for all*, 2001.
33. Ibid.
34. Ibid.
35. Ofcom, *Digital Local: Options for the future of local video content and interactive services*, 2006.
36. Department for Education and Skills, *Wired Up Communities Evaluation: Findings from the Carpenters Estate*, Research Report RR517 by David Devins, Policy Research Institute, Leeds Metropolitan University, 2004.
37. www.regentv.net.
38. Memorandum submitted by Video Networks Ltd to the House of Commons Culture, Media and Sport Committee, December 2005, published by the Committee in *Analogue Switch-Off: a signal change in television*, Second Report of Session 2005–06, Volume II, *Oral and Written Evidence*, 2006, p. 191.
39. DCMS and Chartered Institute of Housing, *Digital Switchover – A Good Practice Briefing*, August 2005.
40. House of Commons Culture, Media and Sport Committee, *Analogue Switch-Off: a signal change in television*, Second Report of Session 2005–06, Volume II, *Oral and Written Evidence*, 2006, p. 192.
41. House of Commons Culture, Media and Sport Committee, *Analogue Switch-Off: a signal change in television*, Second Report of Session 2005–06, Volume I, 2006, p. 15.
42. Ibid.
43. European Commission, *Communication on reviewing the interoperability of digital interactive television services*, COM (2006) 37 final, 2006.

Chapter Ten

1. García Leiva, María Trinidad, Starks, Michael, and Tambini, Damian, *Overview of digital television switchover policy in Europe, the United States and Japan*, in *Info*, 8: 3 (2006), pp. 32–46. This article covers the same ground as our submission to the House of Commons Select Committee, referred to in Note (1) to Chapter 8 above.
2. Antti Sillanpää, *Firm Strategies in the Competition for Dominance of Networked Business Systems*, Helsinki University of Technology, Doctoral Dissertation Series 2006/3, 2006, p. 163.
3. European Commission, press release, *State aid: Commission rules subsidy for digital terrestrial TV (DVB-T) in Berlin-Brandenburg illegal; explains how digital TV can be supported*, 9th November 2005.

4. DTI, *The role of Integrated Digital Television Sets in achieving Digital Switchover*, consultation, 2002.
5. Galperin, Hernan, op. cit., p. 4.
6. Ibid., p. 285.
7. Brinkley, Joel, op. cit., pp. 30–31.
8. Grimme, Katharina, op. cit., p. 57.
9. Ibid., pp. 61–70.
10. Levy, David, *Europe's Digital Revolution, Broadcasting Regulation: the EU and the Nation State*, London and New York, Routledge, 1999, p. 70.
11. Digital UK, DCMS, DTI, Ofcom, *The Digital Switchover Programme, Programme Structure*, 6th January 2006, Annex B.
12. House of Commons Culture, Media and Sport Committee, *Analogue Switch-Off: a signal change in television*, Second Report of Session 2005–06, Volume II, *Oral and Written Evidence*, 2006, p. 160.

Select Bibliography

Books

Birt, John, *The Harder Path*, London, Time Warner Books, 2002.

Brinkley, Joel, *Defining Vision: The Battle for the Future of Television*, New York, Harcourt Brace, 1997.

Brown, Allan and Picard, Robert G. (eds.), *Digital Terrestrial Television in Europe*, New Jersey, Lawrence Erlbaum Associates, 2005.

Chippindale, Peter, and Franks, Suzanne, *Dished! The Rise and Fall of British Satellite Broadcasting*, London, Simon and Shuster, 1991.

Cox, Barry, *Free For All? Public service television in the digital age*, London, Demos, 2004.

Dyke, Greg, *Inside Story*, London, Harper Collins, 2004.

Galperin, Hernan, *New Television, Old Politics*, Cambridge and New York, Cambridge University Press, 2004.

Given, Jock, *Turning Off the Television: Broadcasting's Uncertain Future*, Sydney, University of New South Wales Press, 2003.

Griffiths, Alan, *Digital Television Strategies: business challenges and opportunities*, Basingstoke, Palgrave Macmillan, 2003.

Grimme, Katharina, *Digital Television – Standardization and Strategies*, Boston and London, Artech House, 2002.

Grossman, Lawrence K., *The Electronic Republic*, New York, Viking Penguin, 1995 and New York and London, Penguin, 1996.

Harcourt, Alison, *The European Union and the regulation of media markets*, Manchester, Manchester University Press, 2004.

Horsman, Mathew, *Sky High*, London, Orion, 1997.

Hundt, Reed E., *You Say You Want a Revolution: A Story of Information Age Politics*, New Haven, Yale University Press, 2000.

Levy, David, *Europe's Digital Revolution, Broadcasting Regulation: the EU and the Nation State*, London and New York, Routledge, 1999.

Negroponte, Nicholas, *Being Digital*, London, Hodder & Stoughton, 1995.

Norris, Pippa, *The Digital Divide*, Cambridge and New York, Cambridge University Press, 2001.

Lectures and journal articles

Birt, John, *TV needs more truth and beauty*, James MacTaggart Lecture, Edinburgh Television Festival, August 2005.

Cox, Barry, *TV in the Digital Age*, set of four lectures delivered at Oxford University, 2003 (published in 2004 by Demos, see Books above).

Dyke, Greg, *A Time for Change*, James MacTaggart Memorial Lecture, Edinburgh Television Festival, August 2000.

Elstein, David, *The Politics of Digital TV in the UK*, published at www.opendemocracy.net, 2002.

García Leiva, María Trinidad, Starks, Michael, and Tambini, Damian, *Overview of digital television switchover policy in Europe, the United States and Japan*, in *Info*, 8: 3 (2006), pp. 32–46.

Iosifidis, Petros, *Digital Switchover in Europe*, in *The International Communications Gazette*, 68: 3 (2006), pp. 249–268.

Richards, Ed, *Trends in Television, Radio and Telecoms*, Ofcom Annual Lecture, Westminster Media Forum, July 2005.

Reports by official bodies

BBC
- *The BBC Beyond 2000*, 1998
- *The Future Funding of the BBC: The BBC's response to the Department of Culture, Media and Sport's consultation on the report by the Independent Review Panel*, 1999
- *Building Public Value – Renewing the BBC for a digital world*, 2004
- *Review of the BBC's Royal Charter: BBC response to 'A strong BBC, independent of government'*, 2005
- *The BBC Licence Fee Bid: what does the public think?*, report for the BBC Board of Governors by Professor Patrick Barwise, 2006

Consumers' Association
- *Turn On, Tune In, Switched Off – Consumer Attitudes to Digital TV*, 2001

Department for Culture, Media and Sport (DCMS)
- *The Future Funding of the BBC, Report of the Independent Review Panel, Chairman: Gavyn Davies*, 1999
- *Digital Decisions: Viewer Choice and Digital Television*, report by the Viewers' Panel to the Secretary of State for Culture, Media and Sport, 2001
- *Review of the BBC's Royal Charter*, consultation, 2003

- *Persuasion or Compulsion? Consumers and Analogue Switch-off*, Report to the Broadcasting Minister by the Consumer Expert Group, 2004
- *Review of the BBC's Royal Charter, A strong BBC, independent of government*, Green Paper, 2005
- *Communal TV systems and digital switchover*, NOP World, 2005
- *Ferryside and Llansteffan Digital Switchover Technical Trial: Research on Vulnerable Households*, 2005
- *A public service for all: the BBC in the digital age*, White Paper, 2006
- *Report of the Bolton Digital Television Trial*, 2006
- *Review of the BBC Value for Money and Efficiency Programmes*, by independent consultants PKF, 2006
- *Digital Switchover Help Scheme*, 2006

DCMS and Chartered Institute of Housing
- *Digital Switchover – A Good Practice Briefing*, 2005

DCMS and Department of Trade and Industry (DTI)
- *Digital Television Action Plan*, series of versions from 2002
- *Cost Benefit Analysis of Digital Switchover*, 2003, updated 2005
- *A Guide to Digital Television and Digital Switchover, 2005*
- *Report of the Digital TV Project*, November 2004, published 2005
- *Report of a Digital Switchover Technical Trial at Ferryside and Llansteffan*, 2005
- *Regulatory and Environmental Impact Assessment: the timing of digital switchover*, 2005
- *Government Response to the Culture, Media and Sport Select Committee, Session 2005–2006: Report on Analogue Switch-Off*, 2006

Department of National Heritage (subsequently replaced by the DCMS)
- *Digital Terrestrial Broadcasting – The Government's Proposals*, HMSO, Cmnd. 2946, 1995

Department of Trade and Industry (DTI)
- *Enterprise, Skills and Innovation*, White Paper, 2001
- *The role of Integrated Digital Television Sets in achieving Digital Switchover*, consultation, 2002
- *Paving the Way for a Digital Future* and *Statement on the principles for planning the use of the UHF spectrum once analogue terrestrial transmissions end*, 2003
- *Digital Television For All, a report on usability and accessible design*, in association with the Generics Group, 2003
- *Attitudes to Digital Television, Preliminary findings on consumer adoption of digital television*, in association with the Generics Group, 2004

- *Attitudes to Digital Switchover, The impact of digital switchover on consumer adoption of digital television*, in association with the Generics Group, 2004
- *Equipment needs of consumers facing most difficulty switching to digital television equipment*, prepared by i2 media research, 2006
- *The equipment needs of consumers facing most difficulty switching to digital TV*, prepared by Scientific Generics, 2006

DTI and HM Treasury
- *Review of Radio Spectrum Management by Professor Martin Cave*, 2002

DTI, Radiocommunications Agency and HM Treasury
- *Government Response to the Review of Radio Spectrum Management*, 2002

Digitag (European industry group)
- *Analogue Switch-off – Strategies to end analogue terrestrial television in Europe*, Geneva, 2006

Digital TV Group
- *A Study on the Technical Impediments to Analogue Switchover*, 2000

European Commission
- *Europe and the Global Information Society: Recommendations to the European Council*, report from the High Level Group on the Information Society, 1994
- *Communication on the transition from analogue to digital broadcasting (from digital switch-over to analogue switch-off)*, COM (2003) 541 final, 2003
- *Communication on accelerating the transition from analogue to digital broadcasting*, COM (2005) 204 final, 2005
- *Public policy treatment of digital terrestrial television in communications markets*, Report for the European Commission by Analysys Consultants, 2005
- *Communication on EU spectrum priorities for digital switchover in the context of the upcoming ITU Regional Radiocommunication Conference 2006 (RRC-06)*, COM (2005) 461 final, 2005
- *Communication on reviewing the interoperability of digital interactive television services*, COM (2006) 37 final, 2006

General Accounting Office (United States)
- *Telecommunications: Additional Federal Efforts Could Help Advance Digital Television Transition*, GAO 03–7, Washington D.C., 2002
- *Digital Broadcast Television Transition: Estimated Cost of Supporting Set-Top Boxes to Help Advance the DTV Transition*, GAO 05–258T, Washington D.C., 2005

House of Commons

- House of Commons Culture, Media and Sport Committee, *Analogue Switch-Off: a signal change in television*, Second Report of Session 2005–06, Volume I, *Report* and Volume II, *Oral and Written Evidence*, 2006

House of Lords

- House of Lords Select Committee on the BBC's Charter Review, *The Review of the BBC's Royal Charter*, Volume 1, Report, 2005
- House of Lords Select Committee on the BBC's Charter Review, *Further Issues for BBC Charter Review*, 2006

ITC

- *Discussion Paper on Digital Television*, 1993
- *The Genesis Project*, prepared by NTL and the Smith Group, 2000
- *Go Digital*, report on trial, 2003

ITC, Oftel and Office of Fair Trading

- *Joint ITC, Oftel and OFT advice to Government on Digital Television*, 2000

Ofcom

- *Driving digital switchover: a report to the Secretary of State*, 2004
- *Digital replacement licences to be offered to channels 3, 4 and 5 and public teletext*, consultation, 2004
- *Methodology for reviews of financial terms for Channel 3, Channel 5 and Public Teletext licences*, statement, 2004
- *Ofcom review of public service television broadcasting, Phase 1 – Is Television Special?*, 2004; *Phase 2 – Meeting the digital challenge*, 2004; *Phase 3 – Competition for Quality*, 2005
- *Spectrum management update: technical planning for digital switchover around the UK*, 2005
- *Planning Options for Digital Switchover*, 2005
- *Cost and power consumption implications of digital switchover*, prepared by Scientific Generics, 2005
- *Digital Local: Options for the future of local video content and interactive services*, 2006
- *Summary of research on the ease of use of domestic digital television equipment*, 2006

Ofcom Consumer Panel

- *Supporting the most vulnerable consumers through digital switchover*, 2004

Office of the e-Envoy
- *Digital television – A policy framework for delivering e-government services to the home, draft for public consultation*, 2002

Oftel
- *Digital Television – Consumers' Uses and Perceptions*, report prepared by Counterpoint Research, 2001

Radiocommunications Agency and DCMS
- A Study to Estimate the Economic Impact of Government Policies towards Digital Television, report by NERA and Smith System Engineering, 1998

List of Abbreviations

ACATS (Advisory Committee on Advanced Television Service (USA))

ADSL (Asymmetric Digital Subscriber Line)

API (Application Programming Interface)

ATSC (Advanced Television Systems Committee (USA))

BDB (British Digital Broadcasting)

BSB (British Satellite Broadcasting)

CBA (Cost-Benefit Analysis)

CEA (Consumer Electronics Association (USA))

DAB (Digital Audio Broadcasting)

DCMS (Department for Culture, Media and Sport)

DTI (Department of Trade and Industry)

DTN (Digital Television Network)

DTT (Digital Terrestrial Television)

DVB (Digital Video Broadcasting project)

EPG (Electronic Programme Guide)

FCC (Federal Communications Commission (USA))

HDTV (High-Definition Television)

IBA (Independent Broadcasting Authority)

IPTV (Internet Protocol Television)

ISDB (Integrated Services Digital Broadcasting (Japan))

ITC (Independent Television Commission)

LCD (Liquid Crystal Display)

MAC (Multiplex Analogue Component)

MHP (Multi-media Home Platform)

MPEG (Motion Picture Expert Group)

NHK (Nippon Hoso Kyokai: Japan Broadcasting Corporation)

NTL   (National Transcommunications Limited)

ODPM   (Office of the Deputy Prime Minister)

Ofcom   (Office of Communications)

OFT   (Office of Fair Trading)

Oftel   (Office of Telecommunications)

PVR   (Personal Video Recorder)

QAM   (Quadrature Amplitude Modulation)

TDN   (The Digital Network)

UHF   (Ultra High Frequency)

VCR   (Video Cassette Recorder)

VHF   (Very High Frequency)

Index